WALKING SWIFTLY

Writings in Honor of Robert Bly

EDITED BY THOMAS R. SMITH

HarperPerennial
A Division of HarperCollins*Publishers*

Photographs courtesy of Robert Bly and the contributors to this volume. Every effort has been made to identify and locate photographers and secure permissions.

A hardcover edition of this book was published in 1992 by Ally Press. It is here reprinted by arrangement with Ally Press.

HarperCollins books may be purchased for educational, business, or sales promotional use. For information please write: Special Markets Department, HarperCollins Publishers, Inc., 10 East 53rd Street, New York, NY 10022.

First HarperPerennial edition published 1993.

Designed by Cats Pajamas, Inc.

Library of Congress Cataloging-in-Publication Data

Walking swiftly : writings in honor of Robert Bly / edited by Thomas R. Smith. — 1st HarperPerennial ed.
    p.   cm.
    "Originally published in hardcover in 1992 by Ally Press"—T.p. verso.
    Includes bibliographical references (p.).
    ISBN 0-06-097526-1 (pbk.)
    1. Bly, Robert. 2. Bly, Robert—Poetry. 3. Bly, Robert—Appreciation. 4. Poets, American—20th century—Biography. I. Smith, Thomas R.
PS3552.L9Z95   1993
811'.54—dc20   92-56270

Contents

3. GROWING ORBITS

4. Iron John and Beyond

Preface

THE SEED FOR THIS BOOK was planted by Robert Bly's chance remark that a friend of his had turned sixty-five and he was disappointed that nobody had done a festschrift for him. As Robert was soon to turn sixty-five himself, a freewheeling, spirited collection about his work and one reflective of its many dimensions was obviously in order. Like the hunter in *Iron John* who asked "Anything dangerous to do around here?" Ally Press decided to take up the challenge. Though consulted early on about whom to include in the book, Robert was not involved in the editoral process, and he will be seeing the majority of these contributions, most written especially for this volume, for the first time along with everyone else.

My own association with Robert began in 1973 when I took part in interviewing him for the St. Olaf College literary magazine. It proved to be a rough start, but one illustrative of both Robert's generosity and ferocity. The interview went fine, but after waiting as long as we thought we could for Robert's approval of the transcript, reason gave way to indiscretion and we went to press on the same day we received in the mail a completely edited, reworked version. Rightly outraged, Robert nonetheless had forgiven enough by the following year to offer a couple of poems that helped launch Ally Press, then a small independent literary press of the smallest kind. (The unusual press name derives from the Carlos Castaneda books, in which an ally is described as a power allowing one to transcend the realm of ordinary reality and, contrary to numerous misspellings, has nothing to do with a narrow street behind city buildings.) Given that after eighteen years Ally Press only recently hired its first associate editor, it is a somewhat astonishing leap, as well as a tremendous honor to be the publisher of this vast and wonderful collection.

I've attended many Bly readings and conferences over the years, and to see the enthusiasm and ideas flying between the stage and the audience is incredible. All around, people are out of their seats with ideas, they are lined three deep at microphones to share or shout their insights, and for most, this exchange of energy can't go on long enough. Robert has that effect on people. His writing also wakes people up, and because of this gift for sparking ideas and controversy, no doubt other volumes, some more critical, will follow. But let this book be a gift back to him, and let the stories to follow, begin.

— *Paul Feroe, Publisher*

Introduction

Robert Bly's Gift for Community

IN HIS SELECTED POEMS, published in 1986, Robert Bly saw fit to include an early, unpublished poem called "Snow Geese." The poem's intent is clearly autobiographical, if more symbolic than factual:

> The drunken father has pulled the boy inside.
> The boy breaks free, turns, leaves the house.
> He spends the night out eating with the geese. . . .

Later, in one of his most famous poems of the eighties, Bly had reprised and amplified that image of youthful estrangement from human society:

> He turns away,
> loses courage,
> goes outdoors to feed with wild
> things, lives among dens
> and huts, eats distance and silence;
> he grows long wings, enters the spiral, ascends.
> *Fifty Males Sitting Together*

Only in the past ten years has Robert Bly begun to talk openly about the emotional isolation he experienced in his youth and early manhood, an isolation explicitly linked, as in the poems above, to his alcoholic father. Acknowledging that formative wounding and exploring its ramifications through the poetic image has been one of Bly's chief labors during the eighties. It may seem ironic that Bly, whose own wounds resulted in early separation from the community, should, by encouraging others to acknowledge their wounding, draw about himself the thriving and diverse community represented by the more than fifty contributors to this book. Yet even a superficial glance at Bly's career as a poet reveals a powerful natural gift for community—a gift for encouraging, inspiring, energizing, and acting as what Michael and Milli Quam call a "participant leader" in community.

Indeed, one of the persistent themes of this book is the distance Robert Bly has traveled toward community from those nights "eating with the geese" and those years living "among dens and huts." While several fine critical studies of Bly's work are currently available (certainly with more to come), *Walking Swiftly* is the first anthology to sound the liveliness, breadth, and creativity of the numerous and frequently overlapping communities to which Bly has given his gift during his more than four decades as a public poet. While the tone may vary wildly from one contributor to the next, the voices heard in *Walking Swiftly* are unanimous in one thing, if only that: their deep affection for Robert Bly and his work.

I've arranged the contents of *Walking Swiftly* to reflect the progression or "rings" of community which Robert Bly has enlivened with argument, energy, humor, and warmth. The book forms a rough chronology meant to suggest the particular flavors of each of the four seasons of Bly's work to date.

Section One, "Plains Poet," provides glimpses mainly of Bly's years as a young poet in Madison, Minnesota, when, after Navy, Harvard, and solitude in New York, he'd returned to make the brooding farmland of his boyhood truly his own as an adult, establishing from the family farm an international reputation through poetry, translations, and criticism published in his revolutionary magazines *The Fifties* and *The Sixties*. Among those evoking this period are Frederick Manfred, Meridel Le Sueur, Louis Jenkins, and others who, like Bly, have chosen to live in the Midwest.

Section Two, "A Company of Poets," locates Bly in the expanded sphere of American and international poetry. Here are important poets of Bly's own generation—Donald Hall, Galway Kinnell, William Stafford, and others—who participated together in overturning the dominant formalism of the fifties for a new poetry favoring spontaneity, wildness, and depth. Included in this section are poets, both older and younger, paying homage to Bly with new poems as in the more traditional European festschrift.

The third section, "Growing Orbits," provides a series of vivid snapshots of Bly mostly from the seventies, when he initiated that experiment in community, the annual Great Mother Conference. Still lively and challenging after twenty years, the conference is represented here by Ann Igoe, Andrew Dick, Gioia Timpanelli, and others who have nurtured that small, intense community as teachers and participants. Also gathered in this section are an assortment of friends and colleagues so diverse as to resist brief categorizing, all encountered in Bly's "growing orbits."

Finally, Section Four, "Iron John and Beyond," gauges the impact of Bly's work in the eighties as a leader of what has come to be known as the mythopoetic men's movement. Included in this section are contributions by most of Bly's major collaborators in that work—James Hillman, Michael Meade, and Robert Moore among them—as well as varied reactions to *Iron John* and its place in Bly's oeuvre. These essays are especially helpful in separating the essential Bly from what Michael Ventura has called the "deconstructed" Bly of the newsstands.

I've drawn the title of this book from Bly's prose poem of the same name in *This Body Is Made of Camphor and Gopherwood*. The poem dates from Bly's most ecstatic period, the midseventies, before he'd begun the public labor of transforming his private grief—as a son, as a father, and as a man—into the increasingly unsentimental and hard-boned poems of the eighties (continued into the nineties), to say nothing of the men's work. All of that lay ahead, and anyone attending one of Bly's readings in the seventies was likely to receive a joyous crash course in (the jacket copy of *Camphor and Gopherwood* sums it up) "early Sufi poetry, the animal life of the Midwest, Rilke, the new research on protozoa colonies, and ancient Oriental poetry."

"Walking Swiftly," an expression of the optimistic energies of that time, offers us not only ecstatic language and images, but a model for the evolution of the artist's soul:

When I wake, I hear sheep eating apple peels just outside the screen. The trees are heavy, soaked, cold and hushed, the sun just rising. All seems calm, and yet somewhere inside I am not calm. We live in wooden buildings made of two-by-fours, making the landscape nervous for a hundred miles. And the Emperor when he was sixty called for rhinoceros horn, for sky-blue phoenix eggs shaped from veined rock, dipped in rooster blood. Around him the wasps kept guard, the hens continued their patrol, the oysters open and close all questions. The heat inside the human body grows, it does not know where to throw itself—for a while it knots into will, heavy, burning, sweet, then into generosity, that longs to take on the burdens of others, then into mad love that lasts forever. The artist walks swiftly to his studio, and carves oceanic waves into the dragon's mane.

"Will" becomes "generosity" becomes "mad love"—this is the progression, the sequence accomplished by the soul in overcoming its distance from others.

To those encountering Robert Bly's "mad love" in the eighties and nineties, accounts such as Philip Dacey's of an early Bly reading "shyly, haltingly, without style or conviction, staring at the page and seldom looking at his audience" may seem incredible. Apparently there was another community Bly needed first before he was able to reach out powerfully to his listeners: "The many hours I spent translating Neruda, Vallejo, Antonio Machado and Lorca brought me into a community of poets who believed that it was just and natural to write of important national griefs in one's poetry as well as private griefs." Organizing readings against the Vietnam War around the country in the sixties, Bly discovered the power of the poem, especially when spoken, to encourage, even enact, community: "The community flowers when the poem is spoken in the ancient way—that is, with full sound, with conviction, and with the knowledge that the emotions are not private to the person speaking them." Bly's antiwar poetry drove home forcefully the absurdity of trying to separate the political and the spiritual, the immorality of distancing public from private values. Bly used the occasion of acceptance of the National Book Award for *The Light Around the Body* in 1969 (see Appendix 1) as a forum to publicly indict the war-makers and those complying with them. David Ignatow, who was present, writes, "It was Robert's finest hour, and we who were attached to him through admiration, faith, and common goals were affirmed through him and made to feel our significance before the world."

Bly's activism is often ignored or forgotten by those who reflexively condemn his work with men as politically suspect. Yet Bly has remained constant in his insistence on the falsity of those boundaries we have erected between the spiritual and the political, the inner and outer. One need only examine his response to the Gulf War in an op-ed piece written for the *Minneapolis Star Tribune* (see Appendix 2) to recognize the consistency with which Bly relates the mythological, psychological, and concrete worlds not only in his poetry but in his polemical pieces. During that popular war, Bly organized "grief marches" for the victims (among which civilian deaths are now estimated at over 100,000), granted interviews to anyone who asked, and appeared live on CNN, where he called the slaughter of Iraqis fleeing Kuwait "our My Lai."

My first experience of Robert Bly was in fact one of those legendary antiwar readings at Coffman Union on the University of Minnesota campus in the fall of 1969. That night I heard Galway Kinnell, Robert Creeley, Diane Wakoski, Ed Sanders, and many others—a true showcase of some of the most vital contemporary American poets, among whom Robert Bly astonished most. A formidable and towering presence in his trademark serape, he bristled and spun with ecstatic anger, was a human vortex seeming to embody, withstand, and even draw nourishment from the turbulent, disintegrative energies of the times, spitting forth Mark Twain's devastating "War Prayer" and his own ferocious "The Teeth Mother Naked at Last." Bly's moral ferocity was genuine and "naked," hot, in contrast with the cold, technological, masked rage of the killers he so passionately denounced that evening. Outrage, desire, and renewed strength to act were the great gifts Bly tirelessly gave his audiences during the Vietnam War. Later I discovered and came to appreciate the less attention-getting gifts Bly gives in such abundance in his poems—old boards, bits of oyster shell scattered in a chickenyard, tires on a service station rack, a snowflake on a horse's mane—any one of which, followed to its source, can lead to a rapprochement with the soul residing in matter. Bly gives this gift as freely to stranger and friend alike as clouds give rain to rooftops, or as a sunset gives its colors to trees standing in a field.

In many ways, then, I am grateful to Robert Bly—for his work as poet, translator, activist, teacher, and most recently father of the new men's work. He has indeed "walked swiftly" through a life that has touched and contributed to the spiritual and even material survival of innumerable other lives. This book is a loving and informal tribute to Robert's journey by more than fifty who have walked along with him a way. With my publisher, Paul Feroe, I present to the reader these marvelously individual gifts of the heart, a bouquet of many fragrances and hues for Robert Bly in this year of his sixty-fifth birthday.

—Thomas R. Smith, Editor
Minneapolis, April 1992

1
PLAINS POET

ROBERT BLY IN 1976 (JOHN SEPICH PHOTO).

Overleaf: The farmhouse during the Vietnam War, Madison, Minnesota, 1966 (Minneapolis Star Tribune photo).

William Booth

True Gifts from Robert Bly

Kabekona Lake, Minnesota, February 22, 1975

ROBERT BLY HAS DRIVEN UP from the farm to stay for a few days. He has been coming occasionally since he got word of us and our cabins. It turns out that Kabekona is the lake where he and Bill Duffy, staying for the weekend at an old resort on the east shore, working on an issue of *The Sixties,* drinking and writing rejection slips all night, went out in a boat at dawn to see who could write the best poem. Today the lake is covered with three feet of ice. Our cabin one is poorly insulated, and I think Robert sometimes works on poems and essays sitting up in bed with the covers piled on. The solitude of our place suits him. But by late afternoon he has had enough solitude.

We can hear him coming across the snow to the house singing resonantly, the sound coming up from his belly and chest and through his nose. He knocks on the door and immediately bursts in, still singing. He greets us with much good cheer. He thrusts gifts of books or bottles of wine into our hands. The ceiling in this house built for short people is not far above his head. Big as he is—he refers to "flat stomach types" as if they all worked for the CIA—some energy coming from him is more dominant than his size. He does not sit down but moves around the room, talking, seeming to inspect bookshelves or pictures on the wall that he may not be seeing at all. He makes an announcement: "After we eat I want to read you the Shakespeare article, and then I have to go back to work."

If he is the cook, frying chicken, the skillet smokes and the linoleum floor gets slippery with grease. More often, though, as we get dinner ready, Robert is our teacher. I never met a man who so loves to tell what he knows, as if the purpose of learning were not fulfilled without teaching. ". . . He was the great Sufi poet, you know. Wrote thousands and thousands of poems. I have to work from bad English translations because I don't know Persian. Anyway, when he was young, his father . . ."

The kids are setting the table, Nancy is stirring spaghetti sauce. ". . . That's the way some of the Indians did, you know. They would start with a little insult or dare and build up, going back and forth. So one of them finally said, 'I'm so brave I can kill all the white people in that cabin.' Well, when Little Crow heard about what they had done, he wept, because he knew what it meant—the white man would wipe his people out."

Our boys want to go deer hunting. "So then, after the deer crossed his path, an Indian would wait, absolutely still. And in a few minutes, he'd draw his bowstring, whirl around 180 degrees, and shoot the deer! He knew it would circle and cross the path behind him."

He goes back to his cabin after dark. Snow is falling. In these two years since we moved to Minnesota I haven't yet seen anything like those prairie snows Robert told of at the Santa Rosa reading the day I first heard him: drifts so deep on his farm that he roofed over the trench he dug from the house to his writing shack so the wind wouldn't pile in more snow.

Santa Rosa, California, November 5, 1969

Robert Bly, the poet, was on campus at noon today. Don Emblen introduced him, quoting Louis Simpson, who says he's one of the few poets in America from whom greatness can be expected, and James Dickey, who authorized only a one-word statement about Bly's work: "pitiful." Burbank Auditorium was about half filled with students whose English teachers, including me, had persuaded them to give up a lunch hour for a poetry reading. "Poetry reading" sounds something like "chamber concert," which this wasn't. Bly came on hip, funny, urgent, and brassy. He threatened to read nothing but Tennyson if people didn't move down front to the empty seats. The students moved, and he read the Russell Edson poem about

Martha George, who discovered that her chest was a radio and that by diddling with her left nipple she could turn it on. He read funny haiku. He read a parody of Charles Bukowski by Phyllis Onstott Arone:

> every day I sit around in this maggot-ridden room
> drunk again or maybe still on buck-a-gallon wine
> just settin' fire to the hairs on my chest
> with my 267th cigaret of the day
> and putting them out again with my dirty bare hands
> because life is a sad handkerchief full of snot. . . .

He dropped a few names of antiwar celebrities for us eager campus activists: Ed Sanders, Joan Baez, David Harris ("He's a smart boy"). He read poems insulting Lyndon Johnson's face ("It is a stomach with eyes") and Nixon's ("It's the toe of a footscraper, struggling under petrified hair"). Nixon is dead, he said—he just forgot to lie down about twenty years ago.

No one dozed off. Of course there was in all this no affront to academic propriety that was not fully intended. Just as the haiku he read were, as he told us, intended by the Japanese to "break the hold of the academic poets," his style was a stick rattled along a cage of politeness to startle prisoners awake. "We want to go to sleep," he said at one point. Not with his blessing.

So far this account of how we were entertained by Bly does not begin to explain what went on at the reading. The man did a load of teaching in fifty minutes. For one thing, he kept giving information that people took in because it didn't smell musty—vivid ten- or fifteen-second sketches of contemporary poets, a concise introduction to Issa and other Buddhists of the Pure Land school, book titles and publishers and prices, a bit of Europeans-versus-Indians history from an 1864 commentary on the massacre of the Sioux in Minnesota.

But mainly the risk he took, almost from the start, was to touch the quick of feeling in the listeners. Though he invited us with his brassy style to share in the pleasures of derision, to indulge in a bit of thrilling contempt for Tennyson, Nixon, Johnson, businessmen, and academia, he caught us off guard between dagger thrusts and after wisecracks with invitations to celebrate, praise, grieve, and feel the anguish of someone else's suffering. He was reading tender haiku about insects ("Cricket, be careful — I'm rolling over!") to students who had wanted to sit in the back row. And after explaining Issa's Buddhist outlook, then telling how the poet lost his infant daughter to smallpox, he read Issa's lines, "I know the world is a drop of dew. I know it. And yet . . . " The listeners were very quiet. A year later, he said, Issa had a dream of his daughter — she had her cheek held up to a melon. "Why does that move us so much more than Pope's 'Essay on Man'?" He read a couple of love poems, too.

The last thing was an intense reading from a long poem against the Vietnam War that he said he might call "They Are Dying, But . . ." ["The Teeth Mother Naked at Last"]. He let the poem express his vision and his passion without caution. It made the irony, indirection, and understatement of some antiwar poems look cowardly by comparison. Sometimes in the course of the hour Bly had given us an image of himself as a solitary person, living alone in New York or withdrawing to the farm in Minnesota where "nobody bugs me," but in this poem you can see how compelled he is to come back with a message that he thinks we desperately need to hear.

The applause went on a long time. We walked out under the water oaks of the campus toward the new temporary classroom buildings. It was hard to meet a one o'clock class; we wanted to be better teachers.

Moorhead, Minnesota, May 1975

Robert talked to the Moorhead State students about how he started teaching some classes back home in his farm town. You could tell from what he said that teaching feels to him like a natural obligation — we learn, we teach. Somebody in Madison had caught him by his duty collar: "You go around and tell the college kids everything you know, but you don't tell anybody in Madison anything." So he started an evening adult course called "Discoveries of Freud and Jung and How They Relate to Life in Madison, Minnesota." Thirty or forty people enrolled at four dollars each. As he put it, they were stunned by Freud's ideas. I get an image of their mouths all dropping open at once as he offers a Freudian insight explaining conflict at Madison High School: the kids are the id, the principal is the superego—and where is the ego? "Missing. Naked confrontation!"

Robert said a couple of other things that tell how he looks at teaching. The Madison group went on from Freud and Jung to a short story class, starting with D. H. Lawrence's "The Rockinghorse Winner." They read it aloud for forty-five minutes, then talked. "Man, it was so much more wonderful than a college class. Because they took their guts and laid them right out on the table. Took their marriages and put them right out there."

The main clue to what teaching is all about for him came when he got to telling of this year's course, occult astrology. The whole point of occult astrology is to teach you to work *against* your sign. You swim upstream. There are twelve signs, and so there are really twelve different ways for human beings to grow, not just one. I can see "I live my life in growing orbits" inscribed over the front door of a Bly schoolhouse.

San Francisco, March 11, 1990

That's the place and date of a "day for men" with Bly, James Hillman, and Michael Meade—I'm hearing the tapes from Oral Tradition Archives a year later. What strikes me is the remarkable quality of the teaching by these men. The men's groups are getting plenty of press; the popular images are of drumming, dancing, masks, bonfires, head-butting, roasting in sweat lodges, weeping, hugging, complaining, chanting. Nobody talks about a Bly men's retreat as a place where traditional teaching is carried on with uncommon competence. There is more to the phenomenon than some charismatic quality in Bly, Hillman, and Meade. I see several more or less distinct characteristics in the teaching that make it work.

—They accept the responsibility of imparting knowledge they have worked hard to come by. Robert told the men in San Francisco that the abrogation of authority on the part of teachers is a sickness that started in the sixties, when teachers decided that presuming to teach was all too hierarchical, and that the proper alternative was to arrange chairs in a circle and let students decide out of shared ignorance what to study—such as sandalmaking, or nothing at all. His larger thesis was that we have become a society that so thoroughly despises authority and fears responsibility that no one wants to pick it up—"so we give it to Quayle!"

—But it is apparent that authoritative teaching does not, as conventional wisdom might have it, beget passivity among these men. The point is worth making if you believe that passivity is the occupying enemy force in education. Most collections of students represent a huge weight of passivity dreaded by all teachers and clergymen alive enough to notice it. It is easier to notice among students old enough not to be jumping off the desks. College graduates remember the vacuous silences in "discussion" classes and are frightened away from teaching. Highly paid motivational speakers generate electrical charges that make their listeners jerk and dance with simulated animation, but the deep passivity of the audience is encouraged, not transformed, by the one-way process, and people are conned, not taught. Listening to these tapes, I do not hear passivity. Though Robert Bly courts assent like a Baptist preacher ("Do you hear me? You understand what I'm saying. Can you feel it?"), he also invites dissent ("Does anybody want to attack me?"), as if a thesis always needs an antithesis if anything worthwhile is to be created. He wants a voice coming back at him that does not sound like an echo of his own. That is why his studio readings are flat, and why there is so much life in a teaching session like this one, where Bly, Hillman, and Meade act as both master and pupil to one another, discovering something new in the interaction. It wasn't always so. I heard Bly, Hillman, and Joseph Campbell in San Francisco ten years ago when they acted essentially as three solo performers. Now—and this may have come about while Campbell was still living—each teacher has his own thing to teach, like a piece of music he has worked on (a fairy tale, a group of Blake proverbs, a theme such as "The Hunger for the King in a Time of No Father"), but one man's solo calls up another's improvisation, and then there is music that no one had quite expected, some of it coming from the large group of men who start to pick up their own instruments and play.

—It is taken for granted that the "students" at a men's retreat "put their guts on the table," which is what Robert said made the hometown evening classes so much better than the usual college class, but what comes through from tapes of their sessions is the intellectual content. The teachers do not leave their brains or their erudition at home, nor do they proceed as if one could get at Freud, Jung, Blake, Homer, Yeats, or a complex fairy tale without engaging the mind as well as the senses and feelings. I also hear in this and other sessions Robert's orderly style of laying ideas out for the mind to work on ("I want to give you eight major ideas in Neoplatonism").

—The quality of the teaching in Robert Bly's groups has not been accounted for until one says that the subtext is always "How are we to live?" He teaches as if he believes William Carlos Williams's lines,

> It is difficult to get the news from poems,
>> but men die every day
>>> for lack of what is found there.

Kabekona Lake, March 1990

Phone call, Robert Bly. He has just one more essay to write for the book about Iron John, the hairy teacher. He wonders if the news from the book will be too difficult to get. "But I think I'm going to leave in all the literary and mythological references, and people can swim for their lives." I picture myself on the open sea, one of the swimmers. Coach Bly, bouzouki hanging from a lanyard around his neck, urges us on.

Kabekona Lake, October 6, 1991

Robert comes through our front door carrying bags of potatoes, squash, onions, and carrots bought along the road from Moose Lake. He also brings an October *Esquire,* the "Wild Men and Wimps" issue. In a full page picture he is tilted at an odd angle, as if he had looked too square straight up and down to go with the bold heading on the opposing page, "Robert Bly, Wild Thing." He reads aloud with some relish, as if from a novel, sentences about a Robert Bly who has no time to talk to interviewers or cab drivers and who thinks he's Beethoven.

We use his carrots and onions in the old spaghetti sauce recipe. The children he used to entertain at our table are long gone; our first grandchild is there, not ready for stories about Indian hunters, but appreciative of mashed squash.

Robert reads some poems begun today. Late in the evening I get around to saying that when he and Robert Moore use the phrase "the other world," as in "The King we're talking about here belongs to the other world, not this one," the meaning eludes me. Sometimes it sounds to my ear like a figure of speech, sometimes like an old Sunday school phrase, but either way I am missing the intent. He begins unhurriedly to answer, not with arguments supporting the existence of "the other world," but with images of several other worlds, never trying to draw a line between the literal and the metaphorical. There is the world from which Athena comes to speak to Achilles; the world of witches, giants, dwarfs; the world from which a soul falls into a baby being born; the world from which something comes to take over the body of a Haitian at night, riding it like a rider on a horse; the world of the little people, glimpsed and heard by the Celts, who have none of the gods' power in this world and little concern for human beings. . . . I am at sea among the images, swimming for my life. It is getting past my bedtime. I need a rest. Tomorrow will be soon enough, won't it, for more swimming, and these other strenuous exercises recommended by Robert Bly, such as diving into my own depths, descending into ashes, walking on water where there are no roads but only wind trails, flying up on fiery wings of desire . . . ? My old friend is keeping me awake.

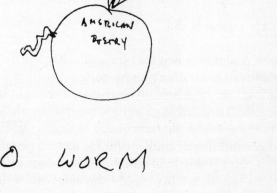

Robert Bly on the state of American poetry, circa 1968 *(courtesy of John Knoepfle).*

Milli and Michael Quam

Talking About Robert

Milli: IT'S INCREDIBLE TO THINK that we've known Robert for over thirty years, but I just realized that I don't know when you first met him.

Michael: Well, even though Robert and I both grew up in Madison, because of the age difference I guess Robert was gone — off to Harvard, New York City, or other remote places — while I was in school. So it wasn't until shortly after I graduated from high school that my parents mentioned something to me about a poet or writer — I don't remember what they called him — who was living outside of town on a farm. They chuckled about it and told me that people said that he sat up in the trees sometimes.

Milli: He probably did.

Michael: And that he flew the Norwegian flag. All those Norwegian-Americans in town didn't know quite what to make of this. Was this subversive, or ethnically patriotic? I thought it sounded fascinating. So, I decided to go out and meet this man. My father must have told me where the farm was. I remember going out there as a stranger and Robert took me in. He seemed genuinely interested in me, a naive young man who had just shown up in his yard. He talked to me about his place — the ramshackle house and the animals — and about his work. I liked the gleam in his eye and his wild hair.

Milli: Wild is a good word to describe my first impression, too. Noah was a baby, and Mary and Biddy were putting on a play. They had rigged up some elaborate costumes and kept us entertained with a steady stream of performances. From the conversation it was obvious that these performances were a daily occurrence. It was such a lively household—I was fascinated—and more than a little intimidated.

Michael: And Robert was publishing *The Fifties* then, so I subscribed. What Robert was writing was something entirely new to me. The fact that the poems in his first book, *Silence in the Snowy Fields,* were set in Madison, in Lac Qui Parle County—my home place—was an eye-opener. I had always thought of Madison as a mundane spot, with nothing that could inspire anything aesthetic. It's mostly to Robert's credit that I don't feel that way about it now. Because of Robert's work, I came to understand it as a place that could provide images that point us to the deeper meaning, beauty, and simplicity of life. I came to understand that because of what Robert was able to see in it AND because of his willingness to live there and not try to escape it. At that point in my life, I was into escaping!

Milli: Wasn't it about then that you arranged for Robert to come to read on our college campus? That was my first poetry reading, and I had no idea what to expect. And then Robert read in such a straightforward manner. His style certainly has changed in the last thirty years.

Michael: I had never seen Robert in a suit before. He stood at a podium, looking a bit uncomfortable, and when he was done reading, one of the earnest young men in the audience asked him if the imagery in *Silence in the Snowy Fields* wasn't all about death— probably a local English major exercising his critical skills. Robert looked a little surprised, and then he allowed as how you might see it that way. When I think about how Robert does readings now, how engaging they are, how he draws the audience into the experience—what a remarkable transformation!

Milli: Do you have any ideas about what brought about that transformation?

Michael: Well, my guess would be that Robert's work in the struggle against the Vietnam War was what shook him loose. When you read "The Teeth Mother Naked at Last" you can feel the fire in him.

Milli: That was about the same time that your father died and you asked Robert to read a few poems at the service. I know it was an experience that touched both of us deeply. Robert says that was the first time he had ever been asked to read in Madison. He had been living there, writing, publishing the journals, traveling around the country giving readings—for over ten years, but had never read in his hometown!

Michael: At the time I had no idea that my request had this significance for him. I went out to his house and asked him to read because I wanted something in my father's funeral that would have some meaning for me. I took along a bottle of whiskey, and we sat around sipping and talking. Robert told me then that my father had stopped out for a visit earlier that year. I was quite surprised, because I hadn't realized that he and my dad actually knew one another. I remember Robert seemed a little reluctant to read, but then he said he thought he had something he could offer. The next day at the funeral he read his prose poem "Finding the Father." It was a wonderful gift. In that moment I felt the loss of my father—it was like a sudden tumbling into grief, but I also felt the comfort of those final lines of the poem: "When you light the lamp you will see him. He sits there behind the door . . . the eyebrows so heavy, the forehead so light . . . lonely in his whole body, waiting for you." You know, when I think back on it, at the time I wasn't yet a father, and Robert was just a young father, not really mature in the experience. And the poem seems to be written for the children of the lost fathers. But when I read it now, twenty-five years and two grown children later, I see how much it captures the longing of the father for his children. And I'm amazed at how Robert was able to write this poem at that time in his life. I know he works on poems, sometimes for years, and he didn't publish this one until years later. Still, most of it was there long ago. How did he know that then, what that feels like? It must be the power of poetry itself to reveal even more than the poet can consciously comprehend, but this poem is also a testament to Robert's great courage and craft in giving himself over to that power.

Milli: After that we started going to any of his readings that were within driving distance—Chicago, St. Louis, Bloomington. And Robert was always so warm and happy to see us. If there was a party afterwards, he would be sure to see that we were invited. His readings were becoming wonderful events, with the music and the poetry— mostly his, but sometimes others, too, like Emily Dickinson—and all that talk about relationships between men and women. It was the seventies, and we were all trying to sort through our shifting identities and broken connections. Then we heard about the Great Mother Conference. Robert encouraged us to attend. After that first one—I think it was in 1979—I was hooked.

Michael: Just what do you think it was that hooked you?

Milli: Well, for one thing the community that had formed around him. There was something spiritual about it, but also something very earthy. That was what I always wanted the "community of saints" to feel like when I was active in the church. I didn't understand it, but I knew I wanted to be part of it. It was at that conference that I really began to see Robert as someone I could learn a lot from—both personally and professionally. I was captivated by the focus that year on the Greek gods and goddesses and Robert's use of the fairy stories. After that I made some important changes in my work. I had my clients reading Greek mythology and fairy tales as often as I could. It certainly opened up my own sense of what life's journey is all about.

Michael: That's Robert, the Jungian. That part of his thinking and work has made him a lot more powerful as a teacher. I don't know if it has made him more powerful as an artist, though. I wonder what he would say about that. I know you admire that side of him, but what has attracted me and continues to attract me to Robert's work and to his presence is the artist in him, and the poet, and also, the wild man. Maybe I should say the ecstatic man.

Milli: What do you mean?

Michael: Well, to me it's the way he uses myth, ritual, and other traditions to ignite something in himself. Not to analyze, just to experience it.

Milli: I think he grabs the anthropologist in you. The way that Robert draws from non-Western cultures, the way he honors their traditions without denigrating his own—surely that's what every anthropologist wants to do.

Michael: Yes, you're right. He's just working in a different discipline.

Milli: You know, that's how I feel as a family therapist. Robert uses the arena of the poet to address the same thing that therapists are addressing in our work. Of course, his work on the fairy stories, culminating in *Iron John,* has been very powerful. His understanding of the human experience, what it means to grow up male in our culture, and the new light he sheds on what is happening between men and women is important stuff. His book has touched a chord in lots of people. Clients who have never before read poetry or fairy tales gobble it up.

Michael: And Robert knows another kind of therapy—not psychotherapy, but the healing power of the ecstatic. I remember several times when Robert was able to get a group to move into another level of feeling in a very tense situation. He seemed to be following his instinct—and that instinct led him to pull the group into an ecstatic experience. One that comes to mind happened just this last summer at the Great Mother Conference in Montana. A major misunderstanding flared up into open conflict. Then there was a community gathering during which people expressed their feelings very sharply about what had gone wrong. The crisis occurred because some people felt wounded by some things that Robert had said or done. Then, in resolving things, I'm sure some more wounding occurred, and no doubt Robert felt wounded, also. A lot of people were feeling pretty raw. Others were puzzled and dismayed by the harsh words that had been spoken. There was a need for some kind of healing. Later that night—do you remember?—David Whetstone led us in Sufi singing. We were in the same building where we had met earlier. We didn't understand the words—we were basically just learning sounds and rhythms. As we were singing, Robert began pulling us—with his body and his voice and his eyes— pulling the group into a powerful ecstatic singing and dancing experience within which he was a participant leader. I remember being struck by how Robert, a Norwegian-American Lutheran man, was able, through that other tradition—that Sufi tradition—to begin the healing process.

Milli: I've always admired the way Robert is willing to be right in the thick of things, listening and thinking, taking the guilt or accepting the blame, but also being part of the solution. I think it must hurt him, and yet he is willing to be hurt and go through the process—that's how we get to the healing. You know, you called Robert a participant leader. It is a hard role to play and not many people can do it well. At a reading Robert lets you know, without it being confessional, that he is reading for or about himself as well as for you. It takes a lot of courage to follow your instincts like that.

Michael: And Robert is usually willing to take some emotional risks whether he is teaching or reading. I remember two years ago when we were in Madison for the "All School Reunion." They asked Robert to come back to town to read. He had been gone for a long time, but his mother still lives there. She was there at the reading, sitting in the front row in a wheelchair. And the audience was primarily made up of townspeople, many of whom had known him and his family throughout his lifetime. When he started to talk about his father and about his father's alcoholism, it just stunned me that he had the courage to do that. He spoke so honestly, straight from the heart, with his mother and all these family acquaintances right there in front of him in that small auditorium—a former Lutheran church—in a farming community where people don't talk openly about such things. Some people probably felt that was insensitive or cruel, but I hope that many people understood.

Milli: I think they did. I was very touched. He was conscious that his mother and his nieces were there. He addressed them directly at times and frequently looked at them as he spoke. Without knowing why, I found myself crying. I think I was awestruck. It felt like a privilege to be part of the experience—after all, Madison wasn't my hometown.

Michael: Of course, one of the reasons why I think of Robert as a mentor is because he grew up in the same town I did, and he never has abandoned his roots. He is very much a son of that upbringing, that place and that tradition, and yet he has never let it limit him. He immersed himself in it all, but he didn't say this is all there is or this is all I'm going to be. That place, that way of life, has always been, I think, at the core of his identity and his personal awareness, and yet he has grown larger and has allowed all of these other traditions to reach him. And then, of course, as we were saying earlier, as a poet and a teacher, he has tried to show people you don't have to abandon your roots.

Milli: Maybe this is a good place to close this conversation. But I'd like to say one more thing. Every time I begin talking with anyone about Robert, I start chuckling to myself. He makes me laugh and my laughter holds my admiration and respect for him.

Michael: Yes, I heartily agree. So here's to you, Robert, in your sixty-fifth year—our love and esteem to a great poet, a fine and sensitive teacher, and a wonderful man. Thank you for taking time with us, for letting us in on your work and life. Have a glass of wine and a few good laughs on us. Lean back and enjoy it.

Louis Jenkins

How I Discovered Robert Bly

IT WAS 1965 OR '66. My first wife and I were living in Colorado Springs, I was working in a library, and I was going to be a poet. I had determined this a few years before, sitting in a car outside the college in my hometown, Enid, Oklahoma, watching the rain fall and deciding not to go to the mandatory religion class . . . ever again, but to be a poet instead. I hadn't, really, the vaguest notion of how to go about being a poet. This was a kind of family tradition, to embark on a big project without training or skill, without the proper tools, but with a lot of confidence. "Let's rewire the house." How hard could it be? I had written some poems by this time. I wrote bad imitations of Byron, of T. S. Eliot, of Robert Frost. . . .

Ignorance and naiveté were, I think, common among young, aspiring poets of the Midwest. There was almost no contemporary poetry available in libraries or bookstores and no one to talk to about it. My case may have been one of the worst, though years later a friend told me that when he was in high school he thought he'd become a poet because no one else was writing poetry anymore. Around 1963 I set off on my quest to become a poet, dragging my bride with me from town to town. I didn't know any poets and I had never heard of a writers' workshop.

Silence in the Snowy Fields seemed like a strange title to me, but promising. I opened the book and read:

> Sometimes riding in a car, in Wisconsin
> Or Illinois, you notice those dark telephone poles
> One by one lift themselves out of the fence line
> And slowly leap on the gray sky—
> And past them, the snowy fields.

It was electrifying. I thought poets all lived in England or New York, someplace far away. This was the landscape I knew and the language I knew, only more, it was poetry. I read:

> We see stiff weeds and brownish stubble,
> And white snow left now only in the wheeltracks of
>   the combine.

I had driven the combine that made those wheeltracks! I loved the poems and read them over and over. I read:

> The strong winds of the box elder tree,
> Plunging in the wind, call us to disappear
> Into the wilds of the universe
> Where we shall sit at the foot of a plant,
> And live forever, like the dust.

I read:

> Beneath the waters, since I was a boy,
> I have dreamt of strange and dark treasures,
> Not of gold, or strange stones, but the true
> Gift, beneath the pale lakes of Minnesota.

It was what I dreamed, what I wanted. I puzzled over the poems. So simple, yet they contained so much. The poems were full of things I knew, barns, farmhouses, fields . . . ordinary midwestern landscape, dull as dirt, suddenly transformed, their mystery lighted up like the gas in a neon tube. As Robert has written elsewhere:

> how beautiful the things are that you did not notice before!
> A few sweetclover plants
> along the road to Bellingham,
> culvert ends poking out of driveways,
> wooden corncribs, slowly falling,
> what no one loves, no one rushes toward or shouts about,
> what lives like the new moon,
> and the wind
> blowing against the rumps of grazing cows.

On the back cover of *Silence in the Snowy Fields* I read: "Robert Bly, poet, editor, and translator, lives on a farm near Madison, Minnesota, in the region where he was born." I thought, "If I write to Robert Bly, Madison, Minnesota, it's a small town, he'll get the letter." How hard could it be? I carefully composed a letter saying something about how much I liked his poems and, of course, enclosing some of mine. I waited. In a week or so an envelope came with a small note that had THE SIXTIES, Odin House, Minnesota, Editor Robert Bly, printed at the top, along with the press logo, Odin on his horse. And some squiggly handwriting. I remember sitting at the dining room table in my uncle's house and my uncle and I speculating about the handwriting and the importance of the note. "He was in a hurry," I said. "No," my uncle said, "this guy knows what he's doing." My uncle knew nothing about poetry or poets, or handwriting analysis for that matter, but it was a touching moment, our serious scrutiny of the letter under the dining room lamp.

It didn't occur to me that hundreds of other young would-be poets were also writing to Robert at the time I was, that the poems had touched other young writers in the same way they had touched me. I met a poet recently who told me her experience. She wrote Robert while she was attending college and, naturally, enclosed some of her poetry. When she read Robert's reply she was devastated by the criticism. She quit writing poetry entirely for the next twenty years. Recently she began writing again and reread Robert's note. In the light of experience she realized that the note contained many more encouraging words than criticizing words. She realized, also, how generous Robert had been to take time to respond to her work, something she had taken for granted at the time.

I was not discouraged by Robert's note to me. I was elated, even though Robert said the poems contained way too much "book language." I felt for the first time I had real direction. I ordered copies of books and *The Sixties* magazine from Odin House. I read translations of poems by poets I'd never heard of, from Spain, Norway, Chile, and I read poems by Americans, James Wright, Louis Simpson, Donald Hall. . . . A new world opened.

In 1967 I was living in Kansas, going to college again, and

slowly learning to write. Now instead of bad imitations of Byron I wrote bad imitations of Robert Bly (and James Wright and others). One day I decided I needed to visit Robert Bly in Madison. I set out hitchhiking with ten dollars and a small packsack. It would be easy, Madison was straight north. Michael Dennis Browne has written beautifully about imagining James Wright long before he met him, his looks, his personality, a picture that was, naturally, completely wrong. I must have had some picture of Robert Bly in my mind also, but after meeting the real Robert Bly that picture completely vanished. I'm sure I imagined that I would be the only one to arrive at his farm like this and that I would surely be welcome. I don't know what I intended to say to Robert or what I thought he would say to me. I learned, years later, that, in fact, so many young poets came to the farm that they had to be turned away. There was a rule. If they came from more than five hundred miles away they could stay overnight, otherwise they were sent packing. I suppose I would have qualified for an overnight stay but I never made it. I spent the better part of a day standing alongside the highway north of Marysville, Kansas. When night fell I began hitching on both sides of the road. Finally, a truck headed for Dallas took me back to Wichita.

It would be after several more years, when events in my life brought me to Duluth to live, that I actually met Robert Bly, almost by accident, and formed a friendship I deeply value. And it was a long time before I wrote anything worth keeping.

Patrick Herriges

My Hometown

Introduction: Robert Bly's Hometown

MADISON, MINNESOTA, IS PLATTED on the Coteau de Prairies, the eastern "coast" of the Great Plains, on land drained by the Lac Qui Parle and Yellow Bank rivers, tributaries of the Minnesota, which wanders southward, through a great valley carved by glacial River Warren, to Mankato—where, finding no outlet, it trudges north again to enter the Mississippi at St. Paul. Forty miles north of Madison, at Browns Valley, is a spring-fed marsh from which originate the Minnesota and the north-flowing Bois de Sioux/Red River of the North (recognizable on maps as an acute westerly bend in the Minnesota-South Dakota border). Robert Bly's hometown was built on buffalo grassland, on sunken Precambrian highlands that were the southern shore of ancient Lake Agassiz. It was founded in 1885 by the trading partners of German and Norwegian farmers. When the railway came west (the Minneapolis and St. Louis, M&StL, or "midnight and still later") it bypassed Lac Qui Parle village, then the county seat, and cut a line through the prairie to Madison and on to South Dakota. Our entrepreneur grandfathers (who welcomed fences, telegraph wires, roadways, and other lines in the prairie) saw the chance to put a governmental base beneath their growing commercial success. On a cold November night in 1886, in obedience to a widely spoken citizens' mandate, they seized the courthouse records, loaded the building itself onto wagons, and, through several days of blizzards and breakdowns, moved it to Madison. (My grandfather, Gerhard Herriges, was one of these pirate pioneers. He also built many of the town's churches and civic buildings, cofounded a milling company, and helped organize the county fair.)

Robert Bly grew up on a farm just west of this town. Like most of Madison's high school graduates, he left home. Unlike the mainstream, he came back. In 1956, Robert moved into a farmhouse near the Bly homestead, converted a chicken coop to a writing studio, and went to work.

He showed up one day at a high school homeroom. My classmates and I weren't quite ready for this intense, earnest teacher. We weren't ready for poetry. We fidgeted. Our minds were on sports, human gender, and whatever else high school seniors thought about in 1957. Robert Bly informed us clearly that he was not there to be ignored; he demanded our attention.

At the end of that year (like most of Madison's high school graduates) I left home, returning only during academic breaks. After two years of good education at St. John's University, I got the picture: there was a real, living, working poet in my hometown. My friend Michael Quam bravely broke the ice. Robert and Carol graciously received us at the farmhouse, fed us food, wine, and ideas, and said, "Come again." I was young and foolish, but not a fool. For years thereafter, my trips home had a routine that my parents learned to accept, if not understand: always an evening at the Blys'. I ate my mother's roasts and hotdishes, and I watched TV with my father; at the Blys', I ate food for my mind and soul.

After college, my first married summer was spent in Madison, working for my father. My wife and I had a second-floor apartment north of the high school. One Saturday morning, a group of children knocked on our door and asked to see the snakes. A visiting friend, Kevin Madden, led them to the bathroom, where I was shaving. "This is the strangest life form we have here," he said. The children described a trail of hand-painted signs worded: "Reptile Gardens," "Boa Constrictors," "Exotic Serpents."

This was clearly the work of Bly coyotes. We retaliated with what we believed to be the ultimate attraction in that Norwegian community. We put up signs pointing the way to the Bly farmhouse, announcing: "Free Coffee."

That summer, and in visits home during the years after, I was given entrée to an evolving literary movement. There were guests

(James Wright, John Logan); letters full of poems for the *Sixties* and *Seventies;* my sister, Nancy, spent a college summer typing and filing for Robert. I was shown new essays and poems. I heard the story of James Dickey's "Crunk" article, rejected by Robert, and later I proofed the Blue Toad award to Dickey. Robert Bly showed me his work, and asked my opinion. This was heady stuff for a young graduate student. It was, I know now, the incredible gift of a great teacher. It was a gift Robert gave to those in the community who took an interest in his work, and who did not distance themselves from his friendship.

In general, however, Madison's people are a passive, inward lot—as if they had absorbed the brooding personality of the buffalo. Maybe the prairie engenders this affect in its children: they present an outward calm and cheerfulness, and say little about their ideas or emotions. But the truth seeps out: Madison folk generally regarded Alice and Jacob Bly's son as eccentric. There was little if any consciousness about his work. Until recently, in fact, Madison residents have been generally ignorant of Robert's contributions to poetry, and of his creation of the mythopoetic men's movement—becoming aware of their native son in about the same way as has American society in general.

But there was a compelling expression of new awareness during a July 1990 "All Class Reunion" commemorating the closing of the high school. Robert read to a standing-room crowd at the former Ness Lutheran Church, now the Prairie Arts Center (one of Gerhard's buildings). The reading was a one-hour masterpiece—a time capsule of Robert's poetry, candid discussion of his relationship to his father, and an introduction to the core ideas of the men's movement. The audience—homecomers and continuing residents (Alice Bly among them)—delivered a standing ovation.

I think that artists and leaders must consciously shed their birthplace skins. Without contempt for Madison and its people—indeed, with love and respect for their good humor and basic decency—I say that its culture impedes the development of art or leadership. The Madisons of our lives dress their children in words such as these: "Don't expect too much"; "don't rock the boat"; "find something secure to do with your life."

Robert Bly met the challenge implicit in such words, discarded the coverings of his community (even while living there; surely an existential victory), and even more than that: this great teacher has created new communities of learning across the nation and around the world. How amazing, as one of Madison's children, to realize that one of us—a native son—has given such gifts to men and women everywhere.

Here is a song grown out of brooding about our hometown. It is a little gift to express the love I feel for this man who, more than any other, is my teacher and mentor.

My Hometown
Additional Lyrics

1. *See music*

2. Endless sky—
   Father of buffalo kingdoms.
   Square-mile farmland
   Fence-line roadways
   Lights from distant towns . . .
   See how they shine, oh they
        shine.

   First chorus: See music

3. God is love—
   Weekly performance of
        churchsongs and
        sermons.
   In Excelsis
   Sola Fides
   Everlasting themes . . .
   See how they shine, oh they
        shine.

And the years roll by
And the dreams all die
And you think of home
When you hear the
     churchbells ring
Sunday morning

4. In his eyes—
   Frail broken child of the
        prairie
   Fear of falling
   Fallen angel
   Caught in space and time—
   My father's eyes, in his eyes.

   And the years roll by
   And your plans run dry
   And you make a home
   And in the ashes of your
        dreams
   Something shining . . .

MY HOMETOWN

WORDS AND MUSIC BY PATRICK HERRIGES ©1991

JAZZ WALTZ, en dehors ♩=120

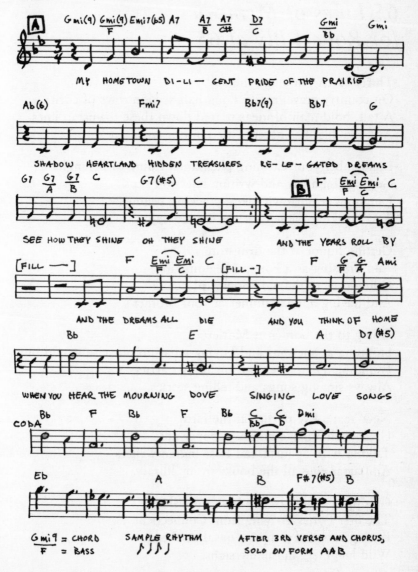

Gmi9/F = CHORD

SAMPLE RHYTHM

AFTER 3RD VERSE AND CHORUS,
SOLO ON FORM AAB

William Duffy

65 Lines of Memories for Robert Bly at 65

Thirty-seven years ago this fall
On country gravel roads along half-section rows of corn
A tall, bold man of ideas roared down these township lines
And the dust has never settled in our souls.

I remember your cleaning pheasants, riding to Bellingham
Getting Jim a car and writing rejection slips
Laughing at our own jokes, cracking peanuts
And drinking pitchers at the old Carcajou.

Getting liquor at the drugstore
And dressing as a Foreign Legionnaire
Going over to the old "home" place
And having Sunday dinner at your brother's.

Going to the border at Marietta
Stopping at auctions and buying what no one else would buy
Founding *The Fifties* and breaking barriers
Always singing songs and telling stories.

New Year's Eve parties at the farm
Greenwich Village and newspaper ads
Talking with Spanish and East Indian writers
And arranging all the books in my library.

Getting censored by the Irish publisher
The first *Fifties* arriving from Connecticut
Petting cats and puppies; nasal snickers,
Wild laughter, and many sighs.

Hearing poetry at the Y in N.Y.C.
Selling ice to L. T. on the phone
Having tea with D. Levertov and calling
On the famed anthologist.

Translating verse, and bringing a corn-cob pipe to Glenview
Picking up a *Fifties* issue on the New York docks
Reading poetry with Louie at NYU while you chaired,
All up till four, talking until the streetlights faded.

Getting nasty comments back on rejection slips
Hearing from a Nobel Prize writer
Frying eggs and bacon for our breakfasts
Listening to sad Civil War songs.

A golden vest in New York, a cup and saucer in Iowa City
A basement door and hammock in Pine Island
A Hudson, wide and roomy, out at Madison
And a hundred waves for the Tangiers train.

Writing and watching at a UMD hockey game
Wearing chesterfield coats and homburg hats
Driving like madmen down the Ave. of the Americas
And correcting lengthy proof sheets.

Floating in a boat at dawn and writing
Picking porcupine quills from a prickly dog
Sleeping late in the old chicken house
And shooting a .22 pistol in the floor.

You're a cellar full of sparkling wines
A garden of wild herbs
A wild rose along the railroad tracks
A tiny grain of sand behind our eyes.

You have changed the seasons of our lives
While riding roaming mustangs,
Have slipped the rusty shackles from our thoughts
And picked the ageless poets clean.

You're as loyal as a good farm dog
As courageous as a roadside badger
As sentimental as an Oslo sailor
And as carefree as a hired man.

My memories of you are in these lines
My prayers for you are in your pockets
My thoughts of you are stored in secret silver files
And my best wishes for you, old friend,
Are whispered only by the angels.

John Knoepfle

A Green Snake Interview:
Speaking of Robert Bly

Q: You are not listening again.

A: yes I was what were you saying
I had to glance at the sports page
see to the cards they are five games out
things heating up in the national league

Q: I was telling you about the hunter in
Robert Bly's *Iron John.*

A: oh yes he had a dog I remember that story
what happened to the dog I wonder

Q: Why, Iron John pulled it down into the swamp
and that was the last of the hunter's dog.
See you can read about it yourself.

A: why this happens on page 5 and the book
lets see goes on for 270 pages
do you mean to tell me a reader
works all the way through this book
and never learns what happens to the dog

Q: Stop being stupid. The dog doesn't matter.

A: thats what you say but I tell you
the whole country must be wondering
did iron john make a pet out of it or did he

eat the dog or what
robert bly should have known better than to
let a thing like that hang by its ears
given the kind of book he was writing

Q: Can we get on with this interview?

A: dogs are important and how about
those dogs of job that licked the poor mans
wounds and there was the little
dog of tobias runs out to meet his good master
coming home and all those years gone by and
himself now with the camels and goats and a big family
and that little dog yapping so the blind
father knows it is his son banging at the gate
and then later the archangel raphael
peels the old mans eyes so he can see his son
yes and what about that great old dog of odysseus

Q: Will you please stop?

A: you cant have decent closure without a dog
bly should have done something about that dog

Q: Just give me a simple answer. When did you
first hear about Robert Bly?

A: oh I was living in belleville
that was on the bluffs in illinois
laurette lane a new subdivision and the young
woman next door had a boxer

Q: Stop!

A: and at the head of the street there was
this huge young dog

Q: I don't want to hear about anymore damned dogs.

A: well I cant speak for the boxer
but the man who owned the puppy was the pastor
at our lady of lourdes and it was
a saint bernard it just cant be
a dog like that would be damned

Q: All right, all right.

A: its not thinkable a saint bernard in hell

Q: Would you please continue.

A: it was in the late fifties
my mind goes to feathers now lets see
the *floating bear* was coming in the mail from
leroi jones and I remember *on the road* how I
could find freedom speeding across the u.s. in a
big car sitting there with my hair blowing
and not a stitch on and yes about that time
came *new world* writing with blys j p morgan poems
and my wife said look at these have you
ever seen anything like these poems and I said
no I havnt because you know those poems
were blowing the fifties away and they were not
anything at all like the museum poems
being hung on the walls of the quarterlies

Q: What do you remember about those poems?

A: well as I was telling you there was that
image of shredded truck tires on highway shoulders
country of slob culture wasting itself
but there was that serene aspect too
I remember it in the soft light of the

shell station in the anywhere dark of blys
rural minnesota or a thousand small towns
I had driven through it myself

Q: You found that his poems were special, then?

A: well the reverence for place
suffering the land into the imagined
world of the psyche and I woke to that because
you were never driven from that
god hungering world really and there are times
when that knowledge is so intense
the hours turn to golden coins

Q: I think you are beginning to put it on with a trowel.

A: well I remember a sliver of moonlight
on a dark evening several years ago
when I drove through pipestone
with peg and linda hogan and you could hear
the country singing to itself over and over
the sparrow has found a house the swallow
a nest for herself psalms for the dark travelers
when I come to battle I shout
I shout as I stand in my place

Q: Peg?

A: my wife we were taking linda to the
festival in marshall

Q: Yes, well, what did you do when you read
the J. P. Morgan poems?

A: I wrote bly a letter and he replied in his
spidery hand sent me some *fifties* also

Q: And you met him shortly after, I suppose.

A: no when was that wait he sent his letter in
july 59 but it wasnt until 63 when he read
at saint louis university that we met
it was an important moment for me

Q: Tell me about it.

A: well I remember he came to our apartment
on heman avenue we were living in
university city then a two bedroom affair
with a solarium the castros moved into the
identical apartment on the top floor but that was
after we moved to trinity

Q: You are wandering off the subject again?

A: well details are important the finkels
were east of us on interdrive and the elkins
were south on leland
but anyway bly came and stood at our door
with a package of fish in his hand not the
frozen kind you know
so we had to eat that for dinner

Q: How was it?

A: it was all right I guess of course
it wasnt like enjoying a plate of squid
on greek independence day 25th of march I think
and lets see peter simpson came over that night

Q: Simpson!

A: you remember pete wrote *stealing home*

probably more national league ball players
have read his book than any poet alive
I mean he does a sports column and the cards
all know him yes willie mcgee
gave him his baseball cap
but he wasnt writing sports then
he was alderman of the 28th ward
I go a long way back with pete we taught
comp in east st louis in the fifties

Q: Is all this important?

A: oh yes you see robert
he had never been to a burlesque show
and he was in his minnesota farm boy role
wanting to experience the big city and take one in
so pete drove and we went downtown

Q: You mean to tell me you went to a strip tease?

A: well we were poets so it was all right
except that pete he didnt want
anyone to notice him because he was an alderman
so he tried to hunch down into his coat collar
like a mud turtle but robert and I
we sat with our heads up

Q: What do you remember about the
performance, if anything?

A: the skits were covered with moss
I can tell you that one with the coxeys army
must have been around since 1895
and to tell the truth the dancers were a
tired boodle old hoofers scarcely able at
holding their smiles except for the one

cheery blonde girl who woke up the audience
that theater was a bit of st louis history
I think frank james welcomed the patrons there
around the turn of the century
and I know the post dispatch did a spread on it
when the building was demolished said the girls
were sentimental about leaving the house
took the porcelain doorknobs for keepsakes

Q: What did Bly think about the performance?

A: oh when we were driving back
he launched into an important monologue
about life and art and vivaciousness
and how the blonde dancer was the true artist

Q: Do you remember anything specific? This
could be important.

A: no it was just refined birdshit really

Q: Please.

A: peter didnt have air conditioning
so the citizens of st louis got a treat that night
robert and I with a rousing on-na-wan-a-ho-e-no
on the way home while pete turned up his collar

Q: What was it you were singing?

A: well you have to be sioux to do it well
but I guess we did not do it too badly
it was amazing I dont know how many people in st louis
could have sung it at that time
but of course now I imagine everybody knows it
what with the new age people multiplying

and increasing but just a minute oh yes
the theater it was the grand theater
pete tells me that jenny lind sang there
a place famous for its acoustics
and the word out is the dancers
took a little bit more off than they should have
a bright showering at the very end
oh the extra marvels and revelations

Q: What else happened during that weekend?

A: well pete took robert to see
the aldermanic chambers there was a brass
cuspidor by each aldermans desk in case
one of them wanted to spit

Q: Don't go any further. Why did you say that the
weekend was important for you?

A: because evenings in the solarium
robert went through all that I had written
challenging the poems line for line
it was the acid test and it burned me
but he did me a good turn you know
gave me the careful edit they needed
the moment for the dispassionate look
and what was polished finally was the copy
for *rivers into islands* which the
university of chicago brought out in 65

Q: I am not sure I could stand that.

A: he softened the blows a little
told me how he had done a marathon poetry edit
with donald hall jim wright and louis simpson and
how nobody got a poem through without hearing

what is this crap how could you have written
a line as dumb as this whoever told you
you were a poet made a mistake and such horrors
he said that he thought by the time
he paraded out his tenth poem it would get through
but it didnt not one poem ever got through

Q: Do you remember anything else about the weekend?

A: no that was about the sum of it
well we did exchange some stories he told me
the wobbly one about the bull and the tin whistle
and I gave him the lady and the kangaroo

Q: I know that kangaroo joke. It is one you have to
tell behind the barn, isn't it?

A: not if you explain it as an allegory

Q: An allegory!

A: why yes the lady is the soul you understand
and the kangaroo represents carnal desire
and the zookeeper is spiritual striving
see he has to catch the roo and cage it again
has to keep carnality within bounds so to speak

Q: If that joke is an allegory, I am a minister.

A: how strange you know I heard that robert
told the story to a conference of ministers and it
spread all over the northern great lakes

Q: I hope you are finished with this matter.

A: it is getting late so maybe
we ought to end the interview now

Q: Why, yes, I am suprised that you should be
so accommodating.

A: as a matter of fact well I should
tell you I was reading through some old
letters notes from robert that go back to the
late fifties

Q: Were you!

A: yes and I found an item in the packet
that I had forgotten you know my memory and
what not

Q: What was it?

A: well why dont I just speak directly to robert

Q: You can't do that. This is an interview.

A: see if he reads this interview as you call it
he will get my message and it will save me some
postage

Q: This is not to be tolerated. You can't
just go around mixing genres this way.

A: yes I can Im retired and I can
do anything I want hey robert are you there
guess what I found in your letters

Q: Oh, this ruins all the afternoon's effort.

A: robert when you are putting your works
in order you know as a bequest to some library
or a foundation I want to tell you

I have the typed transcript of your introduction
for the translations of george trakl yes
two full pages with corrections it looks like
there are two hands or more its good copy
but you should know the pages have suffered
some smoke damage it was a miracle
your letters survived the fire that destroyed
my study some eight years ago

Q: Have you finished your direct address?

A: thats what it was you say
why this is amazing

Q: Yes, and I am ready to leave now.

A: before you go what havnt you noticed

Q: I am not sure that I should answer, but what
haven't I noticed?

A: the dog isnt in the house

Q: That is true. I thought maybe you
had him tied up in the yard so that he wouldn't
bite me again.

A: my dog never bit you but I will let that pass
just ask me where the dog is

Q: I shouldn't, but where is your dog?

A: oh hes gone to the canine chateau

Q: Chateau? Oh, what have I done!

A: why yes dogs are very sociable they
meet from the whole county once a year
and they have a big bark

Q: Where is my coat?

A: they give papers just like mla in chicago

Q: I am getting out as fast as I can.

A: last year this smooth dachshund
presented a paper called "grim hounds in *kinder
und hausmärchen:* animal helpers without honor"

Q: Good-bye.

A: broke all the mutts up oh
they were moaning and crying it was terrible
our dog was depressed for a month

Q: I am not coming back.

A: oh well look out for the badger

Frederick Manfred

A Good Neighbor

ROBERT BLY HAS ALWAYS BEEN a good neighbor to me. When he lived out in the country near Madison, Minnesota, he often invited me up to stay for a few days. This was especially true when Thomas McGrath came down from Fargo-Moorhead or James Wright out from Minneapolis. Robert often came to my home up on the Blue Mounds north of Luverne. Once he brought out that strange shy fellow from Chicago, Bill Knott. I'd looked forward to talking with Knott, but the trouble was the moment Knott arrived in my yard, he looked around, spotted a huge purple Sioux quartzite boulder, asked if he could sit on it. So while the rest of us argued in the house over sandwiches and coffee about mothers and fathers, Knott communed with just-then-found nature's graces. I was never able to find those particular graces. But during that whole day there was no gesture or suggestion from Robert that we interrupt Bill Knott's afternoon worship.

Once Robert asked for a special hour with me. He had a message for me. It was about two women I knew. He said he felt they were doing me harm. Of course he was right. And I had already worked myself around to handle it or them on my own terms and my own times.

I once helped Robert, too. While visiting him one day, I happened to remark that he should prune his apple trees and he'd have bushels of apples. Instantly he asked me how to prune them. So I got a pruning knife and a saw and showed him how. He called all his children around him to watch how it had to be done. This was in the spring. That fall he called me to tell me they had bushels of apples.

I like to think that while we rejoice in each other's poetic jumps and in each other's cadences, we also appreciate each other's suggestions as to how to prune the tree of life in our private Edens.

Meridel Le Sueur

Plains Poet

The struggle of poets on our earth
Enrich the soil
Poet of suffering
You showed me the poet of Dakota plains
No divisions
Embrace of pain
We weigh the grain
Heal the massive wound
On fragile flesh
Come to the meadow of bloom you cried
Abloom together
Gather the seed
You have the bloom of gathered blossoms
Poet abreast the prairie
Appeared to me as a young girl
Out of Dakota
Out of broken soil
Poisoned earth
Bloodied roads
Split continent
Oh poet male a light in bloom
Oh meadow bloom from broken fissures
Despair
Dark son
Dried in dark
We long for you to take the big darkened meadow
Till breaking thundering web
Earth continent splitting
Norwegian poets cry of bringing split into Dakota womb space
Oh come together wheat kernel

Risen to meet the new horizon
We look to you final dark drought
Poet of prairie horizon
Hunger for blooming meadow
Oh tall fresh walker on high horizon
Through broken light
To pit and bloom in Dakota dark
The song is in the earth
Spears, swords of spring
Thrusting up the sword of generation
Poet in the meadow
Come out of split seed
To gather to the earth breast
To spring up bright meadows of lovers and warriors.

Top: *Farm buildings (chicken coop and occasional guest house on left), Madison, Minnesota, 1966 (David Bly photo).*
Bottom: *Converted schoolhouse writing shack, Madison, Minnesota, 1973 (Paul Feroe photo).*

Bill Holm

Why I Live in Minneota:
A Birthday Essay for Robert Bly

AT THE END OF THE FIFTIES, my high school years, western Minnesota looked to me like a mental wasteland, a psychological bowel obstruction. It wasn't, but I had to get outside of it to see that. I wanted to write poetry, play Bach fugues, be politically disagreeable, and skip pep rallies, football games, 4-H, and Luther League. Eisenhower was president, Dulles was preaching, and J. Edgar Hoover was watching. In 1960, I went into the Minneota drugstore, the only place in town to buy books, and rifled the paperback book rack for what news I could find from the outside world. I had already found D. H. Lawrence, Oscar Williams, and R. H. Tawney there, so I knew something was going on somewhere. *New World Writing #15* had arrived, and for only 75 cents, I could have a go at "Contemporary Icelandic Poetry," as the cover announced. I was an Icelander myself, so that meant there was hope to see my name in print before I was dead. I plunked down the six bits and started reading. The Icelanders proved to be poor stuff, so I put the magazine away until a few years later.

By 1962 I had escaped to Gustavus and begun writing tortured imitations of T. S. Eliot and Pound. My teacher, Elmer Suderman, asked me one day whether I'd met my poet-neighbor Robert Bly in Madison, Minnesota. "Can't be a poet there," I said smugly. "They're all devout Norwegians." He showed me *New World Writing #15,* the very book I owned but hadn't explored. There they lay on the page: "Poems for the Ascension of J. P. Morgan" by Robert Bly, "who lives on a farm near Madison, Minnesota," thirty miles north of my misery.

I read with delight. Here was what I wanted from American poetry, culture, politics, daily life—and hadn't found: cranky

attacks on smug Lutherans, respectable Republicans, the "malefac-
tors of great wealth," and the killers of joy in the spirit and the body.

> Here Morgan dies like a dog among whispers of angels. . . .
> . . . With a lily the Pope meets
> A delegation of waves, and blesses the associations
> Of the ocean . . .

> . . . We live among the mountain-high papers
> Of the corporations and the formal insults of the "westerns."

This mad Norwegian brought in the prose world of public stupidity
and venality, quoted it — then left it stand alone to wither in the shade
of the poems around it. Here was the groveling stewardship appeal
from Gloria Dei Lutheran Church in St. Paul, stupid remarks by
Herbert Hoover about the poor, a "count your blessings" proclama-
tion from the mayor of Madison, a defense of commercials and
"soaps" from the head of Proctor & Gamble. This was the dumb
world that hovered over Minneota, that no one dared fight, and a
Norwegian from Madison had stood up to it in a New York
magazine. He was as Lutheran and Scandinavian as I was, and he
had said it! Out of such moments is our frail human courage against
power born.

Against that prose world, he set wild, strange, passionate
images and juxtapositions, the world of history and politics bump-
ing into the world of dreams and intuition.

> The Shell Stations dancing on varnished stones . . .
> Oklahoma is dancing on rotten leaves.

> The gold grasshoppers
> Dive in the flood of Morgan's tears. . . .
> [The Chinamen's] pigtails weave
> A black frame around my grandfather's face.

> The rich man in his red hat
> Cannot hear

The weeping in the pueblos of the lily,
Or the dark tears in the shacks of the oats.

Oats! Imagine them in a poem! I had shoveled them in a granary, choking on dust and chaff, and here they were in a poem! There were no oats or Shell Stations in T. S. Eliot!

Names out of my own history appeared doing strange things in these wonderful lines:

For Three American Heroes

I think of the sour dead
In their kraals of straw,
Which they must move
Often, because
Of the rising water,
That they look out
At times, and see
On roof peaks perched
The soul of Rockefeller
Sorting potatoes,
And the soul of Willkie
Braiding tears together,
And the soul of Altgeld
Nearly covered
With wedding rings,
And the dead in the dawn
Air scratch their heads.

The daily details of a life like my own father's were written down with simplicity and dignity—no ranting against usury or chanting in Sanskrit.

I too am still shocking grain, as I did as a boy, dog tired,
And my great-grandfather steps on his ship.

What choice did I have? I went to Madison to see for myself whether this probably imaginary Robert Bly existed. Madison is half an hour north of Minneota on county roads, past sloughs, corn-fields, red barns, feed lots, silos, the St. Leo church, the Dawson elevator, a few hundred mailboxes with the names of Belgians, Germans, Norwegians, who likely read no poetry. I drove around Madison a little wondering how to find a Bly or whether this was a goose chase. On Highway 75, I saw a "Books" sign and pulled in. What was Madison doing with a bookstore? Inside I found Sunday School books, hymnals, devotional tracts, "Living for Jesus," but no J. P. Morgan. A white haired lady, maybe seventy, eyed me. "Can I help you, young man?" I was nineteen or twenty, a plump, pink, beardless pillar of longing.

"I was wondering if you had any books by Robert Bly. He's a fellow from Madison . . . writes poetry."

"Bly? Bly? Could that be Jacob's boy? I heard he moved home again. Let me call Jacob and Alice. I'll check for you then."

She didn't look exactly pleased at the mention of poetry, but you can never tell about elderly Norwegians.

"Jacob? This is Margaret at the store. A young fellow's in town looking for a Bly who writes pomes." (So she pronounced it.) "Oh, is it Bob, then? He's out on the home place now? I'll tell him."

She hung up the phone and gave me directions to a farm place a mile and a half out of town. I arrived at a prosperous-looking farm with a long driveway, plenty of livestock, a row of grain storage bins and silos, and a bunch of men out shelling corn. I'll be damned! I thought. This looks like a real farm. How can poetry go on here?

I walked up to the house and asked if I could see Mr. Bly for a few minutes. A woman looked at me as if I were a Lutheran Brotherhood trainee and directed me to the corn shellers. "He's the big fellow in the cap," she said.

I walked up to him, and temporarily handing his fork to someone, he acknowledged me. "What do you need?"

"I'm from Minneota, heard you wrote poetry, thought I'd visit a little, but I didn't mean to interupt your shelling."

He guffawed. "Hell, no, that's not me. You've got the wrong place. It's my brother—lives a half mile down the road in the red house. First place on the right after the mile road." He pointed.

I apologized. He laughed affably—but had the look of a man still astounded that anyone related to him could write that or that the big pink lump in front of him was interested in it. I drove down the road, found the red house, Norwegian flag and all, and my life has never been quite the same since.

I think all three of them came to the door, Robert, Carol pregnant with Biddy, and infant Mary. After a brief announcement that I was an Icelander from Minneota, a college student who loved and wrote poetry, admired "J. P. Morgan," and was astonished that anything so intelligent came from western Minnesota, I was ushered inside the red door, handed coffee in a chipped blue cup, and grilled intensively. Who did I read? What was going on in the colleges? Did I know about the bomb tests? I shot back questions. What in the hell are you doing here? Are there better poets than T. S. Eliot? Who should I read? Can you make poetry out of this? I gestured out the window; past the grove and the horse barn lay the great breathing flatness.

Meanwhile Mary crawled on my lap, trying to eat my Camels. We argued, told stories, speculated with such unabated vigor that she ate more than I smoked. Robert recited James Wright and Arthur Waley's Chinese translations. Books piled up next to my chair: copies of *The Fifties* and *The Sixties, The Lion's Tail and Eyes,* the new edition of *Silence in the Snowy Fields.* I filled a notebook full of names to read: James Wright, Louis Simpson, Denise Levertov, Gary Snyder. I handed Robert a few of my poems: "Hmmm," he said, whacking at the page in his tiny squiggly hand. "No good, no good at all, not too bad, hmmmm, there's a couple of lines of poetry here, this is pretty good." He handed me back a three-page epic on pigs, which included attacks on Republicans, Lutherans, and anything generally that displeased me. (Oh, the ego and anger of the young!) All gone but six lonesome lines, spoken by an old boar pig. "There's the poetry," he said. Simultaneously, my ego collapsed while something more intelligent was born. Robert was dead right, and that afternoon he gave me a great gift—that there were indeed six lines left, that it was a man's obligation to use his brains, and to neither humor nor pity himself, but to work patiently wherever he

was—Madison or New York—for those lumbering, joyful blasts from the spirit.

I drove back to Minneota hours later in a daze. I had just had the most remarkable, intelligent, affectionate afternoon of my life—in that shabby red farmhouse with no plumbing, but full of genius, surrounded by five hundred miles of corn and cow manure. If Robert and Carol could live there, a life of high-spirited thinking and talk, then so could I. It was all right to go east or west, or up or down, but not necessary. What you wanted was inside, wherever you were. That afternoon, and the hundreds of subsequent afternoons and nights I descended on them for soul food (and roast beef, too!), gave me a choice: I could go or stay or both. I live in Minneota now, and it's probably the fault of that afternoon.

Silence in the Snowy Fields astonished me in 1963, and it still does. It seems to me one of the great formative books of American literature in the twentieth century. It brings into consciousness parts of our lives and places we had never seen clearly before. My own western Minnesota that I simultaneously hated and loved proved more full of metaphor and mystery than I (or anyone else) imagined. It all depended, as Emerson might have put it, on whether you see it with the transcendent eye or the timid eye of convention and ambition, the American Scylla and Charybdis. The transcendent eye saw "Nearly to Milan, suddenly a small bridge / And water kneeling in the moonlight." It went into old Joe Sjolie's house and noticed the "old abandoned books / And instructions to Norwegian immigrants." It saw not just "gold or strange stones, but the true / Gift, beneath the pale lakes of Minnesota." It went, in the poem I love best out of that book (and have known by heart since I first read it in the car on the way back from Madison almost thirty years ago), to the funeral of Great-aunt Mary:

I

Here we are, all dressed up to honor death!
No, it is not that;
It is to honor this old woman
Born in Bellingham.

II

The church windows are open to the green trees.
The minister tells us that, being
The sons and daughters of God,
We rejoice at death, for we go
To the mansions prepared
From the foundations of the world.
Impossible. No one believes it.

III

Out on the bare, pioneer field,
The frail body must wait till dusk
To be lowered
In the hot and sandy earth.

A little shiver comes over me when I am in the presence of something true being said simply and beautifully. I still feel it in that poem.

Robert's other great gift to Americans is connected to that power, to that inducement to the shiver of truth. He made us feel, in "The Teeth Mother Naked at Last," our unescapable connection as humans and as citizens to the psychic and political life of our community, our country. He did this like no one since Whitman. Our wars take place not only in Vietnam, or Panama, or Iraq, but inside us. Every complaint the academic critics make of "The Teeth Mother" is true; it is excessive, rhetorical, preachy. But watch an audience of Americans listen to it, read by Robert or any passionate voice that can do it justice. They are bolted, fixed, trapped by it. They weep. Best of all, they think, for years afterwards.

These lies are only the longing we all feel to die.
It is the longing for someone to come and take you by the hand to
　　where they are all sleeping:
where the Egyptian pharoahs are asleep, and your own mother,
and all those disappeared children, who used to go around with
　　you in the rings at grade school. . . .

Do not be angry at the President—he is longing to take in his hand
the locks of death hair—
to meet his own children dead, or unborn. . . .

This is what it's like for a rich country to make war
this is what it's like to bomb huts (afterwards described as "structures")
This is what it's like to kill marginal farmers (afterwards described
    as "Communists"). . . .

That's what it is still like, in Panama and Iraq, and wherever we
fix our attention next. To have heard Robert read that poem during
the Vietnam War at one of the antiwar readings was an experience
equivalent, I think, to hearing Bach play the E minor "Wedge" fugue
in your church.

Robert invented the poetry reading for Americans. Ginsberg
and the beats were great readers, but they read for a counterculture audience and their mode was attack and satire. Robert is
probably a failed Norwegian minister, but his great achievement
was the poetry reading as a gift and lesson for an audience, wherever
they lived and whatever literary sophistication they brought to it.
I have heard him read in small Minnesota towns for farmers
who thought Longfellow was a radical and an eastern snob. He read
with tenderness and intelligence, giving them ideas, the gift of
feeling, a sense of community. He gave them, damn it, love and
brains! All of us who give readings and get paid for it owe him a
giant debt.

And now he is sixty-five! Even the plump, pink pillar of
longing who appeared at his door thirty years ago has a white
beard! Given the luck of Norwegian genetics, and his massive
intellectual and physical energy, we can all hope for at least another
quarter century of being hounded, improved, lectured, educated,
irritated, entertained, quickened (a grand old word!), scolded,
and finally—loved. Whatever the carpers argue, as they pick away
at the size and power of his gift and achievement, he has loved
us enough as Americans to hurl his work at us. We haven't had

a poet or a fellow citizen like him since Whitman—garrulous, one
of the roughs, a cosmos. On his birthday, I thank him, and send
him back some love and gratitude.

—*Bill Holm*
Minneota, Minnesota

2
A COMPANY OF POETS

Overleaf: The sixties, with Galway Kinnell and William Stafford (Douglas Hall photo).

Philip Dacey

Not a Television Set: A Celebration of Robert Bly

I FIRST SAW ROBERT BLY in 1969. I am sure of the date because I still have the gift he gave me and the approximately two hundred other people in the audience at the University of Iowa's main auditorium, and that gift—a pamphlet of Issa poems translated by Bly and bearing the words, "This booklet is a gift, and is not to be sold"—is copyrighted. I remember my surprise and delight when he picked up from a table on stage large white stacks of the pamphlets and came down into the audience to pass them out. Soon the auditorium was noisily awash with reaching hands and turning pages and then Bly was back on stage reciting Issa: "Now listen, you watermelons— / if any thieves come— / turn into frogs!" Approximately ten years later, in Marshall, Minnesota, Bly was celebrating his latest book—"A new book always gives me hope," he said then, "that maybe this time I've done it right"—by throwing into the audience about a half-dozen copies of his new work. They fluttered randomly into the hands of happy students. My earliest memory of Bly, therefore, reinforced by the later variation on a theme, established him for me as a gift-giver, a kind of embodiment of Lew Hyde's book on the subject, and nothing in the intervening years has worked to change that perception.

Such large, public gestures as these also remind us that part of Bly's genius resides in his ability to act in the space where theater and sincerity meet—the very verb "act" refers to both theater and to authentically human choices, like cofounding "American Writers Against the Vietnam War." I suspect that the confusion in some people's minds over theater and sincerity—which two may be opposed but needn't be—leads to some of the controversies that have at times surrounded Bly.

Long before Dana Gioia lamented the sorry state of contemporary American poetry in *The Atlantic Monthly* (May 1991), Robert Bly had similarly anatomized the problematic situation and put into practice most of Gioia's recommendations, like reading other poets' work and enhancing poetry with music. Bly's strength can be inferred from how much reaction even Gioia's watered-down version of Bly's values and judgments—largely unacknowledged by Gioia—has caused. For Bly not only "cuts through" to key issues, to nerve endings, but also formulates those issues in such a way as to give them dramatic, involving force. Call it flamboyance; call it outrageousness. I prefer to think of it as the function of an instinctive marriage in Bly between play—high-spirited, self-delighting inventiveness—and passion—feeling for what is most deeply held to be true and good.

Accordingly, perhaps my favorite moment with Bly was his off-the-cuff remark to a predominantly youthful audience that had missed a joke or failed to respond to something provocative he had said: "I am not a television set!" he insisted emphatically as he slapped his flesh-and-blood chest, "I am not a television set!" Of course, he was interested in making people laugh and recapturing his audience, but the remark was the tip—the avant-garde, as it were—of an entire and extensive set of values, a way of life, even, that Bly was embodying and, through his expressiveness, teaching.

Over the years, I have frequently heard stories, no doubt true, of offers to Bly of lucrative teaching positions, all of them turned down. Nor would his declining surprise anyone, given his statements—teasing pokes, really—relating to the academy. Of course, that he has thrived during visits to schools—receiving warm and appreciative welcomes from both faculty and students, to whom he generously reads and speaks longer than other poets would or could—is equally obvious. This apparently anomalous rejection by him of an opportunity he could grandly exploit to everyone's pleasure and benefit is best explained—as Frost says, "I have a theory"—less by his quarrel with academia than by the opposite, a comfortableness that to Bly would constitute a threat to the striving, "heroic," if you will, side of his personality. The example of Yeats helps explain this theory.

I don't think that Bly's earlier use of masks at readings and the centrality of the idea of the mask to Yeats's thought are entirely coincidental. Yeats believed in the duality of the self and in the potential of the undeveloped half to grow and fulfill its promise through identification with masks or personae. Yeats's autobiography is compelling testimony to the poet's ability to create himself as the person he wanted to be. Yeats was made—by Yeats—not born. There are signs that Bly has likewise created himself, deliberately restraining certain components of his personality while stimulating others that he wished to see stronger and more dominant.

Bookishness—this theory goes on—is natural to Bly. From his point of view, too natural. "My favorite room in the whole world," he has said, "is the New York City library's reading room." A playful exaggeration, probably, but a telling one. (The favorite room of the bookish man of action Marx was the reading room of the British Museum.) In addition, he has explained that he first became interested in poetry when he realized that it was not something esoteric and marginal but that within it, particularly within the poetry of Yeats—there he is again—the entire world could be found; refracted, transformed, made over, to be sure, but there. The world in a book. Bly reaching through to the world through a book through the walls of the New York City library. Bly buried like a university don. How nice. How precisely what he chose not to be.

A friend of mine knew Bly at the beginning of his career as a poet and remembers going to one of Bly's very first public readings. If my friend's memory is correct, Bly read like a parody of a bad reader: shyly, haltingly, without style or conviction, staring at the page and seldom looking at his audience; in short, not like Bly. Allowing for the distortions of memory and the instincts of a storyteller, I suspect there's something to the report. After all, Lutherans—even lapsed ones—don't go around draped in a poncho and waving their arms like a ballet dancer.

Bly himself has written of his own early years as a "boy-god," a removed and judgmental being. I titled a 1986 review of Bly "Saint

Robert" to call attention not to anything like piety but to his on-going struggle to "come down" and engage with—"love," say—the earth, its people, and their—including his own—mortal bodies. True ultimately to his Lutheran heritage, Bly is interested in the light, but he wants to arrive at it by going not up but down, as Dante did, discovering in the very center of the earth into which he had descended that—amazing!—he was now climbing skyward, toward purest spirit.

Because Bly loves paradox ("What American poetry needs thrown on it is not more light but more darkness"), he is expert at seeing the topsy-turviness of reality. Thus when—as Bly reminded us in his op-ed piece for the *Minneapolis Star Tribune* during the Gulf War—George Bush declares, "We seek nothing for ourselves," the poet is able to decode the politician and see the truth as a 180-degree reversal of what is being said. The op-ed piece is remark-able for Bly's perspective in the midst of the war. Although "occa-sional," the piece displays a wide and convincing reference of the sort usually possible only after an event has receded in time. One explanation for such an achievement is the fact that Bly has developed over the years a virtual system—as did the aforementioned Yeats and, more obviously, Marx, as well as one of Bly's sources, Jung—which quickly reveals the significance or inner structure of an event placed in that system's context. That is to say, Bly's thinking follows a pattern and forms a large, consistent whole. The street is two-way: the whole helps him understand particular events, and his in-terpretation of particular events reveals his systematic thought. For what it reveals of both Bly and our American selves, the op-ed piece is no less important now than it was during the war and deserves wide circulation.

Mentioning his essay on the most recent war allows me to say something I've wanted to say in print for a long time: Bly is vastly underrated as a prose writer. I've heard readers praise Bly's prose for sounding like his voice. I agree that it is strongly voiced writing, not the obvious product of desk-bound laboriousness. But no one can achieve transparent or forceful prose by simply transcribing tape-recorded speech. The voice we hear in his prose is a composed, created one. Bly makes look easy what is easy only through his artful work (Jack Nicklaus: "The more I practice, the luckier I get").

But perhaps most endearing about Bly is that, in his devotion to craft and truth—a devotion that is all one, not compartmentalized—he knows nothing of half measures, in fact seems to refuse to know them. Etched in my memory—I am happy to say—is his exemplary warning to students many years ago: "Don't trust a teacher who hasn't memorized any poem he or she is teaching." Any counter argument—must we memorize *Paradise Lost* before we teach it?—misses the point that if truth is worth telling, it is worth exaggerating. Bly chooses not to be the kind of person he once sharply skewered as the "on-the-other-hand" man who talks like this: "Yes, the Crusades were land-grabs, but on the other hand . . ." Such a "balanced" point of view is not only boring and predictable but ultimately false, because the person who holds it is interested less in serving truth (an accurate reporting of experience would be closer to chaos than to a simple, neat balance) than in protecting himself. While never self-destructive, Bly—beyond stopping for red lights, and so on—prefers vulnerability to self-armoring. "Armor is fine," William Stafford has said, "but it keeps you from knowing what the weather is like," and Bly obviously concurs in one of his prose poems: "In the snowstorm millions of years come close behind us, nothing is lost, nothing rejected, our bodies are equal to the snow in energy. The body is ready to sing all night, and be entered by whatever wishes to enter the human body singing." So a description of Bly finally arrives—as we should have known it would—at courage, always as precious (i.e., rare) as it is necessary.

Let me end, first, by noting that in countless Bly readings I've attended in over twenty years, at my school and elsewhere, I've never heard him repeat himself—each reading has been wholly reconceived—and, second, by redirecting myself from you, Reader, to you, Robert Bly: You are one of the reasons I and many others are proud to be Minnesotans. It's my privilege to be able to salute you at this time of your sixty-fifth birthday and wish you dozens more anniversaries of your birth, all of them replete with your characteristic vigor and faith.

Galway Kinnell

The Groans

For Robert Bly

When Poet X comes out with a startling
metaphor a melody of appreciative groans
ripples up from somewhere in the front;
and I know Robert Bly is in the audience.
These groans must be an acquired language,
for when I first set eyes on Robert,
in 1957, at a poetry reading, he listened
with great concentration but in total silence.
I remember he stood out from the others.
Perhaps it was the florid health of all
that Minnesota milk and eggs, or the brightness
of the full attention he turned on others.
In listening he seemed actually to glow.
A few days after our first meeting,
which did not happen until a few months after
that first sighting, he came to visit
and we talked for seven or eight hours.
He recited Neruda and Machado and Hart Crane
and produced theories on the sterility
of American poetry, and the need to release
the Unconscious through writing the Surreal.
And he told comical stories about his literary
enemies—I was amazed that somebody almost
as unpublished as I could actually have them—
and I saw he liked having them, it meant poetry
mattered and it also gave him the opportunity
to tell the stories, which he did with much
good humor and as little malice as possible.

I was surprised, and reassured, probably
because I had never before run across
the comic sense of life, to realize that no matter
what subject we took up, if we went into it
far enough we ended up laughing.
He spoke with absolute conviction about everything,
and I was sure he would be an unbudgeable dogmatist.
On the contrary, it turned out he was more drawn
to new truth, even somebody else's, than
attached to old, even his own; and in the middle
of a conversation he could be charmed and won over
by an idea directly contradicting the idea
he had just been expounding. Later, after
he had acquired his vocabulary of groans,
these mid-conversation conversions would be heralded
by bass grunts alternating with falsetto hums,
moderatissimo becoming molto appassionato.
I like to think Robert learned the groans in 1963
in Paris, on a visit we made to Les Halles together
just before they tore the place down, when,
after strolling among the pimientos, mushrooms,
onions, tomatoes, palping them and smelling them,
enfolding them in a hand to know their shapes
and to feel our palms shaped by them, perhaps
half hoping they would speak, that their own
sounds would start coming out of our mouths,
we stopped in a bistro, where a *routard* was
spooning up onion soup with loud mewlings and moans
     . . . and I remember Robert pricked up his ears.
By now Poet X is writhing with pleasure, perhaps
at having his poem heard wholeheartedly
and answered immediately. He seems to have
thrown his manuscript aside and to be
improvising metaphor after metaphor, that call
forth more and more of these growled blats,
as when a screwdriver hits a live wire,

and high rasps, as when you force
gently a light bulb out of its socket.
And it occurs to me—these groans of nearly
satisfied hunger, the mmmmmmmm's and arghs,
like adult versions of the noises babies make when going over
the edge of appetite into play, must be the glow
from the milk and eggs and from the pleasure
of paying full attention to another, made audible.

"Discouraged student" (courtesy of Philip Dacey).

Jane Kenyon

Kicking the Eggs

MY EARLIEST RECOLLECTIONS of Robert date from my under-graduate days at the University of Michigan, in the late sixties. There were poetry readings every Tuesday in the Undergraduate Library—a great luxury, but of course we were not aware how great; we accepted them as our due. One day Robert strode into the room with Donald Hall, Robert wearing a serape, with a blue silk scarf around his neck. He began by reading a few poems from *Silence in the Snowy Fields,* including two permanent favorites of mine, "Hunting Pheasants in a Cornfield" and "Poem in Three Parts." Then he turned to work from *The Light Around the Body,* beginning with poems not overtly about the Vietnam War, but certainly about lives of Americans spent in wrong pursuits— "The Busy Man Speaks" and "Come with Me"; then he read some of the inward poems of the last section— "Looking into a Face," "When the Dumb Speak."

When he read "Counting Small-Boned Bodies," it was as if a sudden squall pulled up a huge tree, roots and all. We fell into his vision of apocalypse. At that reading I understood that W. H. Auden, when he wrote, "Poetry makes nothing happen," was wrong. Here was harrowing public indignation at our atrocities, our sightless, xenophobic, greedy, paranoid warmongering. I understood from that day, from Robert, that poetry is a public moral force, or can be, and not only a path into the individual human soul.

He came almost yearly to read at Michigan, staying with his old friend and confrere, Donald Hall—who by 1972 would be my spouse. I was among the young poets at Michigan who attended the parties after readings, and at these parties I observed the host and his guest tell stories, joke, squabble, show off, and discuss serious ideas earnestly.

Over the years they went through times of separation, even of estrangement, but they wrote endless letters, talked on the phone, helped each other with poems and prose. They couldn't divorce, no matter the schism: they seemed linked at the backbone. Robert went through his changes, Donald went through his—personal, political, aesthetic, philosophical—but they remain profoundly attached.

Once I took a photograph of them working together on each other's poems, sitting on our big yellow sofa in Ann Arbor. At least three people, glancing at that picture, have asked Donald, "Is that your mother?" (Robert turned gray before Don did.) Now what would Marie-Louise von Franz make of it?

In the years before Don and I were married, Don always made breakfast for his guest from Minnesota, or watched him, aghast, as he made his own. Once Robert dropped an egg while removing it from the carton. Donald cast a Puritan look, whereupon Robert kicked the raw egg gleefully under the refrigerator. "I'm a Capricorn!" he said.

It was Robert who urged me to translate Anna Akhmatova's poems, and who, along with Louis Simpson, appealed to Vera Dunham to work with me. Robert had come to visit us for a few days in New Hampshire. He asked what I was working on, read it thoughtfully. "It's time for you to choose a poet dead or alive and work with that poet as a master," he said. That way of reading had never occurred to me. "I cannot choose a man for a master," I said. "Then read Akhmatova," said Robert.

I gathered all the translations I could get my hands on, but felt that the poems remained hidden, obscured. I made my own versions for my own amusement, and as a way of close reading. Then I found a student of Comparative Literature at Dartmouth College, Lou Teel, who gave me literal versions of a few poems.

Next time Robert came to visit, he asked me what I was up to. I showed him my exercises, for that's what I considered them to be. He decided on the spot to do an Eighties Press book of them, and he urged me to work with Vera Dunham as co-translator.

For five years I sat at Akhmatova's feet. What Robert told me was true: whatever work you put into translation comes back to you like the twelve baskets of bread and fish left after the feeding of the five thousand. It's to Robert that I owe the book, and to him the deep changes that occurred in my own poems as a result of that work.

There is no one else on earth like Robert Elwood Bly. He is a cross between William Blake, Ralph Nader, and Mr. Magoo, and I love and revere him endlessly.

Donald Hall

A Friendship

IN FEBRUARY OF 1948 I went out for the *Harvard Advocate* and met the austere figure of Robert Bly. He was twenty-one; I was nineteen. He was skinny, never smiled, and wore three-piece suits with narrow striped ties; he was very very intelligent. If we had not met, how would our lives have differed? My life would have been poorer, thinner, less energetic; there would have been less excitement and less confrontation. For more than forty years we have talked about poetry, politics, and the spirit; we have argued, we have exalted and blasted each other. We perform a friendship of opposites, Heraclitean enantiodromia, as we square off at every crossroads: Plato and Aristotle, Jung and Freud, whirlpool and rock, Don Quixote and Sancho Panza. If neither of us has published anything without showing it to the other, each of us has disobediently published work that the other loathed. Contradiction or conflict is probably more important to friendship than coherence; certainly it creates more. I owe him so much, I cannot imagine my life without him.

The Coalition

If among earth's kings Lord Gilgamesh should remain unreasonable,
if civility refuses to assume citizenship between the rivers,
Sir Agamemnon will assemble a diligent Protestant coalition

to administer death as appropriate lesson and punishment.
We'll station right-thinking King Herod with his updated hoplites
backed by Xin the Emperor's deathless terracotta battalions

beside Mercury, Mars, and Athena from the province of Olympus
to institute, as a deterrent, termination with extreme prejudice.
Young Colonel Bonaparte, upgrading to Alexander, will distribute

slaughter by African blowguns, phalanxes, tortoises from Cipango,
whinnying helicopters from Attila's stables, Cyclopean missiles,
and Greek fire to melt Saracens flourishing their scimitars.

If Lord Gilgamesh should remain unreasonable, we will coalesce
to incinerate retreating Uruki soldiers, furthering the project
of Pharoah Death, Imperator Death, Shogun Death, President Death.

Excerpt from the *Paris Review* interview with Peter Stitt:

Interviewer: Were you ever part of a group of poets? Did you visit Robert Bly's farm in the early sixties in Madison, Minnesota?

Donald Hall: There wasn't anything I would call a group. I did get out to the Blys' a couple of times. The summer of 1961 I was there for two weeks along with the Simpsons. Jim Wright came out from Minneapolis for the two weekends. We four males spent hours together looking at each other's poetry. Of course we had some notions in common, and we learned from each other, so maybe we *were* a group. I remember how one poem of mine got changed then, "In the Kitchen of the Old House." I'd been fidgeting with it for two years. It began with an imagined dream—which just didn't go— and I said in frustration something like, "I remember when this started. I was sitting in the kitchen of this old house late at night, thinking about . . . " Three voices interrupted me: "Write it down! Write it down!" This poem needed a way *in*.

We worked together and we played competitive games like badminton and swimming, but poetry was the most competitive game. We were friendly and fought like hell. Louis was the best swimmer, and Robert always won the foolhardiness prize. There was a big town swimming pool in Madison where we went every day, and Robert would climb to the highest diving platform and jump off, making faces and noises and gyrating his body all the way down. I won at badminton.

Robert and I—he was Bob then, and I feel stiff saying "Robert" —met at Harvard in February of 1948, when I tried out for the *Advocate*. He had joined the previous fall, when he first got to Harvard, but I waited until my second term. After school was out that summer, he came down to Connecticut and stayed at my house for a day or two. I was nervous having my poet friend there, afraid of confrontation between Robert and my father. At lunch Robert said, "Well, Mr. Hall, what do you think of having a poet for a son?" As I feared, my father didn't know what to say; poetry was embarrassing, somehow. So I said, "Too bad your father doesn't have the same problem," and my father laughed and laughed, off the hook.

Robert and I have written thousands of letters back and forth, and we've visited whenever we could. You know these people who hate Robert and write about how clever he has been at his literary politicking? They don't know anything about it. For years and years he was a solitary. I remember a time before I moved on to Ann Arbor, when Robert came back from Norway and stopped to visit while I lived outside Boston. He was talking about going back to the Madison farm and starting a magazine. He had discovered modernism in Norway and wanted to *tell* everybody—but he also wanted to remain independent. Knowing literary people would only make it harder for him, so he did not want to *know* anybody besides me. Then he said, "I don't want to know James Wright. How can I write about James Wright if I know James Wright?" He wasn't being nasty about Jim; he brought up Jim's name because Jim had just taken a job at the University of Minnesota—three or four hours away from Madison. They didn't get to know each other until a couple of years later, when Jim wrote him an anguished letter. Jim read Robert's attacks on fifties poetry in *The Fifties* and decided that everything Robert said was right and everything Jim was doing was wrong. Jim was always deciding that he was *wrong*.

Robert wanted solitude and independence. He was going to lecture everybody, as he always has done and still does, but from a distance. If he wanted eminence he wanted a lonely eminence. He came out of his isolation, I think, at that conference in Texas when he took the floor away from the professors. Do you know about that?

Interviewer: No. This is something I haven't heard about.

Hall: It was a moment. The National Council of Teachers of English invited young poets, as they called us, to a conference in Houston in 1966. They brought Robert Graves over to lecture, and they brought in Richard Eberhart, calling him dean of the younger poets. Dick was fifty-two; that made him dean. Most of the young poets were forty or close to it. There was W. S. Merwin, Robert Creeley,

Robert Duncan, Gary Snyder, Carolyn Kizer, Robert, I . . . and also: Reed Whittemore, Josephine Miles, William Stafford, May Swenson. Young poets! Several of us flew down from Chicago together. We stood in the aisle of a 707 singing "Yellow Submarine" — Bly, Snyder, Creeley, and I. We stayed up all night in somebody's room at the Houston hotel talking about poetry. Creeley had an over-the-shoulder cassette recorder, and every time Duncan spoke he turned it on, and every time Duncan finished speaking he turned it off. We stayed up until six in the morning and Eberhart's talk was at eight-thirty, so we didn't get a whole lot of sleep.

We met in a huge hall filled with thousands of English teachers. Eberhart talked about how the Peace Corps sent him to Africa; he observed a tribe of primitive people and told us that civilization lacked spontaneity. Dick discovers Rousseau! Someone else got up, a respondent, and said something silly. Then Lawrence Perrine, who edited the textbook *Sound and Sense,* stood up as another respondent. He talked conservatively about poetic form, saying something in praise of villanelles — in 1966! — which made it sound as if all poems were really the same; as if nothing mattered, not what you said or how you said it. I'm unfair, but all of us were tired, some of us were hung over, and everything we heard sounded fatuous after the energizing talk of the night before. So Robert stood up in the front row — turning around to face these thousands of people, interrupting the program — and said: "He's *wrong.* We care about poetry. Poetry *matters* and one thing is better than something else. . . ." He went on; I can't remember. . . . Whatever Bly said, it was passionate. It woke everybody up, I'll tell you. Thousands of teachers applauded mightily. As Robert sat down and the program was about to proceed, somebody in the audience said, "Let's hear from all the poets." So we took over, to hell with the program, and one by one each of us read a poem and talked. It was Vietnam time and a lot of us talked about politics. Robert gave the rest of us courage, and his platform life began at that moment: he found his public antinomian *presence.*

A volatile moment with Donald Hall, 1980s (Nicholas Mascari photo).

David Ignatow

Four Poems and a Memoir

The Parting

You are watching me, wondering when
my eyebrows turned white. You stand
brawny with youth, yet with an air
of discreet respect. This meeting
between us must end well.

I ask about your health and happiness,
and both are answered energetically
in the affirmative. I am glad, I reply,
and that I have missed talking with you,
and you respond, Same here.

These are signals to back off
from one another to give room
for each to breathe. I leave
with a wave of the hand. You respond
promptly with a raised arm in salute,
seeing me pass among the dead,
seeing yourself as in an aging mirror.

An Appeal

We need you on TV to tell us the story of your life, holding us with your private thoughts, memories of your parents and of the first day of your marriage, and of your children. Sit there at your desk in the Oval Office before the cameras, drinking from a cup of coffee, as we all do around a table during conversation with friends or with our friendly political opponents and discuss, as we enjoy each other's humanity, content to be human, fallible with ourselves and with others—with a cup of coffee in the hand across a table, and when night begins to wane into daylight we can agree to go to bed, each to his own home or for those who live too far away to bed down in our guest room or on the couch in the living room. And as men are spinning to the ground in death from shrapnel or napalm or fallout set your elbows on the desk and your face between your hands and look at us steadily without speaking, and when you feel the need finally, express yourself in a quiet statement that it is happening, and ask us for help to stop it because you can't do it alone, that it needs more help than you are capable of giving. Since we will know then that you are one of us, we will address ourselves to all sides and in a world chorus demand an end.

I Will Be Gone

What am I if not a pattern of manhood?
What should I be if not a dimension of silence?
I have suffered my pattern, and the last of it
will be the beginning of life in the ground
of ants and grubs or in workings of the rain.
I will have become indifferent and detached,
without fear, no longer envious but happy
as a spark at night. I will be gone into the dark,
my own real mother.

As They Fly

Birds call out as they fly
to keep track of one another.
Each being one, all together
they let each other know
so that none forgets itself
and is lost.

From "Reflections Upon the Past with Robert Bly"

The Light Around the Body brought Robert the National Book
Award when I was back from Kansas and teaching at Vassar. I and
all his friends knew that accepting the prize in front of a huge
audience, as was the custom, would give Robert a superb opportunity to speak out against the war. To Robert, at first, the idea of
accepting a prize in the middle of a war of devastation upon innocent people was obscene and a travesty of the high purpose of poetry
itself. He was for rejecting the prize outright with a written, scathing
denunciation, but talking this out with Paul Zweig, James Wright,
and me, as I remember, he decided finally to accept the award on
the condition that he be allowed to speak as he wished. It was an

unusual request to make to the committee, since it was the custom then simply to accept the prize with a short but graceful thank you and depart from the stage. However, the climate of the times being what it was, and Robert's passionate efforts against the war being already known, permission was reluctantly granted, and Paul, Jim, Saul Galin, and I sat down to rewrite a speech that Robert had begun. After reading through what he had written so far, we realized, as Robert came to realize in discussions with him, that the speech had to be written in a measured and calm rhetoric to be the more convincing to the august atmosphere of the occasion. The speech finally was written among us just hours before the ceremony was to start, and it was an amazing moment in the hall when Robert, after quietly receiving the check, turned to the audience with his speech in hand and began to read it in his measured but angry voice. He denounced the war, those who had begun it and were pursuing it; he denounced the writers in the audience who had been sitting idly by, letting the war take its frightful course without a word of protest or expression of conscience; and, finally, he denounced the publishers themselves who had contributed toward prize money and his own publisher in particular for its silence during the war in the face of its overwhelming significance as an onslaught upon the liberty and civil rights of an entire nation, a fact that could by extension be applied to the developing condition in this country in which publishing itself could be threatened by governmental censorship and intimidation. It was a fact that was already being felt in the publishing world without a word of protest from anyone in the field. He ended by accepting the check only with the intention of then and there handing it to a representative of the War Resisters League, who would then receive it for use in helping to resist the war in whatever manner it saw fit. A hush fell upon the auditorium as he called out the name of the representative to come to the platform and receive the check from Robert's hand. As the check passed between them, Robert offered the recipient a final admonishment— to refuse to register for the draft upon his, Robert's, urging. Such a refusal and the open encouragement of such a refusal was tantamount to a violation of a law that had recently been passed in

Congress. There was silence in the hall for a moment, the silence of extreme tension, until, finally, a small scattering of hand clapping began. We had been forewarned that there would be FBI agents in the audience, and as we looked around we became aware that about ten men dressed in dark suits rose up from their seats in different parts of the hall and walked out in a body. The rest of the audience now had begun an uproar of talk mixed with boos and cheers. The die had been cast for Robert and for us. We had thrown down the challenge to the government. I was apprehensive that the worst was yet to come, but who at that moment would let the fear override the exhilaration, that victory of spirit that swept through us who had helped Robert with his speech? We knew that whatever government reprisal might follow, we could deal with it as it happened. For now we had won the day and put on notice the government and this distinguished audience, composed of most of the major literary figures of the day and their publishers, that this war could not be suppressed in our thoughts, not in our lives, but had to be met honestly and with conscience. Donald Hall and Ted Weiss, two of the three judges who had given Robert his prize, were also seated in the audience. Although they were keeping their counsel, we knew very well what had motivated their decision. And so, for me the moment meant a complete and overwhelming affirmation and vindication of all that Robert stood for as a crusading, visionary figure in the literary world and in the politics of the nation. He had endured insults, threats, and condemnation to make his stand before the artistic and intellectual elite at the full height of his career and poetic talents. He was a man for all seasons. He had done it with all the style, gusto, and political passion on the highest level. It was Robert's finest hour, and we who were attached to him through admiration, faith, and common goals were affirmed through him and made to feel our significance before the world.

James Haba

A Dream and Two Poems

IN JANUARY OF 1975 I invited Robert Bly to Glassboro State College in southern New Jersey to give a workshop and a reading. One Wednesday in early March he took a train from New York and we met for the first time at Princeton Junction.

As we were loading his bags into my car I noticed that, yet again, I had only one of my gloves, and when I explained to Robert that this was why he saw me anxiously looking around (and under) the car, he smiled and said, "You know what they say this means? They say that when you lose things it means that your mother never loved you enough." He smiled still more broadly when I instantly replied, "She wasn't the only one." This first exchange was a gift issuing from loss and I have recently understood its important relationship to a dream I had about five years later.

In the dream I receive a small rumpled package (a kind of padded mailing envelope) which has obviously been on its way for a long time and which has finally come into my hands only after having passed through many others. After studying the delicate, almost spidery handwriting of the address I see that it is for me. Then I also recognize the writing as Robert's. Feeling grateful for the package itself and having no idea what it contains, I carefully open it to discover a cluster of small golden balls (four or five, each the size of a pigeon egg) softly glowing through the fine dust which lies on them. In the dream I remember being troubled by a series of obvious and irrelevant questions: what are these balls? why am I receiving them? what am I to do with them? In fact, another part of my dream consciousness accepted this gift directly and with something like full understanding while also having no intention of ever trying to say anything about it.

This dream seems to illuminate a central dimension of my relationship with Robert and, I believe, an important aspect of what

Robert has brought to countless others. In freely trusting his own impulses and his own instinctive associations, Robert triggered in me and in many others the capacity to begin doing the same. Without pretending that I have yet fully owned the dream gift described above, here are two poems which I am sure derive directly from the deep generosity of Robert's spirit. The first I always intended specifically for him. The second owes its leaps entirely to his example. I hope they honor the spirit which shook them free.

To my knowledge, in 1975 Robert had not yet begun to discuss the Iron John story, and he made no mention of it at Glassboro during his visit. When I began to learn the details of that story about five years later, I was struck with how far impulse and association had taken me in this poem which came while driving Robert to the Philadelphia airport the morning after his reading.

Driving a New Friend to the Airport in Early March
For Robert Bly

A peach in the hand suddenly,
and tall peach colored grass bending over old snow.

Talk is a fountain,
and hearing is a warm gust heavy with fish.

I love these broken cornstalks,
and this muddy windshield.

Let our teeth crack with curses,
and the birds of our wrists feed among algae at the
    bottom of ponds.

When I showed the poem to Robert months later, he read it with pleasure up till the last stanza, at which his face turned quizzical as he said, "But I thought we had always gotten along so well?"

We had, and do. As I explained to him, what I meant by "Let our teeth crack with curses" was that we could share our outrage at the world, the knot of angry energy which propels those of us who have learned distrust as children out of our caves. Once out, we suddenly find ourselves available for life-saving relationships with others. And that kind of relationship, in the car and at the bottom of ponds (where Iron John lives), completely surrounds and contains the violence.

Martin Buber has said that evil is created every time an I-Thou relationship is missed. I think Robert has helped many men and women to move beyond evil. I know that he has helped me to do so.

The other poem I want to offer here came fifteen years later, in 1990. I like to think of it as a small tribute to the gift of himself Robert has so readily given to us all.

Within the Onion

When you follow the spiral
within the onion you always find
something round and something sharp.

One of these remembers purple.
The other worships water.

From them our sun rises.

Michael Dennis Browne

Eating Out: The Three Brains

OUR FOOD CRITIC REPORTS:

Intrigued by rumors that a long-standing Minnesota culinary institution is enjoying a strong revival of interest among discerning diners, we made several unannounced visits and were generally pleased with the results. Though the occasional dish beckons rather than delivers, overall the quality was what one might expect at a restaurant of such firm reputation.

One does not go to **The Three Brains** for the decor. Lutheran Ecstatic is not everybody's cup of tea, and the effect of the four-hundred-foot ceilings is somewhat stark. One of our party considered the dead mariners on the walls a distraction. In fairness I should note that others found the presence of chickens underfoot nicely reassuring.

On a first visit, service was a definite problem. A pale young person approached our table and announced, "I'm Solitude. I'll be your waiter tonight." It was a long evening—at least two hours between each course. On another occasion we were attended by waiters who advanced by whirling; needless to say, that night soup portions were particularly meager. On later visits, service varied between the depressed and the exalted. Acoustics also could use some attention: more than once a server would recite the entire menu only to have to offer to read all the items over again.

By and large the appetizers are winners. The mouth-guilt, caught fresh and faxed in daily from Norway, was served in pleasingly severe slices atop a caustic gruel. The member of our party who ordered the shadow salad declared herself enchanted with the results; a little later she drifted away from our table. The bouzouki chunks were moist, oozing, pungent in their micro-brine. Not everything worked—the masks, for example, were lukewarm. The iron john sounded promising but was sent back after it arrived covered with hair. Among appetizers we left untasted were the blue toad livers, clear-eyed chicken, Chinese cold cream, coeur de loon, and the slimy St. Nicholas.

But it is with the entrées that this establishment really scores. The reptile brain, one of three house specialties, was done to perfection, flaky on the outside but moist and reverberating in the center, just as we had ordered it. The executive power sauce was properly overbearing. The soul/spirit combination, the most costly item on the menu, was also just right, the soul (generous portions) being moist, low, dank, and mossy, and the spirit sprightly and evanescent (though a little hard to keep on the plate). Baked rumi was just this side of bland but pleasingly presented on a bed of private snow. The ant mansion was hearty and flavorful. On one evening the nerudaburger was subtle, lyrical, and moist but on a subsequent visit strident, almost reckless. The camphor/gopherwood platter listed on the menu was not available on any of the nights we dined.

Each entrée comes with a basket of laconic Swedish bread (Ekelöf) baked on the premises. Salads are substantial and drizzled by a low mist. The wine list features a cleverly eclectic range of offerings, and in addition to the workhorses of the wine world includes some real finds from Cathay, Persia, and Macedonia. There is also a good selection of the usual ales; of the several nonalcoholic brands available, we recommend the Kabir.

The Three Brains is open to the universe. Credit cards accepted.

Noel Cobb

"Nearer than Near, Closer than Fingernails" A Tribute to Robert Bly on His Sixty-fifth Birthday

IT IS DIFFICULT TO WRITE about Robert. He has meant so much to me. I could even say he saved my life. More accurately, my soul. Not like Jesus, more like Orpheus. It was 1958. I was twenty—wild-eyed, scared, and skinny—autistically apocalyptic and incoherent as only a 1950s son of a psychotic, Pentecostal family could be.

It was announced that Robert would be giving a poetry reading on the campus of the university where I was an undergraduate. It was to be in an empty classroom at the end of the day.

I had begun writing poetry, though nervously, like a Patagonian spy having mistakenly walked into a novel by Dostoevski. The working-class mythology of my parents damned poets to starvation and a rat's life while their fundamentalist dogma sent such dupes of the Devil straight to hell. Having spent each summer "vacation" working twelve hours a day in order to save money for the next year's studies, I naively demanded that a university degree magic me out of the doom into which I had been born. It was becoming clear that it wouldn't. I orbited in and out of disciplines like an untethered meteor. Organic Chemistry. Greek Tragedy. Logic. The English Novel. Vector Spaces. Aesthetics. Abnormal Psychology.

At home, all literature apart from the Bible and fairy tales had been forbidden. When I discovered Shakespeare, I wept for days. At the university I read indiscriminately all the poetry I could find, but I didn't know where to begin. I had never heard a poet give a reading, except Dylan Thomas on LP. Nothing prepared me for Robert's reading.

For a start he looked different from my professors. His hair seemed to be on fire. And his hands kept fluttering around his body as if they wanted to grow wings and fly off. Here was obviously someone who had "escaped." He walked into the chattering classroom like a logger sizing up a logjam.

If I had never heard another poetry reading, that occasion would still have been enough to inspire me forever after. Beginning with that great poem of puer longing by the early Yeats: "Who will go drive with Fergus now, / And pierce the deep wood's woven shade, / And dance upon the level shore?" Robert went on to illuminate the room with visions of Blake, then darkened it to a flickering candle flame with his translations of Rilke's heartbreaking "Voices": "The Drunkard's Song," "The Suicide's Song," "The Beggar's Song." He had no published book, but his own poems rang with a wild and original sound.

I wept silently in myself. And laughed, free as the child I had never been, at the way he conjured poems out of the dark ground or shook them out of the air, like shining birds out of shadowy trees. Then suddenly it was over, the classroom empty again, the students chattering on their way out, Robert quietly assembling his papers and books. Although, to me, he was a man of ancient wisdom and ten years my senior, desperation demolished my inhibitions. I spoke. He answered! We walked down the long, straight paths over the painfully meticulous lawns, talking in the melancholy twilight. I told of my soul's longing and the great terror that pursued me. He listened. It was such a quiet listening.

Then he said: "It's important to stay close to the edge. That is where poetry comes from. Rilke's whole life was like that. He was like a man skating—black water on one side, ice on the other—seeing how close to the edge he could skate."

The great terror did not leave, but the soul's longing for poetry had been affirmed and that was already much. Within a year I had sold all my belongings and bought a one-way ticket on a steamer sailing out from New York to Oslo. I was going to step off the edge of the world, my known world, into an unknown one, with only the imagination to guide me. Strange. I still had the great terror, but I wasn't afraid. I knew that the imagination would not let me down. And it never has.

That first meeting with Robert was the beginning of a long friendship, but I think Robert will understand if I say that an epiphany occurred the day of that poetry reading. For the soul it was an incontrovertible annunciation. I do not mean Robert personally when I name the Angel. But it was Robert's unique generosity of spirit, together with his natural humility before the cosmos and his enormous love of the imagination, which made it possible for the Necessary Angel to appear. The great Persian scholar and interpreter of Sufism, Henry Corbin, in speaking about the Angel in his book *Avicenna and the Visionary Recital*, wrote, "The epiphany of the Angel corresponds to a certain moment and degree in the individuation of the soul, when, *awakened to its consciousness of being a stranger*, it becomes free from this world and knows that it forms one with its celestial counterpart, the person of the Angel from whom it originates." (my emphasis)

And in his Angel poem "The One Coming Closer," Robert says:

He is no one we know: he is not Jehovah,
Or an obedient ermine-caparisoned king.
He is one nearer than near, closer than fingernails.

Are we all then religious? It must be so.
We know him, we see him, we hold him every day.
He is the one constantly coming closer.

William Stafford

Robert Bly's Working-with-Things Project

THE FOLLOWING PIECE OF WRITING came about at a recent "Great Mother" conference at Little Lake Elkheart, in Wisconsin. This is the way I noted the circumstances of our writing project at the time:

In the afternoon Robert Bly leads about fifteen of us down by the lake for one of his "thing" poems exercises. He tells us to go down to the lake and each one to pick up three wet objects to bring back. We do, and he says to choose one of them— "You'll know which one when you look them over." After that he leads us through a succession of writing exercises, each one to be complete before he tells us the next to do, e.g.: "Describe the object. Did you tell how heavy it is?" "Now tell how it feels to your hand." "Now what is inside it, what it is like." "What shape is it?" "Now compare it to your mother." (This last one shakes us all loose from our plodding ways. . . .) "Now compare it to the princess who sewed shirts to save her six brothers." (A reference to a folktale we had all listened to during the conference.)

I finished a prose description, along with the required comparisons, about a handful of mud with a muskrat print on it that I had scooped up at the lake shore. . . .

Find three wet things on the shore; then describe one—size, feel, smell, shape.

Whiskers of roots brush out from this wet, swarthy glob of mud. It is only a frog-sized piece of the earth—cool and damp, it feels alive almost, or at least ready to be alive if urged by the fingers. It might jump and leave you for its place where you found it.

What right did you have to scoop it away just because a track on this fistful of mud caught your attention? The muskrat that first felt it last night just went on shaking its foot maybe and wondering whether its track would be taken for art, one toe so elegantly splashing a signature separately and as if considering it might become a thumb sometime, should other nights invite a footloose rat for a stroll.

But mud has designs of its own, inside, where pieces of moss have squirmed their own patterns, where a sliver of charcoal dives through old leaves. The smell of the lake lives here, and a faint residue from loon sounds that sank at night and stayed still, hidden from the ice fingers that scrabbled for light.

Now relate it to your mother.

My mother, soft as mud, couldn't survive if we left. She clung with tendrils as fragile as these fragments of root. When she lifted me, my hands imprinted her yielding face as we nuzzled into those last warm days of summer.

Now I have found this mud, understanding on the cluttered shore, except that the track of a muskrat, or my track left over for years, left a print that now reaches my face through the dry air, here, safe but far.

Now relate it to the princess who sewed star shirts to save her six brothers.

Could a princess that steadfastly remained silent to save her swan brothers be more quiet and true than this unnoticed fragment abiding through centuries on the shore? Now the madness of sound — motorboats, loud cars, clashing oars — arches into this day, but the handful of mud has joined my hand to her hand, and the coldness of the deep water is mine, even in the sun.

I have kept silence and woven a star-flower coat for my mother, through the help of a friend who guided me back through tunnels and roots to the dark charcoal hidden too well to be found by the wise or learned or strong.

With William Stafford at the Marshall Festival, Marshall, Minnesota, May 1989 (photographer unknown).

Kathleen Raine

Two Poems

As in a Glass Darkly

Exiles from ourselves,
We, who are in every place our own elsewhere
See as in a looking glass the once and for ever
Blind body stumbles after
But cannot have or hold the fleeting,
The not yet and the gone of time.

Magic of heart's desire,
Who writes these messages in the languages of love,
Indecipherable mountains, stars, sunsets, deeps and distances
Opening their secrets to each alone?
Whom do the loud winds proclaim? Our human cities
Day and night are humming in harmony the cosmic music
Mozart heard, and Schubert, who are ourselves;
Epiphanic wonders everywhere and always
Requite heart's infinite in perpetual arrival
As the mirroring spaces of still water, the swallows,
Bird and image, indistinguishably meet.

Loss of Memory

The holy words: why did we let them go?
Whose are our children, who no longer know
"Our father who art in heaven"?
For words create that heaven, and that Father,
Hallow the holy Name,
Unspoken in a time that has forgotten
The language that peoples unseen heaven
And visible earth with all her creatures,
Tells the thousand stories of our one human story.
What but the word has made kings royal, women beautiful,
Made Mary the Mother of God? God has no mother now,
Nor Eve the far hope of her lost garden.
Disinherited from ancestral wisdom
Whose realm protected once, for us
The soundless voice of memory speaks no more
That used to tell, over and over,
The healing words: "Let not your heart be troubled,"
Of green pastures and still waters
And the twelve signs of love that never fails.

October 15, 1990

Tomas Tranströmer

Museums

AS A CHILD I WAS DRAWN to museums. First there was the museum of natural history, Riksmuseet, in Frescati, north of Stockholm. What a building! Gigantic, Babylonian, inexhaustible! On the ground floor, hall after hall with stuffed mammals and birds swarming through the dust. Then the vaults reeking of bones with whales hanging from the ceiling. On the next floor: the petrified, the spineless . . .

Riksmuseet was a place I visited holding someone by the hand. I was five years old. In the entrance two elephant skeletons greeted the visitor. They were keepers of the gate to the land of wonders. They made an overwhelming impression on me, and I made drawings of them in a large sketching pad.

After some time the visits to Riksmuseet came to an end. I had entered a period when I was terribly scared of skeletons. Most dangerous of all were the skeletons which illustrated the entry on MAN in the encyclopedia. But my fear extended to skeletons in general, consequently also to the elephant skeletons at the museums. I was even afraid of my own drawing of them and did not dare open the pad.

I turned my attention to Järnvägsmuseet, the museum of railways. Nowadays, it is spaciously situated at the edge of the town of Gävle, but in those days it was squeezed into a single city block in Klara. A couple of times a week, my maternal grandfather and I would amble down from the heights of Söder to visit the museum. Granddad must have been quite taken by the model trains himself or he would hardly have been able to tolerate it. The day was complete when we ended up at the nearby railway station, Stockholm Central, where full-sized trains steamed in.

The staff noticed the child's fanaticism, and on one occasion I was invited in to the museum office and got to write my name (with a reversed S) in a guest book. I wanted to become a railway engineer. I was, however, more interested in the steam engines than in the modern, electrical ones. In other words, I was more of a romantic than an engineer.

Later when I was of school age I returned to Riksmuseet. I was now an amateur zoologist, serious, precocious. I sat poring over books about insects and fish.

I had started my own collection. It could fit into a small cabinet at home. But inside my head an immense museum was growing, and between the imaginary museum and the very real one in Frescati there was mutual interaction.

About every other Sunday I went out to Riksmuseet. I would take the streetcar to Roslagstull and walk the last kilometers. It was always farther than I had imagined. I remember these wanderings very well—it was always windy, my nose was running, my eyes were watering. I don't remember walking in the opposite direction. It was as if I was never going home, only there, a sniffling, teary-eyed, expectant wandering toward that giant Babylonian building.

When I got there, I was greeted by the elephant skeletons. Often I would go directly to the "old" section, where the animals had been stuffed as early as the eighteenth century, some quite awkwardly prepared with swollen heads. Still, there was a kind of magic there. Large artificial landscapes with elegantly designed model animals did not catch my imagination—that was make-believe for children. No, it had to be clearly apparent that these were not live animals but stuffed ones. Animals in the service of science. The science of Linnaeus, which was the kind that I felt a kinship with.

The visit of the museum proceeded. A prolonged stay with the whales in the paleontological section. And then the section where I spent most of my time: invertebrates.

I never came in contact with another visitor. Actually, I don't remember there being any other visitors. Other museums which I occasionally visited—the Maritime, the Ethnographic, the Museum of Applied Sciences—were always crowded. But Riksmuseet seemed to stay open only for me.

One day I did meet another human being. No, he was no

ordinary visitor but a professor or something, employed at the museum. We met in the invertebrate section, where he suddenly materialized among the display cases, not much taller than I. He was talking to himself. Immediately we got involved in a conversation about mollusks. He was so absentminded or unbiased that he treated me like a grown-up. One of those guardian angels who appeared from time to time during my childhood and touched me with his wings. The conversation led to my being allowed to enter a section that was not open to the public. I was given a host of good advice about how to prepare small animals, and I left fitted out with tiny glass tubes that looked like part of a set of real professional tools.

From age eleven until I was roughly fifteen, I primarily collected insects and beetles. Then other competing interests interfered, especially artistic ones. How sad that entomology had to make room for them. But I told myself that it was only temporary, in fifty years or so I would start collecting again.

Collecting began in the spring but it came into full bloom in the summer on the island of Runmarö. In the summer house, where we were many sharing a very small space, there were glass jars with small dead insects and a spreading board for butterflies. And above it all floated a stench of vinegar ether, which by the way followed me around as well, since I always carried a jar with the insect-killing agent in my pocket.

For sure, the cool thing to do would have been to use potassium cyanide, as the handbook recommended. Luckily, I did not have access to it and I never had to be faced with the test of manhood in saying yes or no to it.

Many others took part in my chase for insects. Children in the neighborhood learned to sound the alarm when they saw some little creature that might be of interest. "An aaanimal!" The cries resounded in the village and I came running with the butterfly net.

I was always out on expeditions. This was life in nature without the slightest notion that it was healthy. I had no aesthetic notions either—this was science, after all—but I experienced beauty often without knowing it. I was inside the great mystery. I learned that the ground was alive, that there was a vast creeping and flying world that lived a rich life of its own without worrying about us in the least. I caught a fraction of a fraction of that world and nailed it in my boxes, which I still own. A hidden mini-museum that I am hardly ever conscious of. But there they are, the little creatures, as if biding their time.

Translator's note: Klara was an old neighborhood in Stockholm, demolished in the 1960s. Newspapers had their offices and printing presses there, and bohemian and literary life is said to have flourished in the run-down cafés and bars. Söder was until recently the working-class neighborhood of Stockholm, situated on a cliff to the south of the Old Town.

—Translated by Joanna Bankier

David Ray

Two Poems

For Thomas Hart Benton and Robert Bly

The day we brought Bly by to meet you
Rita said you were up to people
for one hour only. But we had a visit
that's endured for fifteen years.
You sipped your bourbon, then walked
us out to your garage, showed us
the painting you were restoring —
and all the while mumbling your memoirs
as we do, circling round and round
younger pictures of ourselves.
In the chat of that brick garage
you let us know who modeled
for that naked woman stretched out lithe
and long upon the golden haystack.
And let us know as well that you
were the leering farmer peeking
around that haystack at her,
like an elder at Susanna. Then
we went back in to take our leave
from her and you — no longer old Tom
or old Rita. Each time I pause
at that painting now that it's back
on the Nelson wall, I think of you,
old farmer in love with the sun
and the hay and the woman,
gazing out from your hiding place
with that straw in your mouth
and your brow cleft by that crack
        I see on my own face now.

Mehr Licht

Mehr Licht!—Goethe's last words

1.
Begin anew with this weeping.
Surely it has purified, allowed touch anew.
Such tears could not have been given for nothing.
They were meant to presage a new beginning.
No matter that these are the same hands
with which we worked and failed.
The earth has been the same earth always
yet with spirit has tried again and again
and has not been content with the darkness.
We too can turn toward the light
in our desperation.

2.
If you have, this day, found nothing
it is because you have not scoured the earth
down to bedrock. A friend may yet turn up.
The trivial chore may yet lead to enlightenment.
But if you make no beginning, rise not
to your tiptoes, searching sky as well as earth,
there will be nothing, as you have said,
as they have shown again and again, nothing—
If you wish to descend to the hell of your choice
you have every excuse. But the secrets were always
there inside the stones, and those stones present
from the beginning, when you chose blindness—
or as you would have it, blindness was chosen for you.

3.
Imagine the man with the stolen masterpiece
who must enjoy it in private, in his own secret cavern,
like that little hunchback Pope who had a grotto
not far from the river. Even so the numinous
truth given by moon or the simple beasts or by trees
must be kept in silence. World will never forgive
such awkwardness of speaking of what was revealed
just as the moon broke through dark clouds,
a truth to keep in its unbearable solitude.
You can with one prayer be the equal of that thief
who carried a masterpiece out of the Prado
or that hunchback who took the words of his poems
as the spiders spun them, inside the grotto.
And there are words men give to others
only with their last breath, give to men, to spiders,
to the great moth beating his wings, swooping near.

4.
"Mehr licht" is the way to say it.
If you are dying, no matter. If you plan
to live forever, your insight may yet be valid.
Joy of this moment is everything.
To see, to accept that the light has been there
all along and you blind to it, that is enough.
You simply forgot to call out.
Your lifetime of blindness has been only that,
forgetfulness, not calling out
to those gods others are blind to. But better late,
better very late than never—to behold,
to cry out for more light.

5.
A year should be caged, not allowed
to take other years with it. If a fire
or a bomb, then that year must not
take other years with it, become
a great fireball rolling toward eternity,
scorching earth's vast field, meadow of years.
Swaddle the years. Some deserve
no more than a bodybag, not chance
for rebirth. Give the years firewalls,
on one side an orchard with fruit,
lover beneath the tree beside the small pond
with sedge and rushes. Be lifted again
as Moses was lifted in that year.
Find it rather than wander lands tangled with thorn,
charred stumps, gouged irremediable earth.
You must insist that a year can kill
no more than itself, not like some berserk madman
take more life than its own, let its fire roll
over the meadows, and the precious past, too.

6.
Calling for more light, you seek
the friend who cannot reach you,
who may not even exist. Yet you are dead
wrong not to be sitting by your phone
or waiting in the public place in sight, not
turning your back on the mailbox, forgetting
to hail the postman, asking him to search deeper.
Your hunger is a part of the landscape, an old ruin.
When you waited for your father, you were better
at it, the waiting, the hunger. Dust settled
over the road where only other fathers arrived.
You waited many years, but his advent
is not a fact of history. You have it all wrong.
He did not descend to you, lift you from dust

by that roadside. He did not come roaring
down that red earth road, yet you still cough
from that dust of his travels! Inside
the great cloud of father and son dust
you embrace and tell him of days and nights
without him. His car should be in a museum—
but his foot on the running board, too,
bronze man—and the boy still looking up.
Compared with that waiting, this should be easy.
Friend, you exist, and you lift me up now.
Is that not what Goethe said to the light?

7.
Westwards, beside his father, a boy jabbers away
to his dad of all those days and nights
without him. Chrome face of the Indian chief
heads into the wind. In your mind,
your face a brave one, too, you moved right along
with your father. The car headed west,
extra wheel inset on the fender, another
on the back, tires and wheels enough
to travel forever. Today when you wait
it is for friendship at most, neither father
nor son. And hence it should be easy,
this waiting, well done, and without tears.
Friend, you exist, and you have reached me today.

8.
Those who have more love in their hearts
than faces confess may forgive you. They too
have babbled to light or dead daughters or sons.
Sky is held up by no more than a twig.
Face glimpsed in a gum machine mirror
has more substance than yours, yet
it sustains you. How could you doubt
your existence, or light's? They do very well,
these twigs that hold the sky up, and one block
of ruins is proof of the Communitas gone,
the passionate voice. Vanished Christ stood
on the stone block, pointed over their heads,
raved, they said—meaning shared what he could
till his voice petered out. Glance
at these men in the streets, forgive them
as they may forgive. They are no worse
than the others on Death Row. Therefore, forgive.
Father, forgive. And dear son, forgive.
These derelict strangers are stumbling
with fire at their backs, too. They too
call out for more light, claw the sky for it.

Reading at Muskego Church, St. Paul, Minnesota, during the videotaping of A Man Writes to a Part of Himself, *1978 (Rick Snider photo).*

Charles Molesworth

Thinking About Robert Bly's Smoke

THE STORY OF ROBERT BLY'S once polemical intervention into the world of contemporary poetry is by now so familiar that it has become prey to the same mental attitudes that he worked hard to change: routinized acceptance of the unusual, the glorification of the normal (or what common sense regards as normal), the de-ritualizing of everyday life. This is a great shame, of course, since that intervention was (and is!) animated by exceptional energy and a genuine concern for poetry and the spiritual values poetry was developed to protect and foster. I say protect and foster, but in fact it is in the distinction between these two actions that we can read much of Bly's meanings. The post-Romantic era in poetry rests so soundly upon the notion that the spiritual must be protected, protected from the invasion of the secular, from the loss of transcendence, from everything entailed in what Wordsworth called "getting and spending" that I think many poets don't even realize what a struggle it was to originate the *cordon sanitaire*. But even more shrouded in ignorance is the idea that such protection could be *fostered*. The notion that a poet in the last third of the twentieth century could go about loudly proclaiming the benefits of, even proselytizing for, the transformative power of poetry is, well, naive at best and unseemly at worst. Naiveté and unseemliness Bly has indeed been guilty of, in fullest measure.

One way to sanitize Bly is to incorporate him into the large and deep current within modernism that wishes to break down the boundaries between art and life. With Bly this would mean finding a way to carry the transforming powers of art back out of poetry into the everyday world, where it could there begin to change the very sense of what it means to be human. Such a deep current has many similarities with wisdom literature, and Bly can also be read as a writer in this tradition. But given the general antipathy that exists between modernism and wisdom literature, Bly can just as readily be dismissed as muddleheaded and contradictory. The most notorious of many such dismissals is that of James Dickey. When asked in 1969 to evaluate Bly's work, James Dickey said that he would "authorize only a one-word statement, and that is 'Pitiful.'" I have always been amused by this response, as indeed I am often amused by Dickey's performances. What I especially like is the use of the word "authorize." This connotes the world of authentic signatures, customer warranties, and advertising claims. Dickey's work as an advertising copywriter has persistently stayed with him, and it has marked his work and life in ways that are breathtaking to contemplate.

Allen Tate has also excoriated Bly, referring to his "misinformed attacks on other poets, his self-advertising through his own journal, *The Sixties*, his boorish public manners." Now when he wrote these words, Tate also explained that if he had thought a little more highly of Mr. Bly he might have been willing to take time away from what he was writing to say more; Tate also insisted that Bly apologize for something he said in public about John Crowe Ransom. In short, Tate could not refrain—in even the simplest statement—from advertising his own work and being boorish enough to call for an apology for something someone said about a third party! To write in publicly accepted forms one cannot help but open him- or herself to the charge of self-advertising (see Rousseau) or the insensitivity that results from self-blindedness (see Derrida on Rousseau). Tate's insensitivity—his mannered way of presenting his opinions on Bly as of clearly less worth than his own writing (but then going ahead to utter very opinionated dismissals of Bly's person and work)—is so tangled up in the structures of the writerly ego that he is perhaps to be forgiven for an inability to see around the corners of the redoubt of his own self-regard.

I bring up these attacks against Bly in what is a context of celebration in part because I think they go to the center of his worth as a poet. Bly has not earned medals for bravery just because he was attacked by people like Dickey and Tate; many American writers have endured far worse, from Melville to Dreiser and from Margaret

Fuller to Richard Wright. But by showing all of us—especially those of us who grew up in the thin air of Formalism and New Criticism and academic poetry—that poets could (and even should) ask questions about values, and about values at the supposedly mundane level of social habits and political choices, Bly opened his art to the warming winds of change as well as the chill air of doctrine. Since I shared Bly's opposition to the war in Vietnam (though not necessarily all the points of his analysis or the logic of his response), it is perhaps too easy for me, pace Tate, to say that his entanglement of poetry and the antiwar movement was the best thing to happen to American writing in the 1960s. And since I share his aversion to the maudlin ethos of confessional poetry (though without subscribing to his addition to the post-symboliste poetics of the deep image), perhaps I am the wrong person to offer a balanced assessment of his role in American poetry. But I take some comfort in realizing that a critic can and should identify his or her political persuasion both before and through the act of criticism, and that we can live with the ideal of disinterestedness and the demands of personal and group commitment without either the ideal crushing us into bland silence or the commitment turning our works into self-righteous bombast. In short, Bly opened up the dialogue about poetry and other values. He has not, as far as I can tell, shifted into a postmodern form of poetry or dialogue, which is another way of saying that he has not become politically cynical or theoretical to the point of emptily rehearsing abstruse positions. But by risking the charge of naiveté in his search for a straightforward truth, he has created much heat, some light, and a minimum of smoke.

I would not want this occasion to pass without talking about one of Bly's poems. But which should I choose? The burden of finding a representative poem is perhaps misguided, and yet I don't want simply to play favorites. If I were to choose only my favorite, I would pick something from one of the prose poems; if I were to talk about his most significant poem, it would probably be "Sleepers Joining Hands." So I will suggest that there is a representative Bly poem (as there is for any poet who works at it for any period of time, and despite the perplexities and complexities of personal and artistic growth, change, and development). We need something, then, that will in some way recapitulate Bly's great themes — transforming the self, reenergizing the sensorium — while at the same time it reenacts the typical Bly sense of aesthetic form — the leaping through images, the plainsong of common words turned prophetic. Here is *the* Bly lyric:

Watering the Horse

How strange to think of giving up all ambition!
Suddenly I see with such clear eyes
The white flake of snow
That has just fallen in the horse's mane!

I realized recently that I had misremembered this poem: I went for several weeks thinking the first line of the poem came at the end. The difference is, of course, crucial. My misreading makes the abandonment of ambition a goal to be striven for, as if the lyric were a straightforwardly ascetic piece of Christian piety, as if the rigor of Jacob Boehme could be versified into a hymnbook format. But by putting it first Bly makes the abandoned ambition something to be imagined, something that exists in the optative mood; he knows that it can never happen, not as long as there are egos and social structures that embody the worst features of ego-structures. The poem's truth depends upon our ability to let that optative hang over us as we read, to hear the torsion in the sentence as the exclamatory mood ("How strange . . .") modulates into something like an optative ("to think of giving up . . ."). The mind is imagining at the same time it acknowledges the limits of its imagination ("How strange . . ."). In this way Bly can be read (allegorically, distantly) as knowing that one can never give up ambition simply by thinking about doing it; indeed, if and when ambition is ever abandoned it will probably be because certain sorts of thoughts have ceased altogether. The poem's gently ironic form implies that having this impossible wish/condition hanging in front of us in fact allows us to see what we could not otherwise have seen. But if pellucid sight can come about from the very *thought* of giving up ambition, what might not the final accomplishment produce! In the meantime, we know that just outside the text (but how far away *that* is!) the body heat of the horse will melt the snowflake, and this brief moment of the snowflake's "life" is the true allegorical center of the poem—the center that tells us that nothing can persist, nothing remains present except, perhaps, the subtlety of the mental ability to know optatively what is not in front of us. But this knowing that which is not present is, of course, the same mental faculty that lies at the very root of ambition, the hunger for the not-yet, the weight of that which is painfully absent yet fully desired. The poem has traces of smoke even as it tries so hard to see clearly.

The other thing to realize about the poem is that its effect is due largely to words like "such" and "just," plain English words whose role as intensifiers is tied up with their very plainness. (But, like the "very" in the preceding sentence, such words can become empty, or nearly so, through overuse.) Those who read Bly negatively or skeptically are likely to be unwilling to grant full force to his intensifiers. And, to be candid, Bly doesn't have the intricate and urgent spoken music of Creeley; his prosody (or antiprosody, perhaps) is rather more like, say, Frank O'Hara's, like that of someone who trusts the purity of his feeling and the immediacy of his response to carry him through the metrical and rhythmic pitfalls—not exactly possessed by Emerson's "meter making argument," but beholden to something of the same Protestant temper, nonetheless.

Robert, you probably don't remember, but on one of the two or three occasions we met, you gave me some advice. I had just published a negative review of a poet and was aware of how you had lamented the appearance of so much mediocre poetry and yet how few negative reviews there were. So I wasn't all that surprised when you told me that you liked my review, and agreed with it. But then you said something that took me completely by surprise: you said my review was insufficient because I should have shown the poet the way out of the artistic dead end that was blocking his ability.

I said nothing at the time, but went through at least three strong reactions over the next few years: first, it wasn't the critic's business to point out the "right" way, but only to assess what was there; second, who was I to even begin to tell another poet how to do it better; third, what was wrong with the Blys of the world is they think they must always be instructing others.

Now I see the virtue of your advice (while also maintaining how wrong it might be). But I think you will know what I mean when I say that I cannot for an instant imagine following such advice.

Flanked by James Wright, left, and James Dickey, right, 1960 (photographer unknown; from Robert Bly collection).

Annie Wright

Joining Hands with Robert Bly

I HEARD MANY STORIES about Robert Bly long before I met him. During the winter of 1967, before my late husband, James Wright, and I were married, I heard about James's visits to the Bly farm in Minnesota, the work he and Robert did, and the fun they had.

I knew about the chicken house where James stayed, and about the day Robert locked him in so he was forced to finish a long-overdue translation. I heard about the barn where Robert and Carol built a stage, and the plays they gave there. I knew about David the swaybacked palomino, and Simon the big shaggy dog. I heard about the children: godchild Mary with hair the color of a new penny, and Biddy, who liked to climb on James's lap, hiking herself up by the hair of his beard. When Noah was born, I was with James when he sent Carol a bouquet in honor of the birth.

After we married, I finally saw it all for myself as we went to the farm for a delayed honeymoon. Robert met us in Minneapolis where we were staying with Roland Flint. He arrived at Roland's house after a fishing trip. My first glimpse of this tall, sunburned man with mosquito bites all over his arms was watching him bend over Roland's freezer to ease in a huge plastic sack of fish caught on the trip. When he saw us, he gave a great shout of joy, hugging us both at the same time.

That night we went to the Guthrie Theater to see an incredibly bad performance of a Greek play. When it was over James and Robert called out, "Bad! Oh, bad!"

The next day we drove to the farm, Robert and James talking all the way. Robert's strong deep voice had a strong deep Minnesota accent. He peppered his conversation with the query, "How does that grab you?"

He thought and acted on impulse. Out of nowhere came the joking compliment to James: "If you keep publishing poems about illegal fishing nets, James Wright, I'm going to have the game warden after me."

Noting a fruit stand by the side of the road, he brought the car to an abrupt stop, leaped out, bought a watermelon, cut it up for us with his jackknife, and drove on. We ate the slices, quenching our thirst in the August heat.

Robert had prepared the schoolhouse for us to stay in. It was an old one-room schoolhouse bought at an auction. The Blys had brought it back to the farm and set it in a small grove of trees down the hill from the field where the big house was. Robert and Tim Baland, a young writer staying on the farm, had cleaned and arranged some furniture in the little building. It was a pleasant room with a beautiful old bed of carved wood at one end and some easy chairs and a writing table at the other.

At an appropriate distance was the outhouse. Robert told us when three young writers came for a visit he set them to work digging the foundation for the outhouse. He grinned ferociously, adding, "They left pretty soon after that."

Robert showed me all around the farm. David and Simon had long since gone. The chicken house was now a study for himself, but in another grove of trees was a screen house for guests.

The main house that James knew from the days when he lived in Minneapolis had been enlarged by adding another house to it. Robert showed us the new rooms. The extra kitchen was an office for *The Sixties* and Odin House publications. There was an L-shaped room for Mary and Biddy downstairs and two little rooms for them upstairs. As we passed the open door of a storeroom on the second floor, Robert pointed to a big fishing net on the floor.

"That's the very net, Annie. That's the illegal fishing net."

Carol and the children were away during the first few days of our visit. Robert and Tim worked most of the morning and early afternoon. Then we all went into Madison to do the grocery shopping. While I prepared dinner, the three men talked in the living room. After we ate, we went for walks along the deserted highway.

One evening as we walked toward an enormous, lone cottonwood tree, Robert told us how the farmers really hated trees.

Although each farm had a grove of trees planted in careful rows, it was only because the government would pay for them that they existed.

"Come on, Annie and Jim," Robert would call out just before we reached home again, "we're going to lie down and listen for animals."

We would lie in the high grass of the ditch beside the road, listening. Robert would whisper about the rabbits, or mice, or owls we might hear. We never did, though. We only heard the hot summer breeze blowing through the wheat.

After our walks, we gathered in the chicken house to listen to records; folk songs, symphonies, or The Fugs. Robert might read us a crank letter sent to him as editor of *The Sixties*. He and James read aloud the translations of the Spanish poets they loved. Often Robert read something he was working on.

When Carol and the children came back, we went swimming in the late afternoon with Mary and Biddy. Robert would buy candy for them, although they weren't supposed to have it. At meal times, the table was full and we were loud with laughter and conversation.

One day the living room was covered with piles and piles of papers. "We're getting out *The Sixties*," explained Robert.

He and Tim sifted through heaps of manuscripts and letters. By the end of the day selections were made, papers were arranged in tidy stacks, and Robert was typing letters of rejection and acceptance.

"Here's my answer to this one," said Robert, holding up a poem typed out in the form of a Coke bottle. "I hate light verse! How does that grab you?"

During our visit, people dropped by constantly. Lois and David Budbill stopped for a night. Fred Manfred came over from Blue Mounds bringing his sleeping bag with him. Hardie St. Martin flew in for a long stay. When Hardie and Fred were there, we had a big fried chicken, potato salad picnic at Lac Qui Parle, spending the day swimming, eating, and talking.

The entire visit was filled with expansive conversation. My head reeled with the talk of poets and poetry, old stories of the farm during the fifties and sixties, tales of Robert's childhood on his parents' farm, visits he and Carol made to Norway and England.

Robert would make outrageous statements and judgments.

"I think he," referring to a mutual friend, "is like an omelette without eggs."

"The reason we have three different races on this planet is because each race came from a different place in outer space. Annie, how does that grab you?"

We were all glum when the visit came to an end. As Robert drove us to the airport he commented, "I feel so sad."

We saw Robert many times after that. He, Carol, and the children stayed in New York for a few months in 1968. We often went to their rented apartment. Sometimes we would have dinner there with the Simpsons, or Galins, or Ignatows. Sometimes, we just went to talk in the afternoons after work. Mary and Biddy came to the nursery school where I was director. Robert might arrive at the school to pick them up, stunning all the children with his height and warm laugh.

That was the year Robert won the National Book Award. We were in the audience cheering and stamping when he read the acceptance speech we all knew by heart.

Over the years, Robert swept in and out of New York City. He might appear at our house, dressed in his Mexican serape, with a group of fans and a bottle of Scotch. He might come alone. Once Layle Silbert came with him to photograph Robert, and ended up taking pictures of both him and James wearing the rubber masks Robert had used for his readings.

Sometimes he stayed over with us. He always brought a present: a roast chicken, a bouquet of flowers, a book, once a pair of golden earrings for me.

We never knew when we might get a call urging us to come with him to the Kinnells', or to join a group at Bobo's in Chinatown, or to see Mary when he brought her.

It was always exciting, always a time filled with people, food, long conversations, and great warmth. Each time we saw him, Robert had new ideas. He talked of Jung and the multitudinous levels of consciousness. He discovered new books by new poets. He talked of his Great Mother Conferences, or new foods, or how some stones could speak, but we might not hear them for a thousand years. He continued to be outrageous with funny stories and comments.

In the spring of 1970, we made one more trip to the farm. It was bitter cold, even for March, even for Minnesota. The small groves of leafless trees, surrounding barns and houses like islands in a flat white sea, looked pitiful and forlorn in the cold.

Carol had sold a story and used the money to build a fireplace in the living room. We read and talked in front of its warmth. The fishnet was still in the storeroom, but there were changes. Mary and Biddy could read, and Noah could walk and talk.

Our schoolhouse was now a place of meditation for Robert. Concerned that we might miss the atmosphere of the first visit, he offered to set up the carved wooden bed for us, even though it was stored away in the barn.

We continued to see Robert when he came to New York. During all the years of their friendship, James and Robert corresponded. Sometimes James didn't answer letters and sometimes Robert didn't. While it wavered from time to time, the correspondence never stopped. Their lives had changed from the time on the farm when James went out in need of quiet and friendship. Their ideas, so similar in the fifties, were now quite different in the seventies. But their feelings about each other were just as strong.

Robert came to see James at the hospital. Earlier in the fall, after a long lapse, their correspondence had been renewed. Robert came into the hospital room quietly, taking James into his arms, IV tubes and all. Although James could not talk, he wrote notes to Robert on a yellow-lined legal pad. Robert talked and James answered him in writing. James was alert and responsive in a way he hadn't been for some months and rarely would be again. After Robert left, James wrote me a note saying:

I was afraid Robert was gone for good.
I'm so relieved he's not.
Today was good.

The winter after James's death, Robert came into New York. I saw him at a party given by Saul Galin. The famous serape had been replaced by a vest stitched in an elegant pattern of roosters, embellished by a flowing black tie. When he saw me he pulled me into the kitchen so I could see our godchild, Mary, now a freshman at Harvard. During the party Robert urged old friends to meet new friends. He praised Jane Kenyon's translations of Anna Akhmatova and recited some of them, accompanied by his dulcimer. As always, with Robert, there was conversation, music, poetry, and friends.

Robert read James's poetry and spoke of his life at the memorial reading organized by Betty Kray and the Academy of American Poets in 1981. In 1991 he spoke with Galway Kinnell at Martins Ferry, Ohio, for the eleventh James Wright Poetry Festival. During the ten years in between Robert started conferences for men, wrote *Iron John,* and became a household name.

At the festival in Ohio, Robert stepped aside from his own gains when he read James's work and spoke of the golden days on the farm. As he joined hands with James long ago in Minnesota, when James needed comfort and companionship, as he joined hands with me on my first visit to the farm, so he joined hands with all of us at that gathering. Joining hands is one of Robert's special gifts.

3
GROWING ORBITS

Coleman Barks

Becoming Milton

AFTER I HAD KNOWN Robert Bly for about ten years, it suddenly struck me that he looked like my grandmother. The readiness around the mouth and chin are remarkably similar. She also wrote poems of a demanding clarity, but hers were about making one's bed *as* one got up, and doing the dishes *immediately* after supper. I wish they could have met, Robert and my grandmother Bryan, Lizzie, both so surprisingly goofy at moments, yet always formidable.

When my uncle Rich, then in his early twenties, came back from World War II, which he spent in Iceland learning how to drink and curse, he was using his new soldier-words totally unconsciously at the homecoming dinner table. During a confused and ominous lull in conversation, grandmother turned to my mother and said, "Bets, pass the goddamn butter, please." That's how she could cut through the amenities, lancing and healing the situation at once.

In the wider arena I have long admired Robert's direct and fearless confrontation of American society, especially the brutish cruelties and the way we deny them. Here's a poem of my own that owes a lot to his stepping out ahead in such matters.

Becoming Milton

Milton, the airport driver, retired now
from trucking, who ferried me
from the Greenville-Spartanburg airport
to Athens last Sunday, midnight to 2:30 a.m.,
tells me about his son, Tom, just back
from the Gulf War. "He's at Fort Stewart
with the 102nd Mechanized, the first tank unit
over the line, not a shot fired at them.
The boy had never even come up on a car accident
here at home, twenty-four years old. Can you
imagine what he lifted the lid to find?
Three helmets with heads in them staring
from the floor and that's just one tank.
He has screaming flashbacks, can't talk about it
anymore. I just told him to be strong
and put it out of his mind. With time,
if you stay strong, those things'll go away.
Or they'd find a bunker, one of those holes
they hid in, and yell something in American,
and wait a minute and then roll grenades in
and check it and find nineteen freshly killed guys,
some sixty, some fourteen, real thin.
They were just too scared to move.
He feels pretty bad about it, truthfully,
all this yellow ribbon celebrating.
It wasn't a war really. I mean he says
it was just piles and piles of their bodies.
Some of his friends got sick, started vomiting,
and had to be walked back to the rear.
Looks like to me it could have been worked
some other way. My boy came through OK,
but he won't go back, I'll tell you that.
He's getting out as soon as he can.
First chance comes, he'll be in Greenville

selling cars, or fixing them. He's good at both.
Pretty good carpenter too, you know how I know?
He'll tear the whole thing out if it's not right
and start over. There's some that'll look
at a board that's not flush and say *shit,*
nail it, but he can't do that, Tom."

Nils Peterson

"The Seeds of Longing:"
Some Words About Robert

I

JANUARY. THE EARLY EIGHTIES. A high house overlooking a deep cut in the Santa Cruz mountains, brush-covered at the rim, but sloping steeply down into a redwood forest. A gathering of writers for a workshop. Robert had read powerfully the night before, work ranging from "The Dead Seal" to his translations of Kabir. Masks and energy. Eros and spirit. Moments of manic extroversion. Moments of what sometimes felt to me a loud performer's quiet. Most of us had been there and at a reception beforehand. I had heard him read at other times and talked with him at other receptions. I had among my things rejection slips from *The Fifties* and *The Sixties* with notes on them like, "These poems are anally oriented," but at least the notes were handwritten. There was a human on the other end doing the work of reading. I had appreciated that.

Some high-spirited chatter. A search for comfortable seats. A settling into a nervous quiet, and now across Robert's animated face, a quieting and a deepening. He picks up his dulcimer (the instrument he used then), fondles it, tweedles a peg as if to tighten it, then runs his thumb across the strings in a chord, and, with the first trembling of sound, I find I am crying. I am shocked, so shocked I do not defend against my tears. Let them come, something in me says. Let them use themselves up, wear themselves out, finish of their own will.

But they do not stop coming—not sobs, mind, but a steady flow of tears. All evening I weep softly in my chair, and through the night, and all day Saturday and Saturday night, and Sunday morning. I do the work, write my exercises, laboring with objects, trying to describe them, trying to get inside to their beings, trying to ride on them out into the cosmos. I talk with my old friends, try to make new ones, pick at my food, feel grateful for a glass of wine, but all the while I am weeping, sometimes more obviously than others. On Sunday morning, during our break, Robert calls me over and says, "Let's go for a walk," so off we go down a road and into the woods toward a moss-covered opening in a rock face, more than a crack and less than a cave, a groin, where we had done some writing the day before, and he asks what is going on with me, and I, not knowing, from some place a thousand miles inside, try to explain.

What can I remember of that walk? I can remember it felt good to stride shoulder to shoulder with him in a slow gray cold almost-drizzle, he in his black wool Minnesota topcoat and Russian fur hat, I in my California parka, descendants of Norwegians and Swedes, little bits and pieces of the old country still clinging to us. I am taller, but he seemed larger and more solidly present. Perhaps a longing for some of that solidity and presence was there in my weeping, but also an awareness of how much I had defended myself against, how much and in how many ways. Part of it was a longing driven underground years before by my early encounters with the Lutheran church where, to my eye, it seemed the strong, powerful Scandinavian males I knew during the week left their strength and energy at the door on Sunday mornings. As I looked from my sullen pew at the face of Pastor Lundquist, something in me knew it was shaped by forces that I did not want to shape my face. When I watched the deepening look on Robert's face at the beginning of the seminar, that same something realized I had made a grave error about the nature of soul and spirit. They did not have to work by way of demasculinization. What I sensed in his face entered me the moment his fingers freed the first shimmering minor chord. I had heard it at the reading on Thursday, though, defended, I had not known I heard it. Now, standing by this split rock, trying to tell him some of this, I felt comforted by the set of his shoulders and jaw, and the soft, thick, strong fingers of his hands. I felt myself paradoxically both softer and stronger.

This was a weekend of working with objects, those exercises he has done with so many of us. This was the weekend that, as we all rooted around outside looking for things to write about, Robert found the stick, "long, bent, ragged, bark gone," that begins "My Father's Wedding," and I think too he began work on "A Chunk of Amethyst," with its disciplined planes that suggest "there is no use in trying to live forever" and the oyster "impenetrable and thuggy" that became part of his small book of translations from Ponge and his own poems in the same vein. So, there was a continual electrical crackling of correspondences just below the air as we tasted, smelled, and touched things and were touched by them in return.

The following summer, after attending my first long workshop with Robert, I wrote the following to a friend trying to explain how I felt when I returned:

> somehow larger,
> somehow carrying great space in my chest
> as if the membrane that separates me from everything
> else had grown elastic, stretchy and freer,
> as if I had taken a longed-for deep breath.

Something in me feels that still.

II

One of the things one learns while working with Robert is to accept the gifts the world sends. So, a friend sends me an essay on *Hamlet*. I am at the same time reading in the works of the French philosopher, Gaston Bachelard. Mostly, I am thinking about what I want to say about Robert's poetry, and the convergence of letter and reading becomes an entrance. There is a lovely mysteriousness about this.

Bachelard talks about "our instinct of verticality, an instinct which is repressed by the needs of everyday, prosaically horizontal life," a cross, then, where the ordinary needs of our ongoingness and the extraordinary needs of something other, which, as Bachelard's use of the word "instinct" implies, is also an inborn part of our natures, intersect (*On Poetic Imagination and Reverie*, Spring, 1987).

He is speaking here of "dreams of height," where, "Living at the zenith of the upright object, gathering reveries of verticality, we experience a transcendence of being. The image of verticality brings us into the realm of values." But he also questions, "May dreams develop in which the above forgets and suppresses the below?" Robert, whose exuberance can carry him right off the ground, has had a fear of this. It is expressed in general in his suspicion of "the California soft male." It is expressed in his own life in a poem like "Fifty Males Sitting Together," where the son

> . . . turns away,
> loses courage,
> goes outdoors to feed with wild
> things, lives among dens
> and huts, eats distance and silence;
> he grows long wings, enters the spiral, ascends.
>
> How far he is from working men when he is done!
> From all men!

But the vertical axis, like a tree, does not just rise from the horizon line carrying us into the cold, pure sky. It also descends into the earth. So, Bachelard, following, says, "The root is the mysterious tree, it is the subterranean, inverted tree. For the root, the darkest earth — like the pond, but without the pond — is also a mirror, a strange opaque mirror which doubles every aerial reality with a subterranean image." "As above, so below." It is the path below Robert has chosen or that has chosen him. He has said again and again we must go downward into grief. To continue from "Fifty Males":

> The males singing
> chant far out
> on the water grounded in downward shadow.

> He cannot go there because
> he has not grieved
> as humans grieve.

This downward movement through the root of grief into the earth becomes for Robert a way into the fullness of humanity.

In "Hamlet's Poisoned Ear" (*Echo's Subtle Body*, Spring, 1982), the essay my friend sent, Patricia Berry, a Jungian psychologist, suggests that verticality is an "anchor," a "connection with some God, principle, tradition." But, by reminding us that Hamlet's connection is with a ghost, she makes us aware that the "vertical axis to the underworld is dangerous indeed." For too far down the vertical axis leads us to death as too far up leads us to a kind of inhumanity.

An awareness of the richness of descent as well as its dangers is the central subject of Robert's unpublished play for two voices, "The Raven Man and the Dandy Walker." In it two characters debate the nature of the world we are most called to. The Raven Man says, "We go down to visit the dead, and join the soul," and, later, "How can I be human if I am not sad?" This is his case:

> Our first eyes see
> children, birds, angels, particles of light—someone gouges out
> those eyes. When our second eyes grow in,
> we see inward and downward.

The Dandy Walker replies:

> When I walk I see
> wind, leaf, and star, lightpoles, old tires, lime trees,
> I walk and praise, so that the soul in me
> can dress, while still alive, in that sweet robe.
> The robe the soul requires to be married
> is that great dress of sun, bright moon, and stars,
> the river bank in shadow, the mountain in light,
> harvest and springtime, husk, seed, husband and wife.

Again and again in Robert's poetry, we find a love for the shinings of things, a marvelous, sensuous apprehension. We also find a suspicion of that love, as if it were an enchantress, and the earth a "bower of bliss" designed to seduce us away from the holiness and humanness of our grief. The tension in Robert's poetry between "The Raven Man," the downward vertical, with its call toward darkness, grief, and the eternal, and "The Dandy Walker," the horizontal, with its call toward shaded light, joy, and the now, is a source of its energy. For myself, I love the names of these two parts of his being. They put a "skin" on the abstract so I can know it. The horizontal and the vertical become embodied and, before our eyes, strut their stuff, argue their cases, and act out their story while we listen, applaud, and choose first one side and then the other.

III

I began with a story. Robert loves stories, and telling stories, and storytellers. He loves to tell and hear jokes that arrive at their point by way of a story. Last spring, while looking through his poetry for a different way of introducing him, I noticed how often he uses a story of one or two sentences in his poetry. Here are some examples of what I mean:

Something homeless is looking on the long roads,
A dog lost since midnight, a box-elder
Bug who doesn't know
Its walls are gone, its house
Burnt.
from "Uneasiness in Fall"

The stiff-haired son has slouched in
And gone to bed.
from "Cornpicker Poem"

The dying man waves his son away.
He wants his daughter-in-law to come near

so that her hair will fall over his face.
                    from "A Conversation"

The mother puts down her rolling pin and makes no more
        bread.
And the wife looks at her husband one night at a party
        and loves him no more.
The energy leaves the wine, and the minister falls leaving
        the church.
                from "Snowbanks North of the House"

These sentences—which in a fiction writer would be no more than entries in a notebook—are enough. Lives summed up. We feel all that has come before and all that will follow. Stories. Mysterious stories. Human presences.

What Robert catches are those moments when the vertical and the "prosaically horizontal life" twist against each other. As we read them in his poetry, we feel in our bodies the reality of that torsion. Our heads nod yes. Something in our throats makes a little sound telling us we are in the presence of a true thing, and something turns us back into the process of thinking about and living our own story. That is one of the gifts of Robert's poetry and of Robert himself.

Winter Day
For Robert

    This wind will not swerve, hurtling straight
down from the north, laying its shadow
on the sundials. How shall we live? Already Mole
has pulled the stiffening fields over his head.
Tucked in, he dreams of the warm seas of Molador.

    Stay inside. Only the fool would leave his house, turn
his face towards this flood, and set forth,
dark coat billowing behind like a wake.

Marv Davidov

You Can Crawl Through Like Mice or Stand Up Like Human Beings

I HAVE KNOWN ROBERT BLY for over thirty years as a friend, a poet, a war resister. I first became aware of Robert during the "quiet decade" when he and James Wright published *The Fifties*. I remember going to readings at which Robert read the poetry of Neruda and his own poetry of the prairie. It was the first time many of us who were students had heard serious poets reading great poetry, and it opened our imagination.

We would drink and talk in the Mixers Bar near the University of Minnesota. Jim Wright would speak in long brilliant riffs and then would suddenly pause to say, "I better not say this. I will write it."

It was the cusp of the sixties. We read poetry, saw the films of Bergman and Da Sica. We sat in the coffeehouses hearing the music of Bob Dylan, John Koerner, Dave Ray, and Tony Glover. We talked politics all night as the cultural explosion which preceded the intense activism of the sixties came on hard.

But it was during the Vietnam years that I came to know Robert better. I learned he had organized the American Writers Against the Vietnam War tour. Also I learned that he won the National Book Award for Poetry and at the public ceremony in New York turned his money award over to a draft resister. Vietnam was the measure of each of us, and Robert rose as much as any artist in America.

In 1968 I started the Honeywell Project, an attempt to take responsibility for the hideous cluster bombs produced in our city. Robert had written one of the most powerful poems about the Vietnam War, "The Teeth Mother Naked at Last." We asked him to read it at a rally before 5,000 people in Macalester College's outdoor stadium. With his usual passion he read his great poem as 5,000 people concentrated, heard the words, got the meaning, and then marched on Honeywell headquarters the next day.

The high points of that rally were Robert's poem and the talk Barbara Deming gave about her trip to Saigon and Hanoi. The funniest moment came when someone handed me a joint to give to Jerry Rubin as he spoke. Jerry sucked in the weed and said, "We have got to force Honeywell to go back to making honey or whatever the fuck they make over there."

In 1980 the Chilean exile "New Song" group Inti-Illimani came to Minneapolis on a national tour. They asked that Robert Bly and Meridel Le Sueur read Neruda during their concert before 1,200 people, and both read beautifully that night.

In the eighties we turned to a campaign of nonviolent civil disobedience at Honeywell because they made guidance systems for Pershing and cruise missiles which the Reagan government planned to deploy to Europe, thereby geometrically increasing the danger of nuclear holocaust.

In October 1983, just before deployment, we gathered 2,000 men, women, and children at Honeywell. Management had put up fences around the entire headquarters compound, and we sat in front of the fences from 6:00 a.m. until 3:00 p.m. on a cold October morning. Robert joined the 577 people arrested that day in a powerful demonstration which closed Honeywell headquarters for an entire day.

Later 100 of us were tried in a mass trial, with 14 people representing the whole group. Robert testified before the jury, quoting Thoreau. In his closing statement he said to the jury, "The prosecutor would have tried to get Jesus for trespass." He said, "The prosecutor has erected a wall. There is a little passage at the bottom of this wall. You can crawl through like mice to the other side, or you can struggle through and stand up like human beings." They crawled through like mice and convicted us, and the judge sent 100 of us to the workhouse for a few days.

The *Minneapolis Tribune* came to the jail to interview Robert for the Sunday magazine section, and he told them what this experience meant to him. It meant a great deal to have an artist of

In the workhouse after Honeywell protest, Minneapolis, 1983
(Minneapolis Star Tribune *photo*).

Robert's stature joining the hundreds of us, whom few people knew publicly. Robert's presence made a statement that one's art, morality, and politics are inseparable.

So, Robert, here we are in the nineties. We are closing down the Honeywell Project after twenty-three years and opening M.I.S.T. (the Midwest Institute for Social Transformation) where we will teach what we have learned over the years about holding on with "our eyes on the prize."

You are turning sixty-five, still writing, and leading a men's movement which I do not fully understand yet. Once again you are in the heat of controversy. Explain to me what you are doing so that I may help others to understand.

Happy birthday, Robert. You have been a good friend to me these past thirty years. I have fine memories of you reading your great poems in the midst of struggles for peace, justice, and freedom. The cultural work you have done with us has given our efforts a dimension nothing else could have done. I wish you a continued long and creative life, and I know we shall work together again as we have done so well over the years.

Love and strength,
Marv Davidov

Rita Shumaker

Portfolio

Introduction

Robert's journey through the image has been to the interior. And the direction has been down. It is neither the dominant mode of our Western consciousness nor the dominant direction of our inherited goals. My response to Robert's life and to his work is predicated on my predicament as woman, as someone preoccupied with symbols, and as a visual artist. It is also influenced by a fundamental turn of mind. For me, the material imagination is Psyche's realm. Psyche guides in the kingdom of soul. The substance of dream, of myth, of art, is one fabric, warp and weft. The web is interwoven, of spirit and matter, life and thought, nature and mind. "In the image, the categories of being and meaning coincide" (Erich Neumann, "Mystical Man," *The Mystical Vision: Papers from the Eranos Yearbooks*, Bollingen Foundation, 1968).

I believe that Robert's work has been as much about soul-making as about making sense of family, nation, politics, or history. It was through the work of Rilke that Robert and others of us approached the grief at the center of the soul. As Robert suggests, Rilke may have been moved by a drawing of Orpheus and the animals because our complaints about life do not intrigue animals. Rilke's sonnets move us from longing's confessional tone toward grief: our darkest hours, our deepest knowing. We enter the shadow, the psyche's dark underbelly, where sorrow works its transformation. And we are moved even deeper, past this personal level, into the underworld of dream, myth, and archetype.

Ancient artists believed the threshold between the worlds was sacred. They carved deities and placed them as guardian figures on the boundary line. Rilke places Orpheus as poetry's personification at the juncture where the two worlds meet, and imagines that junc-

Rita Shumaker, "Bears," pencil, 1988, 18"x24"

ture to occur in the human heart. Orpheus becomes the metaphor for the reconciliation of opposites, in the poet's nature and in human experience. This journey into the depths does not mean rejection of the outer world. For even though the rose does not actively participate in the world, it is still there . . . accepting it, living it, transforming it. This the rose does simply by its presence. In the "Elegies" and the "Sonnets" Rilke would say that the poet does it, too; he transforms the world into word. Both the rose and Orpheus become the symbols for transformation (see H. F. Peters, *Rilke: Man and Mask*, University of Washington Press, 1960).

The kaleidoscopic lens of Robert's thought, his poetry, his voluminous translations (Rilke, Rumi, Neruda, Tranströmer, Jiménez, Machado, and Kabir), and his psychological questing have provided me many vistas. For both Robert and me, our work in the world is at the overlap where Novalis positions soul. The differences in our approaches to the making of art are conspicuous. Robert's poetry is direct and sparse. His syntax reflects the simplicity of everyday speech. There is clarity in his reflections. When he broods there is a Nordic weight. My work is detailed, sensuous, languid, lyric. The meandering line and undulating form is reminiscent of Celtic drawing and Italian mannerism. The interaction between the material and spiritual worlds preoccupies us both, but differently. I see the image as mediator; the movement occurs between them. Robert would distinguish them, to allow each its integrity. As the lyre can make music only because the strings are strung taut between two poles, the oppositions between us and within us matter; they create the dance. For the poet or painter, the opposites are not contradictory, as in logic, but polar; they live by virtue of one another (see Roberts Avens, *Imagination Is Reality,* Spring, 1980).

A life is a collaborative event. Some of the collaborative efforts occur by choice; others by chance. But the interaction is continuous, the interface between mind and matter, self and other, is peopled by the living and the dead. Hermes and Hecate guard the crossroads and bear silent witness to the dialogue, opposition, and resonance.

The soul's substance ferments with the passage of time and the encroachments of the "other." For my creative work, Robert Bly has been a most influential "other."

To Michael Martin for help in revision, my gratitude.

Rita Shumaker, "Hawk: Releaser of Animals," pen and ink, 1990, 9" x12".

Rita Shumaker, "Orpheus," pencil, 1984, 30" x40".

Louis Camp

Being with Bly:
You Must Change Your Life

I SHOULD SAY, of course, how he has changed my life. But that isn't enough. Because when you get to know Robert a new connection between you and the whole world begins. His personal power and his devoted, loyal sweetness are at one with his poems, essays, and translations. This draws you out of yourself, into his world, and into the world. What happens to Robert happens to you and happens to us.

I was lucky because the start of it came from our midwestern origins. He knows the same places I do—Cincinnati, De Kalb, Iowa City, Chicago, Minneapolis. He runs from them and back to them, as I do. Robert has never abandoned the Midwest. That root shows in all his poems, early and late. Just pick up the *Selected Poems* and notice Rock Island, the Sioux, driving at night somewhere, sheds, shacks, and barns.

I could say a lot about the qualities that midwestern origins give us: loneliness, yearning for friends, smallness in the face of nature, fierce independence, hatred of banks—these are some of them.

Now the reason I fled the Midwest for Philadelphia was to get away from the truck stops, the bad food, the repressed sex, the tornadoes, the terrifying women, and the church. I took up, as best I could, Big Time Eastern airs.

I wanted to read, write, go to parties and hang out with poets without fear of being beaten up in the locker room. Strangely, the few people I met talked only about Eliot, Lowell, and Merrill. They had met them, but I never would. Parties there were, but I had to be content with selected reports of how fine and sybaritic they were.

Then in the 1970s comes Bly along to Bucks County Community College, reading his poems and his translations of Rilke, Rumi, Kabir, Neruda. He also talked about Vietnam, Jung, Native Americans, church. What a crazy, out-of-control man: he lives in Madison or Moose Lake or some godforsaken town the likes of which I know in my guts, and here he is dispensing errant wisdom about all the things I'd dreamt of in Ohio reading Dostoevski and Tolstoy, Novalis and Hesse, Crowley and Lafcadio Hearn; listening to Mahler and Hanson, and yes, Wagner (*Tristan and Isolde*).

We became friends, and he reconverted and changed me. Through his poems and our talks I now remembered the Midwest as a place of solace and refuge, a clean, clear, honest way of living. I remember a phone call in the seventies, which I ended by saying, "We'll try to keep your spirit of things out here." The combination of ordinary midwestern images with the images and issues of *world* literature was what I was looking for.

On the other hand, his translations always have that singular, rooted voice. This has troubled some reviewers. For an example, see Erich Heller's wonderful native speaker destruction of Robert's *Rilke (New Republic*, March 3, 1982). Of course, Professor Heller doesn't know of the dozens upon dozens of my students to whom Rilke remained closed by previous translations, and who were changed by the reading of Robert's direct, simple American translation.

This is no place (is there any place?) to offer a theory of translation. The strand I want to draw out is the presence of Robert's voice (and choice of words and images) in his translations. Three examples will do:

Sometimes a man stands up during supper
and walks outdoors and keeps on walking. . . .
      Rilke, p. 49

I have been thinking of the difference
between water and the waves on it.
      Kabir, p. 29

It so happens I am sick of being a man.
And it happens that I walk into tailorshops and movie houses
dried up, waterproof, like a swan made of felt. . . .
            Neruda, "Walking Around"
            Neruda and Vallejo, p. 29

I think that many of us would agree that Bly is here. The translator's voice is always in the translation; that is a truism. But the sheer diversity of Robert's translation—Spanish, German, Russian, on and on, you know them all, is in itself a theory of translation. His vast and unique achievement—not yet fully recognized—has broadened and changed American literature.

Often during the same reading, the voice that ranges through those grieving poems, so often set in the Midwest, noticing the smallest landscape details, translates far-flung, exotic images from Argentina, Scandinavia, Persia, and India into poems that move American audiences to compassion and understanding.

What Robert has done, I think, is to bring together the Jungian archetype in each of us and the principle underlying comparative literature, that all human beings—Africans, Chinese, Germans, Americans—are more alike than different. What happens to him, happens to me, and to you.

But this is not all. I have seen him hold a whole Swedenborgian grade school enthralled for hours with Dirty Dinky. I remember him spellbinding a Conference on Family Therapy as he developed his views of what to do with alcoholically dysfunctional families, with ideas they hadn't even thought of. No discipline is immune to his poking about. All ideas and experience are refracted through his extraordinary genius for compassionate understanding of the other.

So, he is an optimist, a midwestern one, I think, who searches for the connection between the individual and the community. I feel in Robert, as he says of Machado,

. . . . one is moved by his firm and persistent efforts to see and to listen. He does not want to be caught as the narcissist is, in an interior world, alone with his consciousness, but he wants to cross to other people, to the stars, to the world:

To talk with someone,
ask a question first,
then — listen.
>   *Machado*, p. 4

Rarely are we fortunate to have a friend who really listens. Robert saw me through a lot of personal travail, always saying "yes," or if "no," so vehemently that he was saying "yes." Since he believes in me, I have begun to believe a little in myself. He has made me at home in Ohio again, and more in the world.

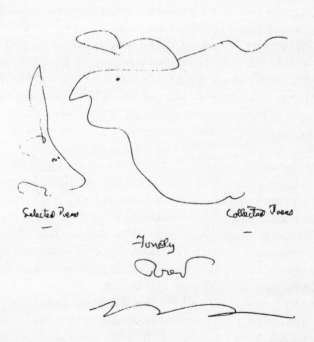

"Collected/selected" (courtesy of Paul Feroe).

Ann B. Igoe

To Meet Robert Bly

OF COURSE I MET ROBERT purely by chance, as most of us did. I was supposed to be having a dinner party for some of my husband's friends, with whom he was planning a trip to Africa. Instead I dropped by a small classroom at the College of Charleston, where I was teaching modern dance. Inside this small room there was a large man standing up and saying things that I had never heard anyone say before. He was using words that were so strong and tender and real, the kind of words that burn up and die in most people's hearts because they don't know how to get them out—the kind of words that kill you if you don't get them out—and the poor words themselves dying to be unlocked and spoken. He wasn't exactly saying these words in a natural tone of voice, but he wasn't saying them in an unnatural tone like a poet, nor was he saying them in any particular logical sequence. In fact the words alone did not say what they meant. There was a weird magic in his choice of words, the alchemic combination and arrangement of them—like "*a leopard leaping to the stars.*"

At the very sound of it I was off the earth, flying toward the stars, my insides rearranged, the sudden takeoff, the dark open space, the wind in my hair, the speed, my heart on fire. Then he mentioned that certain ways of saying things came from certain areas of the body. He named some poets, saying that this one was a head poet, this one a stomach poet, this one a heart poet. He named some and made us guess. How did he know? Suddenly Robert seemed terribly familiar to me. Had I known him before?

And he moved around, breathed deeply, tossed his poncho about, gesticulated and carried on like a madman. We all sat there in complete southern composure. It didn't faze Robert. He went on for over three hours. I wondered why my clothes didn't burst into flames, my skin change color. Here was a poet dancing before me, feeling his words, wording his feelings, not squeezing them to death by the reading of them.

After the reading, I strolled toward the front of the room. I waited in line for someone else to say whatever they had to say in their calm voice, and then I said in my calm voice, "Thank you very much. I like the way you move and breathe while you are reading. It makes a lot of difference. I teach dance." Robert said, "Thank you," and I walked away. I cannot tell you how hard those few steps were to make. In the hall I was dying. "Hey," he called after me, "you say you're a dancer. We're having this conference out in Colorado this summer. Would you come and teach the dance?" I said, "Yes."

Robert picked us up like that, the first Mother Conference people, purely by chance. He had no way of knowing that for twenty years I had been working on poetry and dance, trying to reverse the evolution of the word back into the body, making my students take a poem and look not for the meaning of the word, but for the essence of the emotion that produced the word—exactly how and where the feeling was felt. We were searching for the movement of the emotion and how it danced itself into word. How did he know?

Robert picked up people who had been working independently like this on some idea or project (it's good to have been working on some idea or project before you meet this man), and he brought us all together to see what would happen if we were all thinking about the same idea at the same time. His idea, of course!

I wish I could tell you more about how people feel when they meet Robert Bly. But I can't. I'm too subtle now and sophisticated. It would help if I had the first letter that I wrote to Robert after this reading. I kept a copy of it in a beautiful wooden box along with other transitional treasures of my life: baby shoes, baptismal pins, the fraternity pin of an old sweetheart who died as a fighter pilot, my father-in-law's medals, love notes from my husband (written before we were married, of course), and tiny mementos of my children. In other words, the most important things in my life. The entire box was stolen after Hurricane Hugo two years ago.

Perhaps if I just had the copy of that original letter I could quote some silly unguarded things that I remember saying, like, "I felt I had been dancing forever alone and suddenly someone was dancing with me and they knew me." I felt that someone had given me the chance to put the twenty years of my lonely study into some real work, some real form.

I said that Robert seemed familiar to me. Several years before I met him, I was standing at the kitchen sink and some strange sentences of nonsense drifted into my mind like the lines of an old song have a way of doing and you find yourself saying them over and over. I rather liked the sound of them:

> There was in his finger-tipped radiance
> A world reflected
> Hope unexpected
> Lay angry in the glimmer of a werewolf's tooth.

We met for the first Mother Conference eighteen years ago, people gathered up along the way: writers, artists, philosophers, dancers, musicians, teachers, craftsmen, publishers, a thief, and a fantastic cook, whom, alas, the vegetarians threatened to murder. We met thirty miles out of Denver at Beaver Ranch. When I saw Robert for the second time, he was wearing a rich dark umber sweater and he had on purple tennis shoes. I had never seen a grown man in purple tennis shoes. He was coming down a hill like a great shepherd or Moses, and behind him there was a group of weirdos: the beautiful Ivana dancing in every shade of red, the wild Julia swirling in a costume of ribbons and charms, the mighty Bill Holm, the lovers John and Annie, the mad Papoofnik, Peter Martin the organizer, the steely-eyed Paul, Mary Fell, Mell and Yahuta.

Robert talked that night and read to us. He spoke of rituals, of nature and animals. His hands were beautiful— "*There was in his finger-tipped radiance* . . ." He talked about gods and goddesses, myths and fairy tales— "*A world reflected*" —about us and our relationship to this ancient-present world and how we have the keys to unlock the mysteries— "*Hope unexpected*" —but we must work very hard, we must face dragons and monsters— *"Lay angry in the glimmer of a werewolf's tooth."*

Early the next morning we met in a small round room in the forest. We sat with crossed legs. It was cold. The fireplace smoked. Robert led us in chants. How could this be? The ohooooming was so deep and beautiful. It seemed to be coming from another place, another body.

And it was. Outside dogs from the woods and farm nearby had surrounded our hut. Their heads were thrown back, their eyes closed, and they were howling, their wild bodies happy and easy as though this was the most natural thing in the world. They particularly got with it when we chanted, "Black dog take me hoooooooooommmmmmmmmme."

At lunch Robert talked about sexual energy and symbolism. Somewhere horses broke loose and ran through our camp. Robert and some other people ran after them, their ponchos (ponchos were very popular back then) whipping out behind like great wild manes in the wind.

We did a lot of dancing that first year. Robert's purple tennis shoes, the same ones that Rita eventually made him remove so he could walk in the mud, flashed to the rhythm. His hands danced like mad sparks. In between, nothing moved. He looked like a large dancing bear in a Russian circus. We laughed and shouted for him to move this part and that part and all the in-between parts. He did. It was wonderful. The man's an excellent dancer. Lately I have begun to think that it is the movement inside the poet that counts, the dance that goes on in the great stage of the chest and in the high dome of the intellect.

Sufi dancers joined us and created such a serious magic that sometimes we were moving three feet off the floor. And it snowed on us. In June. . . . It snowed on us and for us and inside some of us.

The sounds of the voices of the first Mother Conference are still clear: they can all be heard, even the words not spoken. They were put there for me by Robert Bly in a great poem of life and language and love. Many of us know this poem by heart.

When you are with Robert, you can never be sure what world you're in. Several times we got so out of space that Fran Quinn had to settle us down by reading some Russell Edson poems. There was so much that year, so much madness and magic and tenderness, mystery—and fierceness. The most important thing that we got from Robert was, GO INTO THE WOODS, DO THE WORK, DO THE WORK, DO THE WORK.

So we left, pushed out on our own into this mythological forest, this tangled wilderness of life. Like little bloodhounds we raced into the woods. We were proud to be doing it. We loved the briars and the branches and the whipping limbs, the dark pools and the wild animals "that sometimes ran beside us." We charged down one uncharted path after another. We have been doing it for years. Sometimes it's terribly frightening and lonely;, but it's always outrageously exciting to be out there wrestling with this great maze of ideas. As Andrew Dick says, every now and then, when we see a flicker of light in this dark forest, we get a huge shot of adrenaline. Our hearts begin to pound. We race faster and faster. The briars stand back. We turn corners never turned before. Just as we are thinking, "I'm working it out! I'm on to it! I've found it! I've found it!" we get a glimpse of the heel of a purple tennis shoe just rounding the curve ahead of us.

Chungliang Al Huang

Knowing the Masculine, Keeping to the Feminine

I FIRST BECAME AWARE of Robert Bly, the man, from reading his interview, "The Great Mother and the New Father" in the August 1978 issue of *East West Journal*. I felt an immediate kinship and deep connection with his words and his expressions. A couple years later, I found myself at Esalen Institute, by chance, participating in his weekend poetry seminar. It was a magical weekend for me. Robert brought out the poet in me, mostly dormant since I had begun writing and thinking in my second language, English. Robert recognized my Chinese metaphoric mind and my yin/yang–T'ai Chi ways of creating poetry through movement. We agreed to continue this East-West exploration with a joint seminar the following spring at the Ojai Foundation, on the theme of "Wild Man and Wild Woman." We joined forces with our reserves of cross-cultural and multidisciplinary methods, using poetry, music, T'ai Chi movement, theater, story-telling masks, and swordplay to illustrate the mythic and heroic journeys both men and women must discover deep within themselves.

Robert and I continued to share our learning and teaching through the eighties, often with another friend-teacher, Joseph Campbell — once in a special celebration for Joseph's eightieth birthday at San Francisco's Palace of Fine Arts, and three years later, sadly, at the memorial ceremony for Joseph in New York City's Museum of Natural History.

In March 1989, to help sustain the traditional Mythbody seminar Joseph and I had conducted at Esalen Institute for nearly a decade, Robert graciously offered to join me in creating a tribute week in Joe's honor. Our seminar, "Stories and Myths for Men and Women: Tales, Discussions and Dancing," encouraged a willingness to listen, argue, and dance both in our minds and in our bodies. We quoted William Butler Yeats: "God save us from those thoughts men think in their minds alone." Ruth Bly was also there, gracing us with her special beauty of quiet reflection, to balance the occasional overly "yang" exuberance in our passionate drumming and whirling. I recall especially Robert's retelling of the "Iron John" myth, masterfully transcending gender identity, and how we managed to create a most poignant session for men and women, learning to listen to one another, with true pureness of heart and mind. Our final dance ritual ended with Robert and I whirling together, spinning out our yin/yang dynamism until we fell to the floor, panting, perspiring, inspired, and wishing to go on forever.

On my friend-teacher Robert's sixty-fifth birthday, I think of what Confucius said when he reached middle age: "At forty, I am no longer confused; at fifty, I learn about my true nature; at sixty,

With Chungliang Al Huang, Esalen Institute, March 1989 (Helga Sittl photo).

I am at ease with what I hear about life; at seventy, I can follow my heart's desire." According to this ancient sage, Robert has reached the midpoint between at-ease-ment with life and the true joy of spontaneity of being.

To balance the yang and the yin, I venture to wonder what Madame Confucius might have offered in her wisdom regarding the Master's reaching sixty-five. I turned to their master, the sage Lao Tzu.

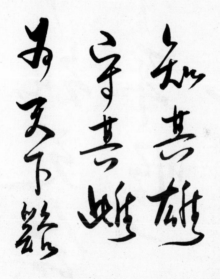

Know the Masculine
Keep to the Feminine
Be the Valley of the world.
Verse 28, Tao Te Ching

Here's to you, my dear friend Robert, Happy Sixty-five!

"Midlife Wisdom," Confucius (brush calligraphy by Chungliang Al Huang).

Barbara McClintock

An Intention Deep in the Man

ROBERT READIES HIMSELF on stage in the moments before an evening reading. He fiddles with the dulcimer, his papers, a music stand, books, cushions, table, microphone, chair, bouzouki. He messes up his hair, quiets himself, turns a page, and looks out at the full house of seven hundred people. A woman comes down the aisle, late, heavy, sad, unaware that her solitary entrance has coincided with the hush of anticipation. Weeks later this woman, whom Robert had met only once before, tells me that at the end of that reading Robert pushed his way through the crowd to find her and say how sorry he was that she was suffering. She said that Robert's astonishing kindness turned out to be the first drop of hope to fall into her months-long dark emptiness.

During the fifteen years that I have worked with Robert at large public events, I have been touched many times by this man's gentle gift of compassion, spontaneously evoked when he encounters a fellow sufferer. However frenzied the moment, he downshifts in the presence of someone who is hurt or ashamed or darkly aggrieved. I am reminded of his own statement concerning his artistic intention: to merge in a poem his personal consciousness with a second consciousness, outside of himself, that "has a melancholy tone, the tear inside the stone . . . an energy circling downward, felt often in autumn, or moving slowly around apple trees or stars." It occurs to me that this "artistic intention" reflects, not surprisingly, the intention of Robert's heart—to merge with the tear in the stone or in the eye.

I wander into his poetry. I am dazzled by the myriad images that could only be born of an instinctive compassion for the particular being. The clues are everywhere in the poems. Here are a very few: *brave alfalfa; insects golden and Arabic; the hair in the ear of a hundred-year-old man; one mousetrack in the snow ahead;*

the blackish stains around screwheads; the big mare's eyelashes; the dog's doubt far back in his throat; an empty corncob on the ground, so beautiful, and where each kernel had been, there was a place to live.

Performing with mask at Old Dominion University, Norfolk, Virginia, 1986 (Rick Alley photo; from Robert Bly collection).

Victoria Frenkel Harris

Received from Robert Bly:
Two Lessons and a Message

"Breathe-in experience, breathe-out poetry." — *Muriel Rukeyser*

WHILE TRYING TO FIND just the right tale to tell in order to properly honor Robert Bly on his sixty-fifth birthday, I have discovered that goal to be inappropriate for, perhaps, surprising reasons. Despite the convenient contexts used to situate the varying phases of Bly's work—neo-Romantic, subjectivist, feminist, masculinist, Jungian, mythological, leaping, imagistic, and so on—Bly's articulations cannot be condensed into any form of essentialism. All his writings are palinodes, rereadings, misprisions—if you will—of cultural inscriptions in which Bly has located some omission, and, therefore, a pathology in a harmonious system.

If, as some have suggested, Bly has always been a programmatic poet, that agenda may best be described by the Hebrew word *chesed*, covenant love. His first volume, *Silence in the Snowy Fields,* for example—in its formal departure from modernism and its attendant humanism—is stunning in its spareness and quietude, in its attentiveness to minute local particulars as vehicle for spiritual insight. A quick tour through this American classic of epiphany reveals Bly joyful—indeed, "wrapped in . . . joyful flesh"—in moments of sensory or more-than-sensory perception. "There is unknown dust that is near us," for instance, opens "Surprised by Evening," in one of many poems that inscribe a milieu darkening while fostering vision. Such vision defies empirical worldviews, as well as Cartesian dualism. A questioning of the deleterious repercussions of dualism is understood by the very title "A Man Writes to a Part of Himself," as well as in its concluding interrogation of damaging division: "Which of us two then is the worse off? / And how did this separation come about?" The flowing out and then back in of energy invigorates the speaker traveling his road in a way that symbolizes Bly's perpetual activity of renegotiating his position in the world. *Silence*, articulating both the gift of inseeing as well its concomitant responsibility, depicts a speaker apparently able "to see / The tear inside the stone," to hear the "Orisons of the stones," and to comment upon the urgency to protest a universe not only in particles, but in historical and political disarray. Desperately lacking rapport, there remains, "weeping in the pueblos of the lily," a world wherein "The stones bow as the saddened armies pass" ("Poem Against the Rich").

Portrayed in increasingly broad compass, the speaker in *The Man in the Black Coat Turns* reiterates Bly's sensitivity to the multiple influx of perceptual material, stating, "I am aware of the consciousness I have, and I mourn the consciousness I do not have" ("Eleven O'Clock at Night"). Such a premise requires accountability, and Bly locates his position in such injunctions as are made in *Talking All Morning*, that we must get out of our "mind hell" (115-117).

Bly's antirationalist, anti-imperialist position permeates the more pointedly political, lachrymal world in his second volume, *The Light Around the Body*. One finds this world to be both badly in need of a center and badly maimed by fragmentation, from the level of consciousness to that of international destruction at the time of the Vietnam War. The desperate question in "Romans Angry about the Inner World" — "What shall the world do with its children?" — is given its frightening reply in a volume in which wholeness is replaced with imagery of disintegration, death, executioners, exhaustion, greed, and a howling for integration from the most disparate and inanimate of sources, such as "removed Chevrolet wheels that howl with a terrible loneliness" ("Come with Me").

In Bly's interactive ecology, when the psyche is fractured the physical world becomes responsively maimed. In *The Man in the Black Coat Turns*, Bly warns,

If a man, cautious
hides his limp,

Somebody has to limp it! Things
do it; the surroundings limp.
House walls get scars,
the car breaks down; matter, in drudgery, takes it up.
                My Father's Wedding 1924

Bly's is not, however, a poetics of despair. His gesture is typically recuperative, envisioning restoration. In *Iron John,* for example, the spirit, Bly states, enters through a wound (209): "the soul enters through the hole of defeat"(210).

While any of Bly's particular positions are always, in themselves, imperfect, invested inescapably with interest, their partiality seems motivated by a desire to reinsert some notion left out of our cultural vocabulary, and thereby our mental systems of acceptances and denials. Bly very well accommodates Seneca's dictum that a poet should be like a honeybee, gathering its nectar from all surrounding sources. While Bly's search for a center seems repeatedly a goal, his sources diverge widely, at times appearing to be mutually incompatible. The givens for Bly are a commitment to address some consciously repressed, perhaps unknown, content and an impulse to correct that which he finds lacking balance in our polity. Thus, his first book quietly sees and connects, the second addresses a warmongering psychic imbalance. Then, for a decade or so, he addresses the diminished female elements in patriarchy (as rendered within a Jungian typology), and gradually turns toward redressing what he sees as the forgotten male. This mythos of a center and inclusiveness propels itself by a constant motive to repair the damage done by subordination. Such repair takes place at both ends of representation: the speaker and the poetry.

Any totalizing scheme always arouses some resistance. Such opposition is seen not only in the reader, but also in Bly. Magnetically attracted to such schema, Bly yet attends to articulations of difference. Consider, for example, the situatedness of the midwestern vista and diction, the repetition of which becomes a source of stability. The deeply private, furthermore, acts as locale for the often-written-about "leap" into the universal. The complexity of this issue may underlie some of his recent work with men. *Iron John* and *The Man in the Black Coat Turns,* as well as some (as of this writing unpublished) poems about his father, depict male initiation, a man speaking and listening to men through both the generations within a life as well as through a collective unconscious.

There is, then, in all of Bly's writing—despite a seeming totalization—a perpetual ideological, and consequently linguistic, negotiation. His longing to restore coherence where he locates disjunction requires the same attentiveness and responsiveness as his poetic inclination to seek the universal through the local, to penetrate more deeply into the visible: "I know what I must do," the speaker states in "Night Journey in the Cooking Pot" (section 5, *Sleepers Joining Hands*), "I am ashamed looking at the fish in the water." Sensitive to and, indeed, at times announcing the continually shifting cultural investments of privilege and power, Bly responds with his own imaging of what appears as noise in a potentially harmonious system. Because Bly's agenda remains constant—to subvert hierarchy, to center the marginalized, and to give voice to the silenced—his focus accordingly shifts in response to changing cultural paradigms.

I see *The Man in the Black Coat Turns* as a gorgeous volume in which the speaker contends with the consciousness that he has, and has contextualized it within generations. It is here that the collective unconscious is made manifest, along with the dialogue of the personal consciousness within its participatory universe. Our temporal moment is but a palimpsest here, where, for example, in "For My Son Noah, Ten Years Old," Bly states, "what is old remains old, and what is young / remains young, and grows old". In "Kneeling Down to Look into a Culvert," a gesture emblematic of the entire life's course—of care, depth, and pause—Bly realizes, "I have seen this lake before . . . it is a lake / I return to each time my children are grown." Bly's trembling sense of a world's containment of large and small elements, past and present generations, within a context of concern and attention at this juncture brings some focus upon his attempt to figure himself into the systemic fold.

Words, too, are hallowed, sounding and resounding with synchronic and diachronic power. Words should be seen as strangers here to any context in a rationalist logic. They report the hieratic, as in "Four Ways of Knowledge," in which Bly seems to be portraying the repercussions as they would be depicted not only in chaos theory, but as such a theory would be if contextualized in archetypal memory:

If we still don't
take in the knowledge,
then he turns to accidents,
disease, suffering,
lost letters, torpid sleeps,
disasters, catatonia. . . .
This time we live it,
and only awaken years later.

Words, then, to Bly, must be attended not with skepticism, but more with the consideration of a gift-giving in a worldview of permanent affect. Bly sets "Words Rising," for instance, in an ambience where "We are the bees then; language is the honey." Here, our verbal gestures become part of the earth's ecosystem: "Now the honey lies stored in cave / beneath us, and the sound of word / carries what we do not." The very act of enunciation is imbricated with time, space, and reverie, as hinted at in his first volume, when "From the long past / Into the long present / A bird, forgotten in these pressures, [is] warbling" ("Awakening"), where a poet "cradling a pen" hears "Strange muffled sounds come from the sea" ("Silence"), where, indeed, "One thing is also another thing" ("Remembering in Oslo the Old Picture of the Magna Carta"). The word is carefully factored into Bly's system of multivalent unity, these early quotations also remarking an aesthetic theory that is more relational than transcendental, more systemic than mystic, because the rapport gained by the word in the world cedes to various aspects of this multivalence their own integrity. Like his rationale for the prose poem — to achieve less separation, more intimacy, by varying from expected pattern — his format in *Black Coat* allows more fluid corridors, the perceptual path segueing from the phenomenal to the noumenal as well as from personal through collective history. I take these perceptions to be the rereadings of cultural reality by a man whose entire being is affected by universal affiliation—posited in both ancient Chinese cultures and postmodern systems theory.

I would like to offer two of so many memories I have of moments when I have seen that Robert Bly knows something that these words of mine must fail to express, that Bly participates in an interactive ecosystem both within as well as beyond the boundaries of the worldly. (One might refer to his essay "The News of the Universe" for a more thorough articulation of this position.) One resonant moment for me occurred at Illinois State University, at a reading being held in an enormous auditorium holding several hundred people. This term *reading* seems particularly inappropriate given the kind of energy with which Bly's interpretations—through his poems, his translations of the poems of others, his commentary, his masked performances—were given and received during this period of the Vietnam War. One person in the audience—off to Bly's right and about twenty rows back—began interrupting the reading with abusive questions and shouts. It seemed clear to me that this individual was under the influence of drugs. That the work of interpreter and reader go hand in hand is never so clear as in the way Bly reads his audience, and, here, read to the person. He responded to this man, who was, to me, disruptive; each response, whether lengthy or brief, soothed wounds while retaining a rapt audience for an unprecedented—in my memory—three hours. I interpret this event as connotatively akin to the holism Bly sought in terms of flexibility, for example, in aesthetic form. Every detail of Bly's life seems imbued with respect for the particular as a portion of the encompassing whole. The audience becomes like a body in holistic medicine, like the paragraph Bly sought in the prose poem—a house of both centripetal and centrifugal energies. A system's ability to gather and extend, to act in fullness, is derived through a rhythmic equilibrium. We all know how easy it would be to dismiss some of the disruption in the system. Robert, however, typically attended to the particular for reparation of the whole.

Another event, which on the surface appears entirely different, I present as an illustration of what I shall try to explain as again characteristic of Bly's phenomenal/noumenal rapport. In December 1979, I attended a reading given by Bly and several other poets in San Francisco—a poetry benefit for Cambodian refugees. After this reading, we drove to the shore. We walked toward the Pacific Ocean and, upon nearing its waters, Bly turned his back for seven or eight minutes before he could "face" it, which he then did—in a way that I did not—for many, many intense moments. Something moved him beyond being, like "all the sailors [who] on deck have been blind for many years" ("Snowfall in the Afternoon"); toward his understanding of the voyage with "the joy of trackless seas," "the joy of sailing and the open sea!" ("Images Suggested by Medieval Music"); toward "thoughts of distant harbors, and new life" ("After Working"), and toward knowing that though "on its road the body cannot march / With golden trumpets—it must march"; realizing, finally, that this "sea gives up its answer as it falls into itself" ("On the Ferry Across Chesapeake Bay").

In a moment of earthly destruction, at a time during which we are robbing our progeny of earth, water, and air, one might look to Robert Bly's life of commitment to interrogate our carelessnesses. He has erased from his life the boundaries of an essential "I" and a world just sitting out there, inert and separated from the perceiver in a disengaged dualism. Perhaps one of the regions of such dualism that may have the most egregious consequences is the passivity underlying all levels of our culture. Bly's "on the road" inductive career is a tireless gathering of that which he finds neglected by himself or in the world at large. Mutuality intenerates dualism and harmony vitiates colonization in Bly's sacerdotal system. Although I do not speak easily to Robert Bly and feel entirely inadequate to situate him, I can with all my heart wish him some of the equanimity he has earned and taught.

Andrew Dick

The Trouble with Robert

A REPORTER ONCE asked President Eisenhower what he liked best about his vice-president. Eisenhower paused. "There are many things about Richard Nixon that . . . ah . . . well, I'll check on it and get back to you next week."

I'd like to say something magnificent about Robert for this festschrift, but nothing comes to mind right now. If I had more time I'm sure I could say something wonderful — and even tell the truth. After all, Robert is generous, brilliant, and prolific; he's done many things for which we should thank him. But all I can think of are stories. Maybe that's not so bad; after all, it's not hard to get praised — all you have to do is die or retire. It's something else to be celebrated in story. You have to be troublesome for that.

As I think of Robert, I'm reminded of a comment William Dean Howells made about Mark Twain. "Among the half-dozen, or half-hundred, personalities that each of us becomes, I should say that Clemens's central and final personality was something exquisite. His casual acquaintances might know him, perhaps, for his fierce intensity, his wild pleasure in shocking people with his ribaldries and profanities, or from the mere need of loosing his rebellious spirit in that way, as anything but exquisite, and yet. . . . One could not know him well without realizing him the most serious, the most humane, the most conscientious of men."

Robert, too, is serious, humane, and conscientious. And like Robert, Twain could be a lot of trouble. Finding himself "between situations," the young Twain jump-started his career by arranging a lecture for himself. He scraped together enough money to rent a hall and hung posters around San Francisco advertising the event. The posters read, in part, "Doors open at 7:30. The Trouble begins at 8:00."

This rambunctious man who reveled in infuriating habits (not the least of which was to say what many people knew but wanted to keep quiet) finally died, leaving with Halley's Comet, the same celestial messenger which had dropped him off. Even so, the trouble didn't stop. Conservatives, who had been trying to stifle his work from the beginning, have recently been joined by liberals, who finally took the time to misread him. Though Twain can no longer answer the attacks, introverted librarians have continued the irritation by defending his work against paroxysms from self-appointed shepherds of morality and the Utopia police.

I like that sort of trouble. And though it sometimes drives me to conniption fits, that's one thing I love about Robert. The bigger sorts of trouble he's started — the revolutions, re-collections and re-visioning — will be around for a long time. He'll be required reading for generations, and letter-writing campaigns will try to ban him from high school libraries. But I worry that the smaller sorts of trouble Robert has caused might be lost in all the hoopla. So I'll try to do a modest service for history and collect a few of the petty troubles for which he is responsible.

Robert has a passion for buildings. At last count he had six in which to live or work. He collected all this property while raising a large family on a poet's salary. God knows how he managed it, but it's something to be proud of. Trouble is, now that the kids are out of school and he has a best-seller to finance this infatuation, I shudder to think what might be in the works. It's not that I begrudge him more real estate, it's just that I always hoped I'd be able to get my own place on some quiet lake one day. But the way things are going, if Robert hasn't bought everything, he'll drive prices so high I'll never be able to afford one.

I understand why he wants so many buildings. He needs a place located on a normal street, where the kitchen door leads to a barn facing a frozen lake, the back door opens on SoHo, and the garage is next to the British Museum. He must have rooms which can hold a conference for three hundred, breakfast for two, and a concert for fifteen. One wing should be a wattle shack with a peat fireplace, and there must be an office, a library, and a small meditation room. There's got to be space for Ruth and rooms where they can argue about walls to paint and furniture to move. It's impossible to get one place that meets all these criteria, so he buys many smaller ones. I understand why he needs so many buildings, but I don't like it. Is there nowhere this man will not buy property first?

That's the trouble with Robert; it's hard to be around him and still have enough room to pitch your tent. His thirst is intoxicating, but you must find your own source of water. People who try to ape him will find themselves becoming something they never were and can no longer be. Those who see only his hulking frame and wild hair might imagine a man laboring in some rude cabin; they'd be surprised. He wants refined, symmetrical space. Oh, there are grotesque masks and strange paintings on the walls of his home, but they're surrounded by Queen Anne furniture and Oriental rugs. He's like that. Wherever Robert finds his passion—on a northern lake, in the heart of the city, at the edge of American poetry—he makes a home, gleefully disrupts city council meetings, and grudgingly pays taxes. But inside, where he lives, there's warmth, order, and delicacy.

Years ago, I visited Robert at his house up north. One morning we walked down to the lake. Joe, his dog, followed us. When we got to the shore, Joe started barking and running in circles. I asked what was going on. "You'll love this," Robert said as he picked up a rock and threw it in the lake. Joe leaped from the dock and disappeared under water. Moments later Joe returned with the rock in his mouth, dropped it, and started barking. We repeated the operation several times with larger and larger rocks. Finally, Robert heaved a big one. When Joe finally dragged it ashore, the game ended. Apparently this was the stone he really wanted. Joe wrestled it into the weeds and started to worry it. He'd stalk it and growl, as if he was trying to open it.

I thought it bizarre that Robert had trained Joe to be a stone-hungry scuba dog, but now I don't think Robert trained him. Joe was simply imitating his master. Robert not only barks until he sees big rocks, he dives to the bottom of cold lakes to fetch them. There must be some food or thick water lying quiet in those bruised rocks—something only dogs and poets notice. Normally, stones keep their secrets, but if Robert gets one in his teeth, I wouldn't bet either way. Both Robert and Joe growl, but Robert opens more stones.

Then there was the time my wife and I stopped at his cabin on our way to the headwaters of the Mississippi. One day, Robert outfitted his little boat with fishing gear and packed a light supper so my wife and I could go exploring. Since it was late afternoon and I was unfamiliar with the lake, I started for my car to get flashlights. Robert stopped me; he wanted us to have something bigger. He rummaged around until he found a beat-up lantern. I preferred the flashlights, but Robert insisted on the lantern, "Much more powerful."

Jeanne and I had a lovely time fishing and watching birds, turtles, and snakes. Night was falling as we turned back toward the cabin. While there was still some light, I tried the lantern, and was surprised to find it actually worked. Reassured by its glowing mantles, we throttled back the Evinrude, relaxed, and putt-putted home. When it got too dark to see, I gave the tiller to Jeanne and stood in the bow with the lantern so she could find the cabin. She told me to hold the lantern lower, higher, left, right. I suggested we switch jobs — as if this was somehow a "relationship problem." But I was alarmed to discover that if the lantern was held high enough to cast light in front, you were blinded by the backlight. Held low, you could only see ten feet — not much help when you're looking for a faded wind sock hidden among dark hemlocks. The lantern was good for only two things: letting us watch the gas gauge dip toward Empty, and reminding us there wasn't an oar.

When we finally got back and told our story, Robert crumpled with laughter. I held my tongue, but I was sure he'd given us that damn lantern on purpose, and I vowed to get him back. Later, however, I realized Robert had given us the same thing which had served him so well: a lantern that illuminates the bottom of one's own boat. As I swore at Robert, he must have sworn at Yeats and Jung when their lights failed to reveal the dim shore hiding a distant home. All told, it wasn't a bad journey over the dark water. It's worth taking — as long as you've got enough gas, and Robert has plenty of that.

Here's a story which takes place in my own house. Jeanne and I invited Robert and Ruth for dinner. Half an hour after dinner was supposed to start, Robert called to say he'd be right over, but asked if he could bring a friend or two. Within minutes, dancers, artists, therapists, and storytellers, a whole circus troupe, knocked at the door. What was supposed to be supper for four had become a party for twelve. When they finally arrived, Ruth was quiet, as if embarrassed by the situation; Robert was gregarious, as if trying to charm away a spanking.

After dinner, I was making coffee when several guests came in the kitchen to apologize. They said they didn't know they were going to be part of an invading horde and were mortified by Robert's rudeness in inviting so many people at the last minute. I wanted to be upset, too, but I'd enjoyed cooking, there'd been plenty of food, the dishes were done, and everyone was having a good time. I wanted to be angry; I felt it was my moral duty. Trouble was, I couldn't figure who'd been injured by Robert's bad manners.

That's the trouble with Robert. He freely breaks the rules, even his own. I suppose it'd make everyone's life easier if someone brought him up short and taught him a lesson, but it's hard to gather enough steam to stop him when the results are so wonderful. Perhaps Robert once broke the rules and food, drink, and lively conversation were exhausted and people starred blankly at the floor or went home hungry. Perhaps, but I've never seen it. Oh, there's often turmoil, tangle, fluster, and commotion, but I've always left the table with a full stomach, and a doggie bag.

Thirteen years ago I attended a conference Robert organized and led. After three days, the initial excitement had worn thin and everyone was sick of something. As we gathered in the lodge for a complaint session, a woman turned to me to say, "God, I hope he doesn't make us get in a circle. I hate holding people's sweaty hands. Makes me wanna kill somebody." I nodded but thought, "Here it comes, two hours of attacking Robert." Unfortunately for me, Robert was late. The lynching, however, started on time—with me as the guest of honor. Maybe I had it coming, or maybe with Robert absent I was just the biggest ass present. Anyway, I tried to respect the liturgical nature of the activity while also protecting my genitals. I did OK, but after Robert arrived it was extremely distracting to hear him giggle as one person after another threatened to jam firewood down my throat for not having been "supportive" enough.

After the ritual sacrifice ended everyone stumbled out of the lodge gasping for air. Robert tried to catch my eye, but I turned away, angry he hadn't tried to slow the feeding frenzy—at least he didn't have to chuckle so much. He came over anyway and put an arm around my shoulder. But, since he couldn't wipe that shit-eating grin off his face, I was quiet. After we'd walked for a time, Robert said, "Hey, good job. Really." (Silence.) "You know, it's only gonna get worse." (Silence.) Finally, he squeezed my shoulder and walked away—only to call back, "Oh, and welcome to the club!"

That surprised me. Didn't seem like an apology, but it wasn't much of a gloat either. Somehow, I do feel like I joined a different club that day. And he was right, everything has gotten worse. I'm pretty sure that's Robert's fault, but I can't prove it.

Even so, there are many things about Robert which . . . ah, I won't go on, and I won't get back to you next week either. I've told all the stories I'm gonna tell. If you want more, ask Robert. He's got lots of stories. Not all of them are exactly true, but then neither are mine. My stories are small, but with more fertilizer they'll grow just fine. For really championship stories I'd need more heat— but other than Robert, who wants to carry burning charcoal in their hands?

Come to think of it, Robert isn't so much a gardener as an ironsmith, one who looks at rock, sees ore, and . . . Well, that's the trouble with Robert. . . .

C. Owen Christianson

From Childhood

Alone on the bluff
he sees the river
flowing by.

The leaves are falling.
Falling.
Soon the crows will gather
to follow the sun.

The sun sets.
The earth grows still
and cold.
In the town nobody waits
and in the home
the soul is numb.

But the earth holds him high
as he lies
alone on the bluff
and sees the river
flowing by.

And sees the river
flowing by.

for Robert on his birthday

In this poem I have set out to salute a balancing of opposites that I have known and loved in Robert. Robert has a

gift for honoring the depths and heights of both these opposites. I have never encountered this same gift in anyone else I've known. I am speaking of Robert's ability to take sadness, sorrow, and loneliness seriously—to look honestly into the bleakness of things—and, somehow, in the same moment of experience, to discern the signs of hopefulness and recovery. Robert sees the sadness of the earth without succumbing to cynicism and he sees the hope for this creation without reverting to sentimentalism. Even as the leaves are falling, the sun is setting, and the world sinks into death, Robert lets the earth hold him aloft. And he sees the river flowing by.

Let me speak more directly. Robert has been present at my side as we have plumbed the depths into which this world's cruelties can sink one. In any time, becoming a mother entails travail and pain. Especially in our times, being a father carries such a burden, too. We stand close by as our daughters and sons fill their "storehouse of sorrows" with grief we are powerless to allay. We refuse to be ineffectual yet we are afraid of becoming overbearing and patriarchal —and what fathers who went before us rose above these weaknesses? In embodying this pain—this fatherly, brotherly, and filial pain—many of us males have come to know what horror is about: the horror of willing for those we love a good we are unable to effect. In facing up to this horror, the horror of having to accompany our own children into "the valley of sorrows," Robert has embodied an honesty that I find heroic. I find this honesty of his heroic not on the grounds that he faces the pain of life with grim, unblinking stoicism. Rather, I salute in him the gift for entering into pain and sorrow and rage without forfeiting humor and hope.

Robert's humor is an earthy mirthfulness to which no single adjective can do full justice. He is Chaucerian in his robust appreciation for the earthiness of us mortals. He is Rabelaisian in his lip-smacking relish for those joys that would gladden even the simplest of hearts. He is Joycean in his almost Celtic delight in the bewitching powers of language.

Robert has been as much a shepherd—a "pastor"—to me as I to him. He has been on hand with the needed insight whether from Hafiz or Grimm, Blake or the Psalms. His critiques of my sermons have cut straight to the marrow—not on any high-toned grounds but on the basis of what the people in Moose Lake most needed to hear. In his blend of the earthly and the ethereal, in his constancy and fidelity as a friend, he has aroused me countless times from my bouts of soul-numbing aloneness. And he has pointed the child lost within to the river that keeps flowing.

Rehearsing with Neena Gulati, Great Mother Conference, Maine, 1986 (Rita Shumaker photo).

Fran Quinn

Three Poems for Robert Bly on His Sixty-fifth Birthday

For Russia and Mikhail Gorbachev, August 19, 1991

It was the rabbit who lost so many feet to luck
that came to mind when I heard of house arrest.

Buffer zone and hills mean nothing
when so much can fly.

I can hear certain hands open with no compassion.
I can see certain mouths refusing song, abandoning words.

Tell me, you leaders of democracy, what are your plans?
They report of Mikhail in rising and falling stock exchanges.

They have him in numbers. They have him
in that purest fiction of Aquinas.

But the archangel's wings still rise in the east
morning after morning, and there is no hint of defeat

in his sword, and no hint of bloodshed in the pink dawn.
And you don't have to believe he's there.

Matins sing his abrupt return
always along the swaying path that mark the seasons.

Woodwinds

The woodwinds have a voice
        that's clear and low,
a reminder of melancholy, or

my mother's aging hand
        smoothing my
brow into its immortality.

Dust gathers on the books,
        wisdom untouched
for so long. The blind poet

is ready to sing again
        at anyone's
scanning eye or touch.

And the new book lies proud
        and bold, brassy
red cover, only half finished.

So many I love have died
        and will die.
Her hand, her kindness

do not compete with those
        of my lover.
Both have their separate graces,

both have their own time.
        A sound clear
and calm, a sound low and

lusty. The sun breaks across
          the old book and
the new. I can hear both voices

reach their crescendo together.
          Listen for a time,
this time, this music. Now

one begins to fade. The woodwinds
          have a voice that's clear
and low, a reminder of melancholy.

Pillow Song

Tired, you learn to lean on tiredness.
The pillow has a hand that moves all night,
washing and washing; first the back of the head,
then the right side of the face, then the left.

Finally it reaches inside to that sticky thought
of yesterday's luncheon where women in men's shirts
sat next to men in women's feelings sat next to the bas-
relief of World War II, and the pillow mixes in the pleasures

of seas and mermaids, the bright colors of fabrics,
lucent and strong, and the picture of your own
heart opening and forgiving. Hearing the beat of wings
inside your breath, that hand and the pillow carry you,

all of you, through twelve centuries of dust that gathers
as filigree behind you, and gems, passing their light
through your skin, gain possession of you until you are
the crown and the king and the poor one ascending
          through new lives.

Thomas R. Smith

Two Poems

Cormorant
For Robert Bly

Buoyant on the chill harbor,
I would live then as a cormorant,

my oily feathers cutting the waves.
I would turn my seeing downward,

reach after only the deepest prey,
and surrender to my unyielding master

without complaint the silver and
elusive catch of each descent.

Around my neck some cunning
surpassing my own had sealed

a ring to force upward my gleaning
of the secretive schools below,

food for someone I'd never seen.
At day's end a few fish left

in the buckets were mine to keep,
enough though neither large nor many.

Listening to Robert Bly at Unity Church

Why don't our heads flop to one side,
pulled down by a grief in earth
that fuses boulders to its titanic ribs?
In this light sanctuary, we must resist
being lifted too readily—there is labor hidden
in these stanzas born effortlessly as we hear them.
The poet has piled the stones of his life
year after year on the unpromising pastures.

Isn't the real work done with a purpose not our own?
I look down, see wrists enter white cuffs
and black coatsleeves as my German grandfather's did.
Behind a wedding ring stands some gold
our eyes have not seen. Childhood goes inside
mute things. My hands do not belong to me
but to someone who has worn and discarded
generations of hands in my family.

Gioia Timpanelli

The Old Couple

Introduction

WHEN I THOUGHT about writing for Robert's birthday, I knew I would like to hear some personal stories from him, give some toasts, and then make some comments about our friendship, which has for a number of years now survived some serious talks, arguments, and general disagreements.

Recently, Robert and I talked about writing, his interest in C. G. Jung's work, and what he thought of friendship, so here I record a bit of two conversations, with his knowledge and permission, of course. I asked him to tell me about the first time he heard the old fairy stories.

"It was at five or six, from a German woman, Maria Schmidt, who worked at our house. She read me 'Hansel and Gretel,' and I remember that I had a fascination with the little stones in the moonlight. I remember feeling a loneliness. I had a feeling that my parents might not want me in the house. Around that time we went on a vacation, and I had a fantasy that if I was left my parents would not be sorry."

In that same conversation I asked Robert when he had first read the work of C. G. Jung and in what way that work touched his own.

"In 1960 or 1961, I met Jackson Matthews at a party. He was an editor at Bollingen. He knew I was poor and so sent me volume 7 of *The Collected Works of C. G. Jung (Two Essays on Analytical Psychology)*. It was a used volume in which he had made notes in the margins. Later, in 1965, I began to read Marie-Louise von Franz, and she became my teacher in the interpretation of the fairy story. I felt an amazement. It was clear to me that I was working, writing, and defining the poetry in which image — not meter, not discursive thought, not narrative—but the image is important (Spanish and South American writing in this century and ancient Chinese literature are interested in the same thing) and, of course, it is the image that carries the dream and the fairy story. Neither social language nor literary language is adequate to carry the image. The image carries everything, and it was wonderful. There was no end to it. I understood from von Franz's discussions that life passes through stages which are particular to a given life and yet clearly millions of people have passed through sequences of stages like 'Allerleirah,' 'Snow White,' and 'Hansel and Gretel.' I had a private life (I was Norwegian and lived on a farm), and secondly, there were invisible markers as well. This was the first time I had a sense of the order of the things in my life—both visible and invisible."

Now I would like to give a few toasts—the first to Robert for his essential contribution to the current resurgence of the oral tradition in poetry. Along with the folk voices, the Beat poets, and others, he has done the tremendous work of bringing back poetry as a spoken art, of making that poetry alive again which is meant for human breath and voice.

Here's another toast—to Robert's ability to remember poems, to say them by heart. Everyone who has ever had a conversation with him knows that at that perfect moment when some other voice is needed, one doesn't have to stop to bring down a volume of poetry—Robert simply recalls lines, stanzas, or entire poems. I sense these are not memorized word by word only, but more by the poem's structure and by some place in his extraordinary intuition. These poems appear in conversation as gifts, not only from the memory but from the mind and heart as well, for they are appropriate to the moment.

When I asked Robert what friendship was to him, he paused a long while—here is some of his answer: "Friends are your second family with which you travel through the woods. A friend is someone who tells you the truth, some action whose shadow side I don't see. I immediately feel an affection for that person . . . someone who gives up certain advantages when he or she sees a soul need on your part. A friend must be aware of your wound. . . . "

While Robert is a generous friend, not stingy or mean-spirited, I wouldn't want to give the impression he's flawless. But then you don't have to know Robert very well to know his willingness to show his "shadow side." John Keats, in a letter to his brother and sister-in-law (April 21, 1819), wrote, "The common cognomen of this world among the misguided and superstitious is 'a vale of tears.' . . . Call the world if you please 'The vale of Soul-making.' . . . Then you will find out the use of the world." I would say that Robert's great heart and desire for knowledge and poetry and intuition and thinking and writing and shadow sides are all part of this great soul-making in him.

Robert and I have worked together telling stories and speaking poems on universal themes, and yet we do not always completely agree on the meaning or way of speaking about stories. Certainly, in the last few years, we have argued and disagreed consistently about gender issues. Ah, gender issues! There is some common ground we have not yet found from which we can discuss them.

These old fairy stories which I have been telling and learning from for many years now are an inner narrative reflecting the literal world and with it our social, cultural, historical, and economic conditions—conditions which can and do change. The stories also bring with them what it is like to be human on this journey: there is at once an inner and an outer story which is felt as a total experience—we see the bird with its feathers. The story's ending is almost always a unifying event, bringing with it a new way of seeing: the sequential parts which we saw and experienced as separate are indeed all working for the common ground, uniting what appeared separate. Often this new sight is the story's gift: it speaks to everyone regardless of age, gender, class—everyone can receive it. There is not one thing that happens to one of us—let alone an entire gender—which does not affect everyone else. In their wonderful and simple way the stories say this again and again. Many women and men, while also working on the inner story, are working to influence the outer story. And then there is the question of what to do with the heart's gift: when the heroine and the hero find this new sight, they bring it back to the community. Robert would agree that the stories bring gifts which are passed on. I put all this down here because it reflects some of our differences in telling the old stories.

Robert and I have gone on to very different paths for now, and yet we still find the right time and place to get together to praise poems and stories, making work and friendship the common ground here.

As I finish writing this, I look out on snow and remember that once, on a wet January afternoon on a country road, I found myself suddenly in an ice storm, fell, and broke my wrist. My ordinary life was changed. When Robert called to ask how I was, I told him that I was not doing more than taking care of the essentials. "Are you not writing?" he asked weeks after the accident. "No," I answered, "I can't seem to get to it." "Well, I tell you what I suggest," said Robert, "you write something each day and send it to me, and I'll send you back what I've written that day. But if I don't hear from you in a week, I'm quitting."

So I went out that day and bought myself an electric typewriter, a nice practical solution for a person who loves options. Now years later I'm sending Robert this story that I started thinking about at that time, honoring a friend who sees wounds literally as well as metaphorically, and who told me he "finds scattering stones in the moonlight with friends a comforting thing." I dedicate this story to him, sending it with love on his sixty-fifth birthday.

The Old Couple
For Robert, December 23, 1991

She thought she had dreamt angels, not a frightening dream but not quite a comforting one either. For, after all, she and her husband were so old, so very old. "We're at the bottom of the hill," he had said just last evening. "But that's where we've always lived," she laughed, "and besides there are many things to do at the bottom of the hill, Sweetheart." She smiled when she thought that after all these years she still called him Sweetheart and he still called her Treasure.

"Why do you call me 'Tesoru'?" she had asked him once, long ago. "Ah," he said, "when I was a young boy wild grape vines grew like treasures in the woods. You are like those vines to me, for I never knew what they would bring, and their value is never what others think." That evening while peeling potatoes she thought of his words and was so moved that tears came to her eyes, so that from then on potatoes, tears, and treasure all shared a common place in her heart.

Now when she thought of this, she laughed and called out to him in a loud voice, *"All'angiuli ci piaciuni li patati?"*

"What?" he shouted back. "Are my brothers coming? Did you say Angelo is bringing potatoes?" He stepped out the door to search the hillside above for their nephew who did come once in a while to look in on them. "No," she said more quietly, "I was just wondering if angels liked potatoes."

When he saw no one, he shrugged and called back to her, "I think you're mumbling. I can't hear you." Later he would ask her. He touched the handle of his shovel and went back to a worry he'd been having since dawn: How long would he be able to pick up a shovel, or even be able to do the most simple thing? A pain which had been lurking became present; he made a fist against it and waited. But by the time the pain left, his worry was gone as well and he felt able again. The animals are blessed, he thought, in *this,* the animals are blessed. Again he shrugged, but this time he picked up the shovel at the door and began to walk down the steps.

How funny, she thought, *patati-frati, angiuli-Angelo.* He just didn't hear me. And then she remembered that her dream angel had not said a word; maybe it knew that they were both quite deaf by now. Suddenly it was all too much for her, and she just *had* to sit down.

At the same moment something made him turn so that he saw her fall back into the chair — as though someone had gently pushed her. He came running in to her. "What is it? *Chi c'e? Chi c'e?* What do you want?" he asked anxiously. She never liked this kind of attention. She waved her hand to put distance between herself and his alarm: *"Nenti, nun vugliu nenti."* "Do you want a glass of water?"

he persisted. "No, please, Sweetheart, I'm all right now; my legs just didn't work for a minute. Thank you." She touched his hand. "Please don't worry, I'm fine. I'm really fine. I'm coming out to finish digging the holes for the new little vines. It's the right time, you know." He paid no attention to this and came back carrying a glass of water shaking in his hands.

She took the cold glass from him and sipped a bit of the water to please him. He made a satisfied sound, nodded, and then waited while she started looking around for a safe place to settle the glass. She found the spot and put it down. What does this mean? she asked herself. He helped her up and then he moved slowly back to the door. She walked over to the stove and picked up a few sticks of wood. "You know," he said, "I was just thinking we might make ourselves a nice plate of potatoes for dinner." "That's funny," she said, "I was just thinking the same thing."

While this was going on in the little house below, by chance two travelers were about to round a bend in the road which would give them a view of the little house and the valley beyond. One was a curious fellow who looked around, taking in as much as he could, gesticulating as he walked in his peripatetic way, hitting first one side of the road and then the other. He spoke the whole time in a running commentary about everything he was seeing. The other walked quietly without curiosity, his step deliberate and quite steady like a native of the place—in this case a Pirzisi—who knew this hillside from birth, walking over the familiar and the unfamiliar with the same solid step. Much escaped the animated walker, and as he talked his sardonic tone could clearly be heard and noted by anyone caring to listen. On the other hand, his companion remained silent, was barely noticeable except for a triangular bit of light which came from the back of his neck, from something which the setting sun caught and reflected. A donkey in the field below turned; the silent man looked up briefly and their eyes met, neither surprised. The donkey looked on, waiting to see if the newcomers were real news for him or not.

As the two men came to the top of the hill, they saw at once the little house and the ancient couple working at something in the field below. The talker stopped and watched. Verifying his suspicion, he turned with a sly smile on his lips and in his usual tone said:

"Teacher, look at that old man. What's he doing planting grape vines at his age?" It would take five years at least to get some grapes out of those new little things, and it was plain the couple were too old, too old, to see *that* vine mature. The Teacher looked up; the donkey turned back, shifted his weight and waited. "Maiestru, isn't that truly foolish?"

The old man had just finished digging; and the old woman was gently placing each plant, with its new, delicate, bright green shoots growing at daring angles from the old darkened stem, into the newly dug hole. Everywhere along the old branches these new buds had burst or were about to burst into the familiar leaf of the grape vine. Now, this done, the old man quickly finished covering the roots while the old woman expertly patted the earth around each plant.

"Why don't you ask them what they are doing," suggested the Teacher, and the student immediately walked down the hill to them. Just as they finished the row, he came up to them and asked the old man:

"What in the world are you planting grape vines for at your age?"

"Buona sera," said the old man.

"Buona sera," said the old woman.

"Buona sera," said the student, looking at them.

He repeated his question: *"Chi stai facinnu chiantannu racina alla vostr'età?"*

A warm spring wind came up suddenly, and the two stood swaying a bit like two gnarled trees grown together in sympathy and place. *"The good,"* began the old man, *"is never lost,"* finished the old woman. She walked away repeating the old saying under her breath, getting pleasure from saying it again, *"U bunu nun e mai persu."* The old man waited a minute, exchanged good evenings again with the traveler, and then went on about his own business, watering the new plants. The old woman came back with more water, and when he finished she slipped her hand under his and took the bucket from him and went to water a bit of wild mint which she had seen growing in the field. A bright reflection off the watering can caught her eye, and she looked up in its direction but could not see the other traveler's face, the setting sun behind him was so strong.

The talker ran up the hill to where the Teacher stood waiting.

"Maiestru," said the student, "the old man said, 'The good is never lost.'"

"And the old woman, what did she say?"

"Teacher, the old man started the saying and the old woman finished it. I guess we can say they were of one mind," he said, thinking for a minute and then beginning to laugh good-naturedly for the first time.

"For their good words to you the old couple will drink wine from that place."

"From that vine, Master?"

"Yes, from there."

The travelers walked out of hearing, the donkey turned away and found something delicious to eat, the old man looked at the row, satisfied, and, humming to himself, drained the last bit of water from the can. He looked up in the distance where the new oaks they had planted five years ago played in and out with the old ones. Maybe he would walk to the woods tomorrow. Maybe.

The old woman looked up at the sky. It was so beautiful: so many running sheep clouds. She started for the steps, felt her dream for a second. There was no doubt, she thought, somewhere the angel of chance was present.

**Robert Bly's
Eleventh Annual
Conference of
The Great Mother
and
The New Father:**

The Orpheus Myth

July 3-July 12, 1985

featuring:
Joseph Campbell
Robert Bly
Ursula K. LeGuin
Linda Leonard
William Stafford
Ann Igoe
Rita Shumaker
Marcus Wise
David Whetstone
Michael Meade
Connie Martin
Fran Quinn
Bill Holmes
Louis Camp
Ivana Spalatin
Andrew Dick
Martin Lowenthal

This conference is ten days of train-ing in how to read myth and fairy story using body, brain and soul. This year our subject will be the Orpheus myth. We will bring the ideas of Rilke, Blake, Joseph Campbell and Alice Miller to bear on the myth; Joseph Campbell will be present for five days to present his views.

A men's group led by Robert Bly and a women's group led by Connie Martin and Linda Leonard will con-vene separately on days two and three to relate the myth to the wild man and the wild woman.

What sort of poetry and art is appropriate for the Orpheus mode of soul? In poetry, is form or free verse appropriate?

We continue to work with how to retain personal power in a nuclear age.

Daily schedules include talks, drumming, dancing, poetry and the singing of Bach.

Place:
A set of cabins
in Mendocino, CA

Cost:
$450
$100 deposit required for a reser-vation (deposit refundable until May 15, 1985).

For reservations contact:
Fran Quinn
31 Lee Street
Worcester, MA 01609
(617) 793-2123

After June 1, 1985, contact:
Fran Quinn
C/o Shecters
Box 621
Point Reyes, CA 94956
(415) 663-8640

Howard Nelson

Loons and Ocean Owls

THE FIRST TIME I MET Robert Bly he was carrying antlers through an airport. Someone had presented them to him at his previous stop. I was the young guy given the job by the English Department (and glad to have it) of picking up the visiting poet. It was 1972, I think. I was only a year or two out of graduate school, with not much of an idea of what poetry readings had been, long ago, and might be again, and I said, trying to make a joke, "Maybe you could wear them for the reading." He responded, neither sarcastic nor ingenuous, "I might do that."

Robert Bly is a great teacher. Many people know this now, but it's been true for a long time. I want to say something about him here as teacher, critic and prose writer, and poet, and I'll start with his teaching. It's one of his gifts — gift, as in "ability"; gift, as in "something given to others."

Recently I attended a three-day conference he conducted on the subject, "W. B. Yeats and His Father." It was a conference for men — there were about a hundred of us — and on the first night Robert polled the group. How many of us knew Yeats well, and how many knew his work a little and had come to learn more, and how many had come primarily because they had seen the Bill Moyers program or otherwise become interested in the men's movement? When hands were raised there were five or so in the first group, five or so in the second, and the rest in the third.

One might have thought that William Butler Yeats and John Butler Yeats and poetry would drift to the sidelines, but that wasn't the case. There was talk of many things, but W. B. and J. B. Yeats remained the curriculum, and the poetry of W. B. Yeats was the spine of the weekend. A hundred contemporary American men, very few of them specialists in literature, spent many hours together listening, talking, and reciting — studying with seriousness and pleasure the life and work of a complex, challenging Irish elk of a poet. To me that seems more than refreshing.

I'm a teacher by trade, and I've thought a lot about what makes good teaching. Seriousness and laughter, I think, and planning and spontaneity; staying on the immediate subject and getting off it in proper ratio; being able to recognize a real opening or connection when it appears. Wanting to listen to one's students. Knowing one's subject well, and loving it. That weekend the subjects were John Butler Yeats—sweet intelligent man, painter, master conversationalist and letter writer, "prodigal father" — and William Butler Yeats— great poet—and men's souls and spirits, and Robert Bly taught about as well as anyone could ask a person to teach.

The second night there was some drumming and dancing. Some of those who had been to men's conferences before had brought drums, and we formed a band of ten or so and started drumming. The other men stood around, talking, sipping beer or soda, some swaying or tapping a foot maybe, but no one was dancing. Then Robert came in. With his arms and his slightly maniacal smile, he encouraged the drummers, exhorted us to crank it up a notch, and then urged the men standing around to make a circle, and pretty soon men were dancing, taking solos out in the center—the minister, the financial consultant, the psychotherapist, the carpenter, the hairdresser, the insurance man, taking their turns as supple and turbulent men in boisterous devotion to the sun and the moon. Maybe it doesn't speak well for us that we needed Robert, who had a right to be tired after lecturing six or seven hours that day, to come in and stir things up and get us moving, but that's the way it goes. Many of the men there probably hadn't danced in a long while. As has happened many times and in many situations, Robert might have been tired, but he had more energy to offer, and he called forth energy in others as well.

It was the kind of scene that has been made fun of and condescended to in various articles about men's gatherings. Neither the drumming nor the dancing was of professional quality— no Olatunjis or Baryshnikovs in our group. But in this culture we rely too much on others to do our music making and dancing for us. Also, it's all too easy to lose sight of how closely connected the willingness to perhaps appear outlandish or ridiculous is to what is sometimes called "higher consciousness," but might also be called "extravagance" or "giving yourself a little more credit as a human being." Extravagance is among Robert Bly's important gifts. Heed it well, ye journalists: dancing and drumming is a good way to end the day.

What did the men who attended the weekend gain? It's hard to say. Probably there would be a hundred individual answers. But here's my thought. We men who sat together listening intently to Robert Bly and W. B. Yeats may well have increased our ability to follow to its source every event in action or in thought, and may have opened ourselves a little more to the possibility of feeling so great a sweetness flow into our breasts that we must laugh and we must sing. We may have learned a little better how to sit down in the rag and bone shops of our hearts. And we may have improved the likelihood of our coming—when the time arrives—proud, open-eyed, and laughing to the tomb.

Well, maybe I hope too much . . . it was only a weekend. But you never know. It could be true.

So many times I've been startled by sentences, insights, and judgments in Robert Bly's essays. He has a remarkable talent for saying the penetrating thing. His descriptions of poets, for example. In a short piece on Robert Frost, he wrote, "If you ask him: 'Do you visit the other world?' he would answer, 'I wouldn't tell you if I did.'" And I say to myself, "Yes, that's exactly right." One can read a vast amount of criticism on Robert Frost and not find anywhere that essential, subtle quality in Frost, or combination of qualities, caught so cleanly.

Somewhere Robert once used the phrase "sober and spontaneous," and he brings those qualities together well in his essays and his prose sentences. Maybe it's the combination of intellect and intuition that I'm describing here: he doesn't sacrifice one to the other. On Pablo Neruda:

. . . Neruda, like a deep-sea crab, all claws and shell, is able
to breathe in the heavy substances that lie beneath the daylight
consciousness. He stays on the bottom for hours, and moves
around calmly and without hysteria.

On college teachers:

Teachers and therapists often have a strong Cook, Mythologist,
or Magician inside. But if a teacher has not developed the Wild
Man or Wild Woman, that person becomes the strange being
we call an "academic," whose love of standards is admirable
in every way, but who somehow filters the wildness out of
Thoreau or Emily Dickinson or D. H. Lawrence even as he
or she teaches them. Not all teachers do that, thank God, but
universities shelter a lot of them.

Intelligence flows in such observations and such prose like blood
flowing in a brain.

One of my favorite Bly essays is "Being a Lutheran Boy-God
in Minnesota," which is in large part about his father and which
lies near the beginning of the thinking that went into *Iron John*.
He tells a story of his father coming to the aid of a hired man vic-
timized by circumstance and community indifference, and saving
him from an unjust jail term. After the story, Bly writes, "I learned
then that the indignation of the solitary man is the stone pin that
connects this world to the next." What a strong, beautifully worded
sentence that is. It's a sentence that I carry around inside me along
with certain other permanent sentences, like "Yes, as every one
knows, meditation and water are wedded for ever," or "In wildness
is the preservation of the world."

Before I met Robert Bly at the airport I had met him walking
through fields of corn stubble. I was a senior in college. Who was
this poet who noticed how snow glows in the ditches, who exchanged
gazes with horses, who thought of giving up all ambition, who used
so many exclamation marks, who was reminded by old boards lying
on the ground of the decks of ocean ships, and looked out at a barn

through falling snow and saw a storm-tossed hulk on whose deck stood, not just sailors, but sailors who had been blind for many years? I was fascinated and moved by the simple pleasures, and also by the images and undercurrents my mind couldn't quite understand—not rationally. This was *Silence in the Snowy Fields,* which I still think of as a single poem, and a powerful one, all its quiet notwithstanding.

Then I looked up the other book that Bly had published, *The Light Around the Body,* and found something very different. Churning, dense surrealism, moral outrage, the war in Vietnam, which was at that very moment raging and grinding on, politics, history, denunciations, smoky caves, hands developed by apes with terrible labor hanging from the sleeves of evangelists, fatigue, fury—a raised, angry voice. It was an anger that contained conscience, imagination, and citizenship, and hearing that anger was of great value to a young man.

I remember sitting once in a group of people reading and reciting poems together. We began after midnight, sitting in a circle on the floor, in a room lit with lanterns and candles. As we began, Robert suggested that we invite in some of the poets from the past that we loved, and we did that, inviting them with a simple phrase and naming. It was a small ceremony. I don't know anyone else but Robert who would have made that suggestion. It isn't important who was invited, but I'll say that I felt them in the shadows. It's in the spirit of that circle that I've mentioned and borrowed words from various poets in this essay—to set Robert among good company.

Robert did a good thing when he learned to play the dulcimer and the bouzouki. They've brought an old, delicate, twanging beauty to his poetry readings. I remember sitting with him one fall evening in the kitchen of my house. I read some passages from Whitman while he improvised on the dulcimer, and Walt never sounded better, if I say so myself.

I love Robert's capacity for pleasure and content, and his capacity for discontent, outrage, and restlessness. In his poetry we are allowed to stand at ease or with joy in "what is." And we are brought also into the realm of what is not; what might be, but for the most part isn't; what we struggle for and don't get. How we are filled; and how we are broken, fragmentary, ordinary, lonely as if abandoned.

Standing in a barn where thirty steers are milling, he says:

> These breathing ones do not demand eternal life; they ask only
> to eat the crushed corn and the hay, coarse as rivers, and cross
> the rivers, and sometimes feel an affection run along the heavy
> nerves.

Along whose nerves is that affection running? A man stands in the dusky barn looking at the cattle. The lines are praise for being alive on the earth, among other creatures, in the clay jug of the body.

And he also speaks — as in "Snowbanks North of the House," a poem of great plainness, sad mystery, and power — of the failures, breakdowns, and refusals we can hardly understand, let alone overcome: "And the sea lifts and falls all night; the moon goes on through the unattached heavens alone."

Robert Bly's assessment of the human condition encompasses roughly the Song of Songs and Freud's reckoning, "We consider that we have succeeded when hysterical misery turns into ordinary unhappiness." I'll set down a few more lines to show a span of moods. First, out in the cornfield, near a solitary willow tree in late fall:

> The mind has shed leaves alone for years.
> It stands apart with small creatures near its roots.
> I am happy in this ancient place,
> A spot easily caught sight of above the corn,
> If I were a young animal ready to turn home at dusk.

It is one of the responsibilities of poets to take us to ancient places. Not all poets may care or be able to do this, but we had better have some who can, or a taproot dies. Robert Bly guides us to such places often in his poems. The solitary tree. The tide pool. The ferns on the stream bank, where the deer's hoofprint is pressed into the sand.

Next, lines from one of the poems he quarried and shaped from the flowing work in *Sleepers Joining Hands:*

Some beings get used to life underneath.
Some dreams do not want to move into the light.
Some want to, but can't; they can't make their way out,
because someone is guarding the posts of the door.

Have you seen those Chinese tomb guardians
left at the closed door? They stand with one knee raised;
they half-stand, half-dance, half-rage, half-shout—
hot tempered muscle-bulgers, big-kneed brow-bulgers.
They scowl for eternity at the half-risen.
What do you have that can get past them?

A person might never be able to get past the likes of those.

But an ocean owl might get past them, swooping over their
chalky red shoulders. In one of his love poems, we perch calmly
on some crag among the sea-mist of desire, ready to spread our
wings:

Standing by you, I am
glad as the clams
at high tide, eerily
content as the amorous
ocean owls.

Praise the Lord for amorous ocean owls! And praise the Lord for
vowels.

Another poem, one of his very short poems, a poem that Issa
smiles on somewhere:

The Loon's Cry

From far out in the center of the naked lake
The loon's cry rose.
It was the cry of someone who owned very little.

The age-old job of the poet: praise and lament. To reveal and remind us how rich the human soul is, and how poor; to express both
in words that have inside them some imponderable, singing thing.

Robert Bly's poetry is full-blooded, original, and encouraging. In his books of poems he undertakes certain tasks. For example, he learned through conscious effort the discipline of looking and describing with care and accuracy. He learned to do that, and then to push off from an inner surface of the thing described, moving from there into one's own past and half-hidden thoughts. These particular tasks are parts of a larger one, one that takes a lifetime at least to complete.

He hasn't rested on his laurels. He has written some weird lines. He has made poetry more useful in his time. He's preached the fiery sermon, and written the poem of three or four lines as private and mysterious as a creek in a ravine that no one has ever seen. His imagination likes to wear bright green and brilliant blue, and it also likes the colors of oats stored in shadowy bins and sea-water running back over stones. He's played with bony fingers the dulcimer of the mind. He loves words, and has a special feeling for some of the simplest of them, placing them in plain syntax and thereby somehow restoring to them their original weight and freshness; words like "snow" and "brood" and "stump" and "reed" and "joy." And his poetry has grown warmer as he has gotten older.

All these qualities and labors have been important parts of his accomplishment and his art, and I value them all. But possibly what I value most is the way his poetry contains the hooting of ocean owls and the cry of the loon.

News of the Universe

"Man with snake and birds" (courtesy of Thomas R. Smith).

4
IRON JOHN & BEYOND

Saul Galin

The Third Male

IN THE LATE FIFTIES I was publishing a magazine of Latin American and European literature in English translation, and I needed a translator for a Swedish poet. I asked friends to recommend an American poet with a sharp ear for the finer values of Swedish tone and mood. One afternoon Louis Simpson took me to a small apartment on Charles Street in Greenwich Village and introduced me to Robert Bly.

We talked all afternoon. We talked late into the evening. I remember his esteem for poets, particularly Machado, Lorca, Jiménez, and his loathing for dry, fussy, reasoned attitudes toward poetry and for the complacent scientific conceptualism that made contact with any poem a body odor with few remedies. Above all I remember wild, passionate words about poetry taught in universities and sold by publishing houses. Poetry was treated as cool alabaster, bathed in ironical radiance. To oppose this, Robert published *The Fifties,* an outspoken, often rebellious magazine which helped readers to understand that by turning from Auden and Eliot they gained the rare privilege of escaping a colossal fiasco. I had met one of the most interesting minds of my generation.

Since that meeting Robert has produced poems that embrace the inner and outer worlds of fathers and sons, husbands and wives and lovers, the earth and life above it where dawn often breaks crooked. He has also done translations—clear, precise, rhythmical, in American English—that never double-cross the original. And I will never forget those magnificent poetry readings (I can only speak of New York) to which all of us came from different streets of the city to get high on words and thoughts. Not only Robert's (he never read many of his own poems), but those of Rilke and Machado, Goethe, Jiménez, and Vallejo. English departments had always treated these giants with slight derision and fear. Robert read their poems with respect and passion.

One reading a few years ago changed my life. Struck by something a young woman in the audience said, Robert went into Rilke's "You Darkness That I Come From" as if his life depended on it. Suddenly mine did too. I had always been in Sartre's pocket. After hearing Rilke, Sartre's words seemed to be on the same level as "Father Knows Best," and at that moment he became a grisly relic. Most of the English and American poets I had read since childhood now gathered around me like a drift of pale, uneasy shapes. And so much of what the psychological brotherhood calls outer reality quickly became a cluster of meaningless particles. I didn't know it then, but I was getting ready for *Iron John*.

It is no accident that the Gulf War and *Iron John,* savage and wild male energies, brother souls in the American psyche, sped into our lives at about the same time. Opposing male energies had arrived to do battle on the plains of America. A poem's worth of blue sky stood against a radiant bulldog commander-in-chief, trying very hard to look like Randolph Scott, who in his best milk-and-scorpion voice proclaimed to the world that punishment for aggression by liberty-loving people, themselves toiling up the hill to paradise, was honorable and just. The savage energy of the war spread madness over a vast area with superb surges pitched at perfect angles. Directed by cold, unwavering reason never subject to compassion, it glorified its two highest attributes: power and serial murder. "Shooting Iraqis was like shooting ducks in a pond," one pilot told CNN. No scalding remorse harrowing the soul, no grief, no weeping, no senseless rage, no heart on "a wheel of fire." The infallibility of the just. Truth, judgment, science, morality, the four horsemen of madness in reason, accompanied this savage male energy.

Wild male energy feels and pictures itself in a different way. It celebrates sexual love as part of a grand divinity. Spirituality and sexuality lift their legs, join hands, and dance in consort. Wild male energy is not seduced by the sympathetic pressure of government, industry, or the church. It honors ancient rituals that protect the earth, the waters, and all living things. In the presence of grief and sorrow it knows that "the human eyelid is not teartight." Finally the wild man understands that the merging of wild and savage energies means one thing in our civilization: meat and potato sex and the desire for fiscal distinction in corporate Gehennas throughout the land. No more music.

Iron John is a brilliant, compact, lyrical poem evoking certain possibilities for men. On such hinges as Machado, Wordsworth, Kabir, Rilke, Shakespeare, Lorca, Al-Muntafil, Rumi, Dante, Yeats, and many others of time past, Robert has put up doors, each opening into a room where males can sit with their past and feel the pulse of their present life. The poem asks males to join hands with their ancestors and found a new life. This is Robert's call for the second male. I like this male, without rhetoric, without cant, without sentimentality, unself-pitying, disciplined, and alert to the flow of his mythic life. And yet I am not fully satisfied. The outer world of green earth, sky, and water is distant, muted. The second male essentially concerns himself with male rebirth, male feelings and love, male destiny. I need these things but I also need something more. I need the third male.

Unlike the first male, who crushes the world with murder and terror and "does great damage to the soul, earth, and humankind," and unlike the second male, open, caring, feeling, never bullying, refusing emotional injustice and the power to inflict shame, the third male chooses to confer a different destiny on his life. Because he knows that America no longer loves life, he dedicates himself to living things that cannot defend themselves — water and air, fish, birds, insects, animals and grass, trees, flowers, and earth. He insists on giving his life meaning by sustaining their life again and again.

In the fiftieth year of his life (his life before belongs to himself, his family, his community, his nation), the third male tells his wife (if he has one) and grown children (if he has any), without arrogance or pride or missionary zeal, in an ordinary voice as if he were telling them the simplest of facts, that he is quitting his job if that job sustains the commercial, industrial, or military life of the nation, and that he will come together with others like himself, a band of outsiders, to work at jobs they choose for food and shelter. Refusing any longer to be a lonely witness to the crucifixion of innocent life unable to defend itself, he will give his remaining days to them.

All living things are now his first and last love. He still loves his wife and children and friends—may even live with them—but the action of his life is elsewhere. That vast collective agony, humankind, is no longer his chief concern. It can arrange its own salvation. We all breathe and die under the same sky, and each of us has his own destiny. The third male chooses not to turn his back on the murder of the innocents. His whole being sanctifies life. He knows that the real tragedy of our time is not the tragedy of men and women but the tragedy of nature.

Should the third male turn his back on nature, should he fail to give it the last full measure of devotion, should he submit to the delusion of consensus and power and the mirage of human justice, then must he refuse to give birth to existence. "I will no longer father any children, and I call on all males to do the same," says the third male, without malice or anger, without self-pity or the tyranny of impotence. "All undefended life merits our protection and love, and if we cannot cherish and love all life, what good is our salvation? If we, the protectors, commit the definitive crime against the life it is our duty to protect, then we must pronounce sentence upon ourselves: Extinction so that the planet may live."

The third male knows that he must live out his life and embrace oblivion. He does this with grace, even joy. Injustice, oppression, murder, words always used for humankind, are now more fitting for nature. It is up to him to refuse injustice and allow the green earth and all life on it, allow the desert sands and the mountains, the fish in the water and the air and the sky that comfort us to live as long as the universe chooses to breathe.

As I finish these words to honor a dear friend, I remember all the mornings and evenings in my kitchen opening cans of tuna and devouring Russian pumpernickel bread and scrambled eggs. I think of his courage, his clear lucid vision, and how much of my sense of justice and freedom I owe to him. *Iron John* changed the direction of my life. There is much suffering and terror now, and we are at grips with our destiny because we have become great masters of death. Our task is not to end life but to create it. If we cannot do that, then it is our duty to absent ourselves from the future.

With Saul Galin and Ruth Bly, Kabekona Lake, Minnesota,
circa *1980 (Bill Booth photo).*

Robert L. Moore

Robert Bly and True Greatness: Some Musings from the Study of Leadership in Human Culture

FOR MANY YEARS NOW I have been pursuing the historical, anthropological, sociological, and psychoanalytical study of leadership. One of my mentors in this study was the great German philosopher Wilhelm Dilthey. Dilthey was one of those incredibly broad and deep intellects who focused on the magnificent complexity of human history and gave us intelligent ways to interrogate this "blooming, buzzing confusion." He helped us use insights from the past to come up with ways to map our way through our present and to understand the most significant challenges of our future. One of Dilthey's most cherished ideas was that great men—not merely impersonal forces—shape the critical twists and turns of human history. Another of my intellectual mentors, the great Erik Erikson, shared many of Dilthey's central assumptions. Many years ago I used their insights to evaluate the significance of the life of the great reformer Wesley and published my first book on the psychology of leadership.

Little did I know at that time that I would have the opportunity to know and work with *in my own time* a man whose leadership has opened the possibility for some truly great things to happen in the human community. That man, of course, is the poet Robert Bly.

Erikson believed that the way great cultural innovators act upon their age is that their own personal issues and problems coincide with some of the central problems of their age. In seeking to deal with their own problems, great men—cultural innovators—help their culture address these issues on a wide scale. It is my belief that Robert

Bly's contribution to our culture and our time may—when evaluated by historians of the future—prove to have been an example of the dynamic that Erikson has noted. Robert is, I believe, a great poet. But his true greatness lies in the way in which he has, in struggling with his own masculine wounds, enabled an entire generation of men around the world to begin asking some of the most significant questions of our time.

These questions, of course, revolve around the task of helping the males of our species become consciously masculine in a way that can lead to healing in the human community. When the cultural and intellectual history of our time is written, Robert will be recognized as the catalyst for a sweeping cultural revolution. This cultural revolution will one day not only reroot the masculine in its primordial depths, but open the way to the maturation of our gender and the empowerment of its potential contributions to the well-being of our species and our planet.

We celebrate today his past and present contributions to our common life. We anticipate with great hope that his generativity will continue to grow in the coming years. We wish him peace, power, wisdom, and passion as he continues his work.

Terry Dobson

Robert Bly

ROBERT BLY IS A CURIOUS and chimerical force of nature. A cloud, say—now a proper, stately fleece, now a twirling, puckish wisp, now a thunderhead full of piss and clangor, now a purpled evening empyrean meant to drape your eyes with glory. How can one relax around such a man?

For the past ten years he has showered me with kindness, leavened with the occasional mordant observation of some flaw or lapse I thought I'd papered over. I'd gladly be his footman, working for tablescraps of conversation. He won't have it, though. No Mr. Chips, he. He likes push-back, and I've learned to keep my hatchet scoured and my walking shoes supple.

It's easy to love the man, easy to be awed by him, but what compels me to respect him as I do is his consistent willingness to jump out of bed. At one of the first men's retreats, I was leading a bunch of guys through a pain containment exercise. I had men slapping each other's forearms full-force with open palms, those slapped then thanking the slappers for the very painful experience. Bly happened along. He watched for a while. "He's the boss," I thought, "and a poet—he'll stay at a safe, proprietary distance." Not Robert. He walked right up to me, rolled up his sleeve. "Hit me," he said. I did, as hard as ever I could. He returned the favor as smartly. How wonderful to meet a sage in a clearing, slapping and grinning, slapping and grinning, his eyes glinting like oysters open to the moon.

John Stokes

The Poetry of Land Rights: DownUnder with Robert Bly

FOR ABOUT A WEEK in 1978 I helped Robert Bly and poets from many different countries to meet the Aboriginal Australians during Writers' Week of the Adelaide Festival of Arts in South Australia. In addition to his time with urban and tribal students at the Aboriginal Community College where I was working, Bly also took part in a large land rights march and rally with hundreds of central desert Pitjantjatjara people. These are a few memories from that time.

For Robert

"You don't belong in here!"

Those were Robert Bly's words to me as he stood in front of my desk at the Beacon Press in Boston. My boss, the senior editor, and I were preparing *The Kabir Book* for publication, and Robert had come for one of his rare visits. As he shook my hand, he continued, "You belong out here with us."

Taking him at his word, I began to tag along when he came to town, attending the Great Mother Festivals of 1976 and '77, sitting in on college campus readings and talks, meeting Etheridge, Gioia, Saul . . . and "all those nice American boys who smell of soap, love their mother *and* their girlfriend and would never start a nuclear war." Bly was speaking at the time of the great need in America for *grounding,* of the weak rope over the chasm between the unconscious and the conscious, of the *"infantilization of America,"* and of the need to *not* use acquired language like "collective unconscious," but to let our own psyches rise and slowly devour those terms in order to make them personal and original.

Answering the call of a great snake deep within my own psyche, I left cold Boston in late 1977 and moved to Adelaide, South Australia.

Australia, the southern land. Land of the Rainbow Serpent. When Gondwanaland, the original land mass, broke apart into seven pieces, the great Rainbow Serpent coiled beneath also broke seven times. A portion still sleeps beneath each great land mass. Aboriginal Australians continue to remember this long-ago event. Forty thousand years of Dreaming, the people singing and dancing the land. "White people sometimes think we make up all these sacred sites. We didn't make 'em. God made 'em. We just found 'em and knew they were sacred."

One day in a pub, I heard a low droning growl and turned toward the sound to see a black man on television painted white, cockatoo feathers in his hair, cheeks puffed as he blew into a long log. As I watched, an Aussie standing next to me turned to the TV and laughed, "Bloody Abo." Setting my pint down on the bar, I headed out the door toward the source of that sound. Looking in the phone book under "A" for Aborigine, I found a listing for an Aboriginal Community College. The world being a funny place, within a month of my first visit, I found myself teaching country western guitar to adult urban and tribal Aborigines from all around Australia at the college. "Okie from Mootwingie." A secretive tribal man from the Kimberleys named Michaelangelo for his painting abilities noticed my attraction to the didjeridu—the log I had seen the man on TV playing—and began to sit with me in a corner of the students' Common Room each day. With my hand touching his throat as he played, I learned the breathing and mouth sounds used to make different rhythms. Dadeeron Dadeeoron. Didjemro didjemro didjemro. Like the Hanged Man in the Tarot deck, I began my education in learning to see the world upside down.

"Like looking at the back of your head without a mirror" was how I used to describe being in Australia. At that time the Community College was located in a run-down mansion in a flash part of North Adelaide, just beside the four-star Oberoi Hotel. The proximity of so many black Australians to wealthy overseas visitors proved to be a constant source of embarrassment to the hotel management, eliciting many difficult questions from startled guests. Some warm days I would sit outside with classes on the grass, looking at these two buildings which somehow seemed to epitomize the cultural chasm between the Aboriginal people and the new Australians. The distance from one door to the other was about twenty-five yards — or forty thousand years, depending on how you walked.

> We are fighting a big fight for the right to be Aboriginal in Australia. Our bodies must keep doing the dances and living in the bush. . . . These are the things we need to help us keep the head and body alive until we are given back our land and the land can make us whole again. We need the land to be Aboriginal in our minds. Without it, we will die.
> —*An elder, now deceased,*
> *from Mornington Island*

Secret rainfall and hidden canyon springs can swell a river to overflow. In the spring of 1978, two streams of people made their way in to Adelaide. As Robert and other writers and artists began to arrive at the Oberoi, where they would camp during the Adelaide Festival of Arts, the council executive of the Pitjantjatjara people, a large tribal language group from the central desert, drove into town for land rights talks with the state government. Only a month before, two hundred Pitjantjatjara elders had camped in town on the Victorian raceway for an unprecedented "public" tribal meeting, hoping to show non-Aboriginals the careful, patient manner in which they make their collective decisions. With imminent mining leases on and near sacred sites, the people had come once again for a big land rights rally. Understanding that this might be their last chance, these people who had survived the last two hundred years in remote silence had decided to change their strategy. "Help will come from outside," they knew. "We will be the folk heroes of tomorrow's history books. We have been talking, but no one here has been listening."

Robert and I met up at the Oberoi shortly after his arrival, laughing at this strange scene we had chosen for our next meeting. Later that night at a "get-to-know-you" dinner we met many of the other writers: China's Yang Xianyi, Yu Lin, and Wang Zualiang, Chinua Achebe from Nigeria, Darmanto Jatman of Java, Kazuko Shiraishi from Japan, Professor P. Lal, poet and editor from Calcutta, as well as Joan Aitkin and Elliot Anderson from the United States. Peter Brook's international theater company flew in from Paris for a series of plays including *Ik, Ubu,* and a filmed performance with tribal Aborigines. Robert agreed with me that a poetry reading for the Aborigines was a good idea, so I began to recruit the interested poets. "Would you like to meet the people who really 'own' Australia?"

Poets and singers are the people who remember what everyone needs to know. Changing little over thousands of years, the poet's role has been to sing from the earth, from the peoples' heart, from the heart of the community, reminding everyone of the origins of things, of the land, of words, of the human beings. As Uluru meets Manhattan, as the great serpent curls around to bite its own tail, healing itself with its own poison, the task of remembering means going back to the old stories, recovering the symbols, recreating the myths, and rebuilding mythic mazeways. Deep in thought as we walked back from a writers' party one afternoon, Robert sat quickly on a low stone wall.

"It must be very difficult to be a writer in this country. They see all the value in a thin strip that goes around the coast and the whole interior as nothing but a wasteland inhabited by a few scrawny dark figures. The Dead Center."

The more we thought about it, the funnier it seemed. "But the Dead Center is really the Living Heart," we joked. And the Outback is really Infront.

Robert crossed the chasm to the Community College many times. While meeting with the students, amusing them with imitations of Kali, fangs dripping, necklace of skulls, one asked him "'Teeth Mother Naked at Last?' What does that mean?" One afternoon, dispensing with "Christian nicknames," the students introduced themselves by giving the name of their home country or community—Pipalyatjara, Mimili, Kununnurra, Amata, Point Pearce. Adelaide itself was once called Tandanya—place of the great red kangaroo—by the Kaurna people. Kazuko Shiraishi and Darmanto often joined us for these informal sessions, everyone sharing their cultural ways. For the Unlucky Australians the problem is not a lack of *grounding*, it is a lack of *ground*. The sacred land, cared for by their people since the beginning of time, fed by the blood of countless generations of ancestors now stolen and parceled out. Massacres, poison, epidemics, assimilation, mining. "If they gave us back the land, I reckon the cities would nearly empty out of our people."

"Strange that there are no Aboriginals here today," Robert noted to the audience at a panel discussion downtown entitled Myth, Symbol, and Fable. "Some of the best storytellers in the world." As the discussion turned to "good" and "bad" myths, bad myths being those which were perpetrated to persecute others, a voice from the audience stated that all myths were bad and that only by destroying all myth could Australia progress. To this Bly responded, "Sounds to me like that old American saying—'the only good Indian is a dead Indian.'" When he mentioned that we had gone to see the movie *Picnic at Hanging Rock,* the audience was anxious to know what Robert thought had happened to all those pleasant young schoolgirls who disappeared in the movie.

"Do you know why those girls all disappeared at the rock? Because no one will acknowledge that that rock is Aboriginal country. And until someone does all your little girls are going to disappear. We've already had it happen in America. First, they become black swans, and then do you know what happens? They become B-52s."

Wednesday morning at the college, the Common Room was filled with students and their friends, lying on the floor or sitting around the room beneath bark paintings, woven mats, and other implements of traditional life. Chinua Achebe's hushed whisper opened the reading with passages from his book *Things Fall Apart.* Robert tuned his dulcimer, telling the Aborigines, "This is an American instrument, but no one knows where it came from. It might be Icelandic. Or African. Who knows?" After a few Kabir poems with the dulcimer, he prefaced a story: "An interesting thing is happening in the United States. We're going back and instead of writing all new words we're looking at fairy tales of Europe from say three hundred to four hundred years ago. And we're retelling those stories to our children and to adults because there's a lot in those stories we haven't noticed."

Kazuko read animal poems in her samurai movie voice and Darmanto danced and sang several *kalatida*—the traditional songs of Java. Maureen Watson, noted Aboriginal storyteller, joined us, as well as K. C. Das from India and Faye Zwickey from West Australia. One of the Aborigines later told me, "That friend of yours was just like one of our old songmen, the way he made the pain disappear with his words. You know, sometimes, the best thing you can do for us is just to make us laugh. It helps us to go on."

After the reading, Robert came over. He seemed upset. "John, I have to tell you something. Don't be angry with me. Who was that man sitting under the television set?" One of the students had sat through the reading on the lower shelf of the TV stand we used to wheel the set from room to room. He had dark black skin, a high forehead, and broad Aboriginal features. I told Robert his name. "Well, when the reading started," Robert continued, "I couldn't help looking at him because he was the ugliest human being I had ever seen. But by the end of the reading, I realized he was the most beautiful human being I had ever seen. And I'd like to give him something."

I spoke with the other teachers and found that this student could not read English at all. His grasp of English grammar was "A,B,C . . . shit, what's that next one?" Great, I thought, since he can't read Robert could give him a book that his teacher could use as a primer. Robert wrote out the inscription, "For Peter . . ." The book—*This Tree Will Be Here for a Thousand Years*.

Later that evening, we attended a talk by Professor Lal, who continued a theme he had developed in other talks on cultural identity—compassionate love. During the trouble in Bangladesh, he pointed out, millions of refugees had poured into Calcutta, swelling that city's population far beyond the saturation point. Yet, for nearly six months, those millions were cared for and fed by people whose situation was little better than those they helped. I wondered to myself what the history of Australia—and for that matter, North and South America—would have been like had the same compassion been practiced by the Europeans in their initial and subsequent meetings with the native peoples they encountered when they happened upon these vast populated continents. In his book, *The Unlucky Australians,* Frank Hardy writes that if Australia is the "Lucky Country," then the Aboriginal Australians must be the unluckiest people of all. In the foreword to that book, historian Donald Horne writes: "To be an Australian is, in part, to be an Aborigine. The Aborigines are part of our Australian-ness, part of ourselves as a nation. To treat them like dogs is, to that extent, to treat ourselves as a nation of dogs. . . . To the extent that we still tolerate the de-humanisation of Aborigines, we take some of the humanity out of ourselves."

That Saturday, Robert, Darmanto, Kazuko, and I walked arm in arm down King Williams street with several thousand other people, Aboriginal and non-Aboriginal. On the outside, just four more people. But to the students from the college and the people from Pitjantjatjara country, it was a sign of international solidarity and a hope that word of their plight and ongoing struggle would somehow reach beyond the conspiracy of silence that enables Europeans to claim an entire continent using the doctrine not of Manifest Destiny, but of "Terra Nullius"—empty, uninhabited, desolate land. From Captain Cook to the King Ranch, from massacres to mining, "until we are given back the land / and the land can make us whole again."

One day we will all have to make peace with the land and with the indigenous people. Without their help and blessings, no one is going to get very far. It is now many years later and Robert and I have met many times—in Manhattan, Mendocino, Santa Fe, Tesuque Pueblo. I'm still making that walk from the fancy hotel to the Aboriginal college. In an *East West Journal* interview in 1976, speaking of the book *Man-child: A Study of the Infantilization of Man* by David Jonas and Doris Kline, Bly states: "The gist of it (the book) is that each generation of Westerners after the Industrial Revolution has been more infantile than the one before. The authors define an adult as someone who can exist in the physical world without a lot of supportive devices. Many Eskimo in old times were probably adults. . . ." If we live in a society "without a father, or models for maturity," then perhaps the grounded, self-sufficient stance of native peoples such as the Pitjantjatjara, the Lakota, the Ainu, and the Hawaiians can act as the models lacking in technological society. Twenty-five yards or forty thousand years . . . whichever comes first. *There are still people who know how to live here,* and by helping them retain and regain the land, we also help ourselves.

Robert, whether you knew it or not, you made a big difference in Australia. And you were right about me not belonging in there at Beacon. I belong out here. From the bushes, Happy Birthday.

—*John Stokes*
Corrales, New Mexico

Ted Solotaroff

Captain Bly

GORE VIDAL HAS REMARKED that instead of politics Americans have elections. One sees what he means, but it's not quite on the money, because elections matter mostly to the politicians, their PAC groups, and their dwindling party loyalists. For the rest of America, elections are a peculiar form of TV entertainment in which the commercial has become the program. The affiliations and ideologies people care about are elsewhere, in what Theodore Roszak fifteen years ago termed "situational groups," the politics of the personal. "In less than a generation's time," he wrote, "every conceivable form of situational belonging has been brought out of the closet and has forced its grievances and its right to exist upon the public consciousness." He was writing about the mitosis of the counterculture, but his observation was no less prescient about its opposition — the pro-lifers, creationists, apocalyptics, neoconservatives, school vigilantes, et al. There are also the expressive therapeutic groups. The most influential ideology of change in America today is probably that of AA, not only because it works so dramatically but also because it provides a model of psychological and spiritual community, which is what the ethnic, racial, gender, sexual, and other situational groups are partly about. The most interesting recent example is the men's movement, a complex phenomenon that appears to derive from AA, feminism, New Age religion and therapy, environmentalism, and the culture and charisma of Robert Bly.

That a poet has become the spokesman of a broadly based movement as well as an author at the top of the charts has, of course, struck many readers but not, I imagine, many poets. They are used to Bly the group leader, publicist, ideologist, translator, mythologist, guru, and scold, he having played these roles in the American poetry of the second half of the century, much as Ezra Pound did in that of the first half. Poets are also used to Bly the showman, his hit performance on Bill Moyers's program, which sent the men's movement into media orbit, having been preceded by hundreds of his sold-out poetry readings and seminar star turns.

Like most literary careers that last, Bly's has been formed from the ongoing play of oppositions, but his have been particularly intense: Lutheran and pagan, rural and international, reclusive and engaged, austere and grandiose. These contending traits and inclinations have generated Bly's high energy and also created a certain rhythm to his career that makes his present celebrity and function almost predictable. Also they are compacted into a strongly lived life that personalizes the mythopoetic structure and far-out counsel of *Iron John* and gives the book, for all of its discursiveness and high-handedness, an overall staying power and a kind of charmed ability to hit pay dirt about every third page.

Iron John is less about male identity than it is about what Jungians, following John Keats, call "soul-making." Much of Bly's soul has been forged and refined by his relationship with the Wild Man, the tutelary figure in "Iron John," the fairy tale that he unpacks and embroiders to tell the reader how boys psychically become men and men remain psychically boys.

Bly grew up, as he says, a "Lutheran boy-god" in Minnesota, being his mother's favorite, and in good Freudian fashion, drawing from that a heightened sense of entitlement as well as a tendency to see the world through her eyes and feel it with her heart, which means he didn't see or feel very much on his own. In Bly's terms his soul or psyche had a lot of conducting "copper" in it, which would come in handy for Bly the editor, critic, and translator, and not much of the "iron" of autonomy that he would later have to extract on his own from the mines of the archetypal warrior king in himself. In short, he grew up "soft," like the males of today to whom *Iron John* is mainly addressed. Bly's brother appears to have been his father's son, the one who took up the family occupation of farming, the hairy Esau to his tent-dwelling Jacob. His father was strong, kindly, intensely moral, and alcoholic, creating a particularly poignant remoteness that broods over *Iron John*, as it does in some of Bly's later poetry: "the man in the black coat" who appears only to turn away again and whose haunting absence, along with his mother's haunting presence, has created Bly's lifelong project and process of fathering one's soul, the fruit of which is his particular contribution to the men's movement.

For the rest, Bly was a well-raised product of Madison, Minnesota, a small plains community with a Norwegian cultural accent. He was properly clean and godly, cheerful and repressed, "asleep in the Law," as he puts it in his major autobiographical poem, "Sleepers Joining Hands." A Lutheran boy-god who remains in this state is likely to become a minister, his grandiosity put into the service of interpreting doctrines and counseling the flock. Bly has, of course, taken the opposite road, "from the Law to the Legends," as he puts it in *Iron John,* but the deal he apparently made with his psyche is that the nascent preacher has gone with him and adapted to his various stages and purposes.

Bly doesn't talk about his Harvard experience in *Iron John*—he seldom has in a career otherwise rich in self-revelation—but it was a determinate stage in which this wounded boy-god and naive "ascender" was both endowed and banished, a literary version of the prince of his fairy tale. Here he is as an editor of the *Harvard Advocate,* reviewing a collection of British poetry edited by Kenneth Rexroth. One sentence tells the tale: "Perhaps it is unfortunate that Rexroth should have been let loose on the Romantics; there is, I think, a difference between the desire to express personal emotion by increased direct reference to the world of nature, and the desire to overthrow all external discipline of morals of government."

This is, of course, the T. S. Eliot act that many young literary men in the postwar era imitated to put themselves on what they took to be the cutting edge of modernism. In Bly's case, it suggests that he was turning over in his sleep from the Lutheran law to the Anglican one. The literary air at the time was thick with conservative authority and decorum. It had an archbishop, Eliot; a set of bishops, the New Critics; a martyr, Pound; and lots of acolytes, who were becoming half-paralyzed by the dogma that poetry was a hieratic vocation, that the imagination lived, worked, and had its being within The Tradition. As Eliot had laid it down, The

Tradition was mostly Dante and the metaphysical poets, who were high Anglicans like himself. The dogma came equipped with Eliot's emphasis on the impersonal, objective image and with a set of literary heresies and fallacies that were meant to nip any revival of Romanticism in the bud.

To subscribe to this ethos typically led a young writer to graduate school or to the pits. Bly chose the latter, having become "overcommitted to what he was not," as Erik Erikson would say, and badly needing to find his way to his own "inner tradition." He ended up in New York, where he spent the next three years being mostly blocked, depressed, and poor: the state of "ashes, descent, and grief" that forms a major early stage in his mythic prince's initiation. According to Bly, life reserves this "katabasis" particularly for the grandiose ascender, putting him in touch with the dark, wounded side he has tried to ignore and evade and ministering to the naiveté, passivity, and numbness that come with the apron strings of his entitlement. The road, in short, that leads "from the mother's house to the father's house."

The one poem that Bly published from this period, "Where We Must Look for Help," is based on the three birds that were sent forth from Noah's ark into the flooded world: the glamorous peaceful dove and the graceful swallows find no land, only the crow does:

> The crow, the crow, the spider-colored crow,
> The crow shall find new mud to walk upon.

As Bly was to tell Deborah Baker, who has written an excellent biographical essay about him ("Making a Farm: A Literary Biography," *Poetry East,* 4 and 5, Spring/Summer 1981, pp. 145-186), "It was the first time . . . I ran into the idea of the dark side of the personality being the fruitful one." After a year at the Iowa Writers' Workshop, Bly went to live on a farm his father had bought for him, and a year later, while visiting relatives in Norway, he discovered his new mud lying adjacent to his inner tradition.

In primitive societies, as Bly tells us in *Iron John,* the male initiations are viewed as a second birth, with the elders acting as a "male mother." Bly's were first Georg Trakl, a German, and Gunnar

Ekelöf, a Swede. From them he began to grasp the subjective, intuitive, "wild" side of modernism as opposed to the objective, rationalist, "domesticated" one. In their work, as in that of the French and Hispanic surrealists—Char, Michaux, Jiménez, Vallejo, and Lorca, among others—Bly sensed the missing water, the unconscious, for lack of which he believed Anglo-American poetry was suffering a slow, choking death. Increasingly dry, ironical, exhausted, remote, it was itself The Wasteland, while the European poets were still fecund, passionate, and present. Returning to the family farm, Bly started a magazine, *The Fifties,* to say so as aggressively as possible and to provide translations of the European and Latin American surrealists in three or four languages, as well as to give welcome to his contemporaries who showed signs of new life and to put down those who were dead on their feet. Flying a woodcut of Woden as his logo, Bly almost single-handedly led the charge against the reign of the "Old Fathers" in the middle, joined by the New York School on his right and the West Coast Beats on his left. Neither wing was anywhere near as relentless, reductive, and brutal as Bly himself was. He was out to deauthorize as well as replace the Eliot-Pound-Tate tradition, stamping on it well into the next generation—Lowell, Berryman, Delmore Schwartz, Jarrell, Karl Shapiro, whomever. In *Iron John* he chides himself for contributing to the decline of "Zeus energy," attributing it to the demons in his father-wound: a false note from someone who has repeatedly insisted that literature advances by generational strife and repeatedly deplored the absence of adversarial criticism among poets.

Be that as it may, in the late fifties Bly entered his warrior phase, developing the strategy and service to a cause that in *Iron John* distinguishes the warrior from the soldier. Though his magazine was known mainly for its demolition jobs, it also blazed, paved, and landscaped the first section of a new road. Bly wrote many essays that developed his idea of "leaping" and "wild poetry" both in concept and prosody. In "Looking for Dragon Smoke," Bly hooked together a countertradition to the Christian-rational-industrial one, providing a kind of culture of the Wild Man. It begins with *Gilgamesh,* in which the "psychic forces" of an early civilized society created the hairy, primitive Enkidu as the adversary and eventual companion of the golden Gilgamesh (a harbinger of *Iron John*). After *Beowulf* (Bly's Nordic touchstone), the "dragon smoke" of inspired association with primal memories is not much in evidence until Blake arrives to give the lie to the Enlightenment, as do the associative freedom and "pagan and heretical elements" in his German contemporaries Novalis, Goethe, and Hölderlin. With Freud and Jung the unconscious is back in business again, and the romantic/symbolist/surrealist wing of modernism provides Bly with a whole range of leaping, dragon-smoke poets from Scandinavia south to Spain and across to Latin America to translate, publish, and emulate.

Compared with Trakl's images ("On Golgotha God's eyes opened") or Lorca's ("Black horses and dark people are riding over the deep roads of the guitar"), Bly's own early leaps as a poet did not take him very far inward. About a horse wandering in the moonlight, he wrote: "I feel a joy, as if I had thought / Of a pirate ship ploughing through dark flowers." The poems of his first collection, *Silence in the Snowy Fields,* are noticeably restrained, wishing to be admired for the integrity of their mood, mostly a meditative one: a young pastoral poet getting his act together rather than a mantic bard with snakes in his hair or a revenant from the depths of surrealism.

Then, in the midsixties, Bly got caught up in the antiwar movement. He became a leading mobilizer of the literary community and provided one of the great moments in the theater of demonstrations when he gave his National Book Award check for his second collection, *The Light Around the Body,* to a draft resister on the stage at Lincoln Center. Auden said of Yeats, "Mad Ireland hurt you into poetry"; the Vietnam War hurt Bly into writing the kind of poetry that he had been calling for and that in places matched Neruda's in its measured balefulness. Evoking the fallout of evil that has settled in Minnesota, he ends:

Therefore we will have to
Go far away
To atone
For the suffering of the stringy-chested

And the short rice-fed ones, quivering
In the helicopter like wild animals,
Shot in the chest, taken back to be questioned.

In the course of writing these poems and of editing a collection of antiwar poetry, Bly developed his concept of the intuitive association to reconnect literature with politics, two realms that most criticism and most experience of their "bloody crossroads," in Lionel Trilling's phrase, counseled to keep apart. Bly's position was an early version of the statement, long before it became cant, that "a modern man's spiritual life and his growth are increasingly sensitive to the tone and content of a regime." Since much of our foreign and domestic policy comes from more or less hidden impulses in the American psyche, and because that psyche is in the poet, too, "the writing of political poetry is like the writing of personal poetry, a sudden drive by the poet inward."

Along with strengthening his own poetry, Bly's involvement turned him into a performer of it. His high-visibility poetry readings developed into a countercultural event, the Lutheran boy-god and warrior now reappearing as the bard. I first caught his act in the early seventies, when he entered a symposium on literary editing dressed in a serape and tapping a Tibetan drum, as though he were a cross between Neruda and Chogyam Trungpa, the meditation guru Bly studied with. After his poetry reading, complete with primitive masks, the other Bly, the literary caretaker, appeared on the panel of editors—sharp, shrewd, and no less dominating.

He supported himself by his public appearances; otherwise he remained on his farm, tending to his chores as an editor, publisher, critic, and poet and using his solitude to nourish "the parts that grow when we are far from the centers of ambition." Through the writings of Jung, Joseph Campbell, James Hillman, and other psychic/cultural explorers, he developed his encyclopedic command of the great heuristic myths, legends, and folklore that understand us, concentrating on those that involve the female side. He gave lectures on Freud and Jung, as well as on *Grimm's Fairy Tales,* in the church basement in Madison, his trial by fire in making the esoteric vivid and meaningful to the public. He turned from America's shadow to his own, producing eleven collections of poems, most of them inward, associative, naked—Bly fully joining the tradition he had been staking out. He put out only one issue of *The Seventies,* a noticeably temperate one. The warrior was giving way to the gardener and the lover, two roles that Bly lived through and that noticeably "moistened" his poetry in the eighties. They also provided two more stages in the process of male initiation that he took into his work with the men's movement. So did certain personal experiences of shame, guilt, and loss, along with the aging process through which the holds that a father and son put on each other can turn into a yearning embrace. So, too, did his awareness that the young men in the literary and New Age circles he visited and who visited him on his farm had been weakened by the feminism of the era, and that male consciousness was in short and despairing supply. It was time, as Bly would say, to do something for the hive again.

Iron John, then, grows not only out of Bly's experience during the past decade in the men's movement but out of the central meanings of his life. If he has bought into the confusion and anxiety of many younger men today, caught between the new sensitivity and the old machismo, he has done so with the capital he has earned from his own growth as a man, a poet, a thinker, and a husbandman of the culture. The souled fierceness that he prescribes for staking out and protecting the borders of male identity has provided much of the motive energy for his career as a literary radical. By the same token, his devotion to asserting and cultivating the primalness and primacy of the imagination in a highly domesticated and institutionalized literary culture has led him to view the condition of men in similar terms and to apply the learning he has acquired in the archaeology and anthropology of the imagination to remedy it. This authority is finally what makes *Iron John* a serious, ground-breaking book.

The startling public appeal of Bly's therapeutic sermon is not hard to fathom. Based on Jungian psychology, it takes a much more positive measure of human potential for change than does the Freudian model, whose Great Father and Great Mother are pretty strictly one's own and give little quarter to altering their influence: a foot of freedom here, a pound less grief there. Bly's pagan goodspell is that the gods are still around and within each of us, able to be mobilized or deactivated, as the case may be. Like Rilke's torso of Apollo, they search us out where it aches and command us to treat it and thereby change our lives.

Also, *Iron John* has a lot of specific insight and lore to teach men and employs a very effective method. It takes an old story and gives it a new spin, thereby enlisting the child in us who is still most open to learning and the adult who is keen to escape from his own banality. Along with combining therapy for men, or at the very least clarity, with a course in the world mythology and ethnography of male initiation, *Iron John* is also a spiritual poetry reading in which the words of Blake and Kabir, Rumi and Yeats, and many others join Bly's own poems as a kind of accompaniment to the text.

The prominence of poetry in the men's movement is perhaps its most surprising feature; none of the other situational groups seem to be particularly disposed to it, and most poets would tend to agree with Auden that poetry "makes nothing happen." Perhaps it's only an aspect of Bly's influence, but I see it as part of the same reviving interest in the imagination signified by the increasing popularity of poetry readings.

Some people say that the men's movement will have to move into national politics as the women's movement has done if it is to survive its trendiness and become socially significant. I'm not so sure. As the bonanza of the Reagan era recedes and the midlife crisis of its favored generation draws on, there are a lot of men in America who have mainly their imaginations to fall back upon. As a social analysis of male distress, *Iron John* is pretty thin stuff; but that's not why it is being read. It's not the *Growing Up Absurd* of the nineties but rather a deeply based counsel of self-empowerment and change. Like the men's movement itself, it offers the sixties generation another crack at the imagination of alternatives they grew up on, right where they most inwardly live and hurt and quest. This is the imagination that they turned in to become baby boomers; if it can be let loose in America by this broad, influential, and growing situational group, there's no telling what can happen.

Michael True

Celebrating Robert Bly, but Taking Him to Task as Well

ROBERT BLY'S GIFTS are many, and I remember, with gratitude, his generosity to my students and me over the past quarter century, at Assumption College. In 1971, with Stanley Kunitz and Denise Levertov, Robert helped to launch the Worcester Poetry Festival, now celebrating its twenty-first season. And for seven summers, he drove from his cabin at Lake Kabekona in Northern Minnesota to nearby Bemidji, to read and to suggest writing exercises during the Upper Midwest Writers Conference, where I taught nonfiction and the teaching of writing.

Although I first read Robert Bly's work in *New Poets of England and America,* edited by Simpson/Hall/Pack (1957), our real "meeting" was through his remarkable pamphlet anthology, *Poets Against the War in Vietnam.* Coming across that booklet in 1965, at Gordon Cairnie's Grolier Bookshop at Harvard Square, was a bright moment in a dark time, and I gave many copies of the valuable collection to young men facing the draft. That year, less than 25 percent of the American people opposed U.S. policy in Vietnam, so it was encouraging to find one of the country's most interesting younger poets exposing the lies and cruelties of our government in an artful way.

When Robert received the National Book Award for Poetry for *The Light Around the Body* (1967)—and committed civil disobedience at the award ceremony—many of us felt part of the celebration. Several poems in that collection and in *Silence in the Snowy Fields* (1962) remain among my favorites in all of American literature:

Oh, on an early morning I think I shall live forever! . . .

I have suffered and survived the night. . . .

These suggestions by Asians are not taken seriously
We know Rusk smiles as he passes them to someone. . . .

Every day I did not spend in solitude was wasted.

Like many people, I live with and love Robert Bly's early work, including the prose poems: "We love this body . . . as we love the gift we gave one morning on impulse, in a fraction of a second." I still enjoy, also, the irreverence of his and James Dickey's reviews in *The Fifties* and *The Sixties,* when they were "doin' Daddy in": that is, presenting the Blue Toad Award to poets of the previous generation (e.g., Robert Penn Warren) who failed to live up to the high standards of young mavericks just beginning to dominate the poetry scene.

With Allen Ginsberg, Robert Bly helped to return poetry to the public platform thirty years ago. Through his translations of Pablo Neruda and César Vallejo, among others, he turned our attention from the French to the Spanish poets, thereby enhancing the possibilities of American poetry after 1970.

Robert Bly's gifts include an ability to philosophize on the spot and to make convincing generalizations that stick. His insights are quick and authoritative, and his powers to carry an audience, even in the most difficult setting (including the barny All-Purpose Room in Assumption's Student Center) are impressive. For this reason, he has remained a visible and entertaining performer, even as his later poems have become, for me, less interesting—sometimes forced, didactic, emotionally uncertain, even sentimental. Has his muse turned away, or does he just refuse to listen and transcribe accurately?

More troubling is Robert Bly's fame (what Milton called "that last infirmity of noble mind") as a guru of the "men's movement." *Iron John,* a file folder of sometimes interesting, mostly nutty ideas, resembles gleanings by earlier American writers—Hemingway's *A Moveable Feast* and Pound's *Jefferson and/or Mussolini*—though *Iron John*'s prose is slacker than theirs.

A common fate of aging American poets and novelists is to lapse into cynicism (Twain) or apocalyptic visions (Whitman), rather than to push on with the difficult task of aesthetic and moral education. Because American culture hates artists and intellectuals, they often wear themselves out (as Fitzgerald did) or go crazy (as Pound did) trying to sustain themselves in a hostile environment.

Iron John is a tired book; my heart sank as I read the windy, abstract prose, the disconnected and arbitrary meanderings about a myth that could mean just about anything, with reflections that clarify nothing. Exhausted from trying to "keep on keepin' on," as Etheridge Knight used to say, American writers (and their readers) prefer muddled thinking and diversions to the hard task of addressing the real work and of building value-laden communities.

All of us, including a poet-turned-essayist, get lost in the maze occasionally, then recover our way; at sixty-five, it's not too late. Stanley Kunitz, at eighty-seven, retains his powers to discriminate and to rabble-rouse—as in his brilliant essay, "Poet and State," in *A Kind of Order, a Kind of Folly* (1975); so does Denise Levertov, at sixty-eight, as in her recent collections of poetry and her remarkable essays, *Light Up the Cave* (1981).

With characteristic insight, Robert Bly recognized a serious dilemma among middle-aged men, our inability to age as gracefully as women or to grow into wisdom. In addressing "the problem," however, Bly talks nonsense much of the time. For the early poems, he deserves the Bollingen Prize. For *Iron John,* he gets the Blue Toad Award.

So Happy Birthday! Huzzah! Gratitude! to Robert Bly. Now let him return to his proper work, as poet and critic, in the years ahead.

Judith Weissman

A Woman's View of Iron John

As a woman and an academic, I have been overwhelmed with joy at the amazing success of *Iron John*. When Robert wrote me that he was working on this folktale I thought he would produce a book for a small and devoted audience of Jungians and people who love his poetry. When I bought my copy—at an occult book store in my neighborhood—and saw that it was published by Addison-Wesley and not one of the big New York Houses, I was even more sure that this was a book for a fit audience, though few. And then I saw the best-seller lists, week after week, and started reading Robert's name in new places, as a commentator on patriotism for *The Nation,* as someone whose opinion on the Clarence Thomas hearings mattered. Something very important is happening in this country; I am doubly sure of this because I have not heard one word about *Iron John* in the English department of Syracuse University, where I teach.

The old centers of intellect and power—universities, New York presses, mainstream politics—have become empty and hollow, unable to recognize a new leader when he appears. I had lost hope that a wise leader could break through the walls built up by money and coldheartedness in this country, as I had watched the American public revel in the defeat of Jimmy Carter, the only halfway moral human being to be president since Eisenhower, and watched the few presses that stood up for the humane Left either die, as North Point did, or be absorbed by a bigger and less scrupulous press, as Pantheon and my own beloved Wesleyan have been. I thought that never in my lifetime would a small press reach a big audience— but Addison-Wesley knew more than I did.

The one other book I own from Addison-Wesley is almost as miraculous as *Iron John. Victorian Cakes,* an unpretentious memoir of a girl's childhood in Chicago in the 1880s, in a community of eccentric and strong-willed women who loved to bake, to eat, and to share, is in fact a feminist Utopia. It is about how women once gave each other exactly the kinds of practical skills and ethical rules that Robert believes men must rediscover for themselves. Blessings on you, Addison-Wesley! May you have a long and happy life. I rejoice that a new press has arisen to fill the moral emptiness left by the old ones.

But what can I say about universities, where Robert is pointedly ignored? In them I have seen no such upstart movement of good faith. English departments, where Robert should be a major presence, are frozen in obeisance to a set of deadly untruths which *Iron John* could bring tumbling down — if English professors would only read Robert. One of the surest ways to get yourself bashed by a university press or by an English department is to say that men and women really are different in an absolute, biological way that can be only partly altered by culture. The dirty word you will be called is "essentialist"; you actually believe in a human essence that is not "socially constructed." That's right, all you gender-theorists out there, I do believe in essences, and I'm glad to see that Robert does, too. English professors no longer believe in evidence; anyone who does gets smeared with another dirty word, "empiricist." It matters to them not a bit that every single human culture known throughout history has had rules, ceremonies, initiation rites for men, and that in every single culture men have been lawgivers, the ones who upheld a code of conduct. (I thank feminist historian Gerda Lerner for having the guts to admit the latter fact in *The Creation of Patriarchy,* Oxford University Press, 1986.) It matters not a bit to English professors that Jane Goodall has never found a single group of chimpanzees in which little girls were not more fascinated with new babies than were little boys, and in which males were not fighting for dominance. In a secret, unacknowledged affiliation with creation scientists, English professors of the fashionable sort deny both history and evolutionary biology in order to declare the dawning of a new cosmic freedom. Words have no referential meaning, but are free to circulate in endless play; men and women are not bound by any genuine differences from each other; and all the old ethical rules, grouped under what is supposed to be a loathsome name, "the law of the father," can and should be ditched.

Well, folks, Robert has hit you between the eyes, if only you knew it. All the people who are buying *Iron John* recognize it as the articulation of truths that have been denied by the contemporary business world, which has been well supported by both academia and the most arid forms of feminism. Despite the left-wing French Marxist blusterings of academic poststructuralists, you can bet your life that they are spiritually at ease in the business world, the world that ultimately controls both presses and universities. And feminism has gotten along very well with capitalism for the last twenty years or so. Of course we still hear plenty of complaints about the absence of women at the very very top levels of corporate management, and about the need for more feminist "progress." What we do not hear about is the absence of women in the resistance to the business world. Where's the woman Ralph Nader? Where's the woman Dave Forman? Where's the woman Kirkpatrick Sale? Where's the woman Wendell Berry? Where's the woman Jesse Jackson? Where's the woman Robert Bly? There are some women, certainly, in important resistance movements like Cultural Survival and Earth First!, but feminism has produced far more accommodation than trouble for the powers of the state.

Both men's and women's communities of work are now being destroyed by money-makers who do not know the truths of *Iron John*. Robert says that men could no longer see their fathers work after the industrial revolution of the nineteenth century—as Wendell Berry says that you don't have a good farm until you have three generations working together. Actually I think that this men's community survived into the industrial age, recreating itself in family-owned union workplaces, where owners were proud of what they produced, not how much profit they made, where fathers and sons could still work together, where words like loyalty and solidarity still meant something. I never thought I would look lovingly at capitalism in any form, but just as Robert has modified his Jungianism in the light of human experience and historic evidence, I have had to modify my bookish Marxism and admit that capitalism, when checked by unions, did not have to be evil. What kept it from being evil was the feeling of responsibility—of fatherhood—on the part of those in power, who were not quite as programmed to destroy as Marx believed they were. Ideally I would prefer absolute equality, ownership by workers; but compared with the multinational companies, the leveraged buy-outs, the junk bonds, the corporate raiders of the Reagan-Bush era, some of the old companies which have been destroyed look mighty good.

I think the single event which opened my eyes on this was the hostile takeover of a major Syracuse company, Carrier Corporation, by the demonic Harry Gray and United Technologies Corporation. Night after night workers who were fighting the takeover appeared on the news saying that Carrier had been like their family. I believed them. Men and women were both part of this community at Carrier, which now looks as precious to me as the loving women's community of domestic work recollected in *Victorian Cakes*. The new captains of industry, men for whom the family is no longer the foundation of human relationships, who do not think of building something for their sons and adopted sons to inherit, have spawned a world in which women do have a kind of power that very few women ever had before. Isn't it wonderful that Jean Kirkpatrick can make foreign policy and Sandra Day O'Connor can vote against abortion rights? A few women are free to pursue great power; many more are free to starve and freeze on the streets as women were not free before, when men and women lived in communities still bound by codes of conduct. The liberation of women into abject poverty is one terrible by-product of the destruction of the laws of the father, the rules of male conduct. The rediscovery of male rules and rituals in our culture probably will not help any women CEOs of the multinational corporations which are so busy moving jobs to countries without labor unions or environmental laws. But I believe it will be a blessing for those women who want something besides their piece of the postindustrial capitalist pie. It will be a blessing for future generations of girls who are likely victims of heartless young men who do not feel any responsibility for the children they carelessly beget, just as it will be a blessing for future generations of young men who are in danger of not knowing their fathers. (Perhaps one of these days Robert will team up with Spike Lee, the brilliant filmmaker who is also remembering how much we need the fathers we have lost.)

I hope women are reading *Iron John*. I hope they can see that Robert can be a mentor, a male mother, for women as well as for men. He has certainly been that for me. I do not think I have ever in my life received another unexpected gift quite like the note Robert sent me over ten years ago, telling me that he liked an essay on Yeats that Mark Rudman (another gift-giver) had published in *Pequod*. I was astonished that someone so famous would write to an obscure English professor out of sheer generous goodness. I wrote back a note of thanks—and Robert has been a friend and mentor ever since. The old saying "a friend in need is a friend indeed" does nothing like justice to Robert's importance in my life these ten years, as I have struggled to get my unorthodox books published, as I have unsuccessfully fought against the transformation of my department into the Department of English and Textual Studies—Textual Studies meaning deconstruction, French Marxism, and gender theory. To know that someone in the world outside was hearing me has enabled me to live.

And Robert has been far more than an intellectual ear. When I wrote him two years ago in despair to tell him I had breast cancer, he wrote back, "Breast cancer may conquer some cloudy goof, but it won't get you." So far it hasn't got me—and who knows how much difference those cheering words have made in my immune system.

I have only met Robert once. When he came to Syracuse to read his poetry five or so years back, he also came to dinner at my house, and utterly transformed my understanding of him. I had read only his letters and his poetry, and was terrified that he would walk into my modestly comfortable house and tell me that my precious, tattered Oriental rugs and old country furniture were a materialistic impediment to my spiritual life, and would demand distilled water and brown rice for a properly purifying dinner, instead of my country French beef and lamb stew and bean salad and ginger cookies. Imagine my relief when the first words he uttered—prelude to the section on hunting in *Iron John*—were, "There are too many fucking vegetarians in the world." My sentiments exactly.

John Densmore

"Don't Get a Massage, Finish that Poem!"

THE SECOND-TO-LAST chapter of my autobiography *Riders on the Storm* opens with the director of my off-off-Broadway play saying, "You should check out Robert Bly. It might help your writing." Help my writing! It changed my life, or rather—Robert did.

I went to a weekend seminar and found myself teary the whole time. What's this? My New England genes aren't keeping my upper lip stiff? OK. I'll try one of these week-long men's retreats. Wow. I've got a bottomless river flowing under my psyche.

Since then I've been to many conferences and had the joy of accompanying Robert, his wife Ruth, and a small group of people on a trip to Ireland. I've also enjoyed accompanying Robert musically, as he reads Rilke.

But what attracted me initially to Bob (I know he hates this and I don't want to inflate him too much!) was his openness in showing his shadow. He criticized my men's group, then wrote a second letter saying, "I take *most* of what I said back." Robert is *still* making fun of my vegetarianism and rationalizing *his* diet of red meat. As I introduced him in Los Angeles at a reading of Kabir and Rumi: "Robert Bly is a mensch. He says that 25 to 40 percent of what he says is B.S. (It's nice to know what's up ahead!) Robert Bly is a real man."

And Robert did help my writing. "If you've got a backache, don't get a massage, finish that poem," Robert snarled one evening. It stuck with me. I struggled for ten years trying to get down on paper what I'd been through in the sixties, and I did it. And I almost chased Robert up the charts. So thanks, Bob. Hey, if we learn a couple of more poems together, we could make a record!

love,
John Densmore

James Hillman

Some Psalms of Davis

For Robert Bly

A BUNCH OF Connecticut-grown posies as a grateful contribution in kind to the festschrift for that wily old darling fox whose good poems and person got me back to reading, reciting, and even trying again to write poetry—such as it is. Thank you, Robert, for your foolhardy courage, and your intelligent carefulness, from your friend and companion of that superb year, 1926!

—*James*

Awakening

One Wednesday Davis woke to see
He was not so very different
From Harry or from Everett
Or from you and me.

He took his turn and worked
The garden earth, an ordered worm,
Gathered wood and worry from
The usual brown of Thursday's trees.

The claim on Davis: to simply be
An ordinary man, half slave, all free,
A thank-God Friday man who sees,
And does not see.

Cooking

In the gloaming O my darling
When the lights are soft and low
—At the stove, Davis humming,
Drops an onion in his stew.

Romance rises, steams his glasses;
Aromas of sweet melancholy
Stir up ancient fragrant folly.
He can't see for loveliness.

Garlic, pepper, bayleaf, clove
Dance and bubble, merge and drown,
Sacrifice and sink on down.
To the meat they give their love.

Tho' up the way and down the way
May be, as Heraclitus said, the same,
For Davis, forward and going back
Have each a very different name.

The urgency of time requires
An arrow-point to things ahead,
The pungency of thyme desires
Savored memories instead.

Driving

Sure, he had thought of it—dying.
He had thought of it while driving
Close beside the broken yellow line.

Lying down in the snow
To be as good a way as any way
To go. Some rum and then a walk
White into the woods, hips deep
In soft drifts,
                just lying down to sleep.

When Davis slammed the brake
It was too late.
The yellow dog shot from the bush.
Bumper. Fender. Hub. Under the rubber,
Crushed.
          Did the dog want to die?
Davis let it lie.

Davis Declares that Birds Still Sing in the Morning

I

Those who live where I do not
Who come at night to brush their wings
Against my walls, my stony deafness,
Can be turned from, can be left.
I will not hear their clamorings.

We do not need to always yield,
To meet halfway and find forgiveness,
Another hearing, another clearing.

The sun has risen, tho' the day is dark
And I am leaving to not be left;
It is morning, the birds are singing,
They sing and sing as if they wept.

II

Not one moment do I stop to think
On death. Will not pause or change.
At Grandma's house the palm plant
And the rubber tree stayed long after she
Was gone. The settee that stood there with them
I'm recovering now, the same dark-weaved cloth.
I will not listen for footfalls, or that chariot,
Nor will I rage, nor trust black ink to outlast
A fading mansion—
                            The rubber leaves despite the dust,
Still, stubborn, thick and dull, still grow,
Their tub of roots still full of ground—
Nor will I turn these lines
To any other end than the rising palm
Here, not in the mind.

III

Nothing more than meets the eye
A staring wall and on the wall
A white-faced clock and one black fly
Prepare—
                Breakfast!
"Mornin', Davis,"
                "Morning, Rock."
"Same as ever?"
                "Yep, just like the last."
The constant fare.

IV

The loveliness of images exiled from this verse
Are carried to the Met in a little dealer's hearse.
The bits left over, fragile, slight,
Yet shine with daybreak's dazzle light;
These, Davis hammers into place,
Makes his shield and joins the race.

Michael Meade

Rocking the Boat

I.

WE WERE IN A SMALL wooden ferryboat in South Puget Sound. We were crossing from the mainland to Tanglewood Island. Crowded into the open boat were the Irish music band No Comhaile, the poet Erica Helm, and myself: sometimes drummer in the band and sometimes storyteller. Packed in with us were fiddles, flutes, drums, and the misgivings, fears, and ferocities that accompany poems and tunes. In truth, the boat barely contained the arguments that we carried on board. All was in disagreement and going out of tune like the instruments that swelled or shrunk as damp shadows unevenly battled the early June sun. We argued over the primacy of place between poetry and music, over the capacity of the as-yet-unseen audience to hear either one with a true ear, over the time of escape after the gig, over the whole thing, again.

No Comhaile (No-come-all-ya) is Gaelic slang for "no fooling around, no bullshit." It was a band that poured out a tune for your ears to imbibe, or pitched one at your feet as a challenge to dance. Each playing was an attempt to catch the tune, hold it firmly, but let it go before it became domesticated. Irish tunes are like flights of birds, full of sudden turns, graceful bendings, and spooked eruptions. They are full-speed interpretations of the voices of the wind. The musicians must stand like old Cuchulain himself when he was trying to lasso a flight of geese with silken ropes, thrown from the brink of a chariot, tearing across an unsullied plain. It is not the slaying of the geese that is intended. Rather, it is the binding of wild geese and people that is attempted. It is a temporary wedding of wings and musicians' fingers, the display of animal, human, and unhuman sound, uncertainly caught on silken strings, so that for a moment, fingers, wings, earth, air, breath, and song are one. It slays daily time, rends stiff speech, cracks hardened thought, and wounds any excuses that obscure the heart.

Once No Comhaile, while playing at an open-air festival, got into a battle with another Celtic band. The two groups were trading sets of tunes back and forth. The crowd grew, filling the hills around the stage as the air warmed with the fire of the music. After the battle had heated well up, No Comhaile let loose a set of reels that fair flew out of the instruments. Just then a flight of geese appeared from behind the hill, flew straight at the stage, and passed directly over the players. The crowd leapt to its collective feet, hands clapping, mouths whistling and cheering, eyes pulled wide with excitement. The people didn't know that for the old Celts, geese flying over you when something was in doubt was a blessing. Many of the crowd couldn't see the geese clearly. But everyone was pulled to standing and cheering in the middle of a tune, and the outcome of the battle was settled right then. Someone walking in upon the scene at that moment could readily surmise that the listeners, the players, and the geese were all part of the same surging tune. Afterwards, people lingered right there, as if the music was still coming out of the hills and grass.

What is sought after in tune or poem is temporary and elusive. Because it is certain with beauty, yet mutable as the timbre in a lover's voice, chaos surrounds the seeking. A willingness to battle is required, a willingness to fight one another, to fight beauty itself. A willingness to hurt and be hurt surrounds this seeking, and the willingness to accept the abundance of a proper feast or to sit empty and alone. Because all this was being sought, our little boat was as full of argument as it was of people.

II.

For a time I had been struggling with the story surrounding the oldest known fragments of Irish poetry. In ancient times a poet would speak verse before any important undertaking. The words are attributed to the poet Amergin, when he spoke from the bow of a ship about to lead an invasion of Ireland. A poet of the indigenous people chanted poems from the shore to drive back the invading ships with wind and wave. Whoever won the war of words, prayers, and spells inevitably won the war of deeds.

The poet of the island people was a woman, Cessair. None of her words have been recorded or handed down in history, though there are various versions of the words of Amergin, a man. Erica was quick to point out that this was a typical suppression of the female voice, perpetrated by the patriarchy, emblematic of the need to dominate at any cost. We argued about this various ways, and finally decided to go to the seashore ourselves and rewrite the poems with two voices interacting. My job was primarily to adapt the old language; on the one hand, to keep the traditional sense of it, on the other to make it more tolerable for a modern ear. Erica's work was to make entirely the words and images of the poet Cessair. The difference between tasks led to another argument. I complained of the severity of being restricted by traditions and conventions, of having to uphold all the history of a tribe. Erica argued the suffering of having to create and invent with no preordained source for self-grounding and self-esteem. Soon, any arguments became possible through the mouths of male and female, invader and defender. We roared up and down the beach for days, sometimes arguing in earnest, sometimes simply enjoying the poses we struck.

In the poem, Amergin rides the uneasy waters of the sea as he reaches for the depths of his people's knowledge and memory, and shapes what he finds into totem images. He is recreating himself and his people and calling their ancestors present at the bow of that ship. The carved prow figures of later ships, the hood ornaments of cars, the emblems on flags are faint echoes of the voice chanting tribal memory at the front of an event. Cessair stands the ground of indigenous people, calling on the land they inhabit and the spirits that animate its shores and skies and winds. She calls present all the mysteries and powers of her culture as a repelling gale, a bulwark of spells, a force of memories that pushes the very waves from the shore.

Ultimately, a poet is required to tell the truth, and what finally is named is the true powers of person and place. All that each poet can do is name the inheritance truly. When that is done, the destiny of the battle is clear to both sides. The rest is the acting out of the destiny for the reassurance of the bodies involved.

In this incantational battle, the two poets escalate rapidly, each calling out their tribal powers and totems. At a certain point, Cessair shifts from the fierce words of battle to gather elusive images of stars and lilies and wordcraft itself. The battle de-escalates. Tumultuous waves settle to still waters of a lake, and the final lines speak of harmony, words of skill, finally silence and a secret. A sense of mystery comes at the end, and the question is never truly answered: Did the invaders conquer and dominate, or did the indigenous people absorb and integrate them? The question remains unanswered, or is multiply answered, or is a secret. One version of the story says that Amergin and the Gaelic invaders met the goddesses Banba, Fotla, and Erin. Each goddess requested that the island retain her name. Amergin consented to the request of each. Ireland has retained all three names, but because Erin was last it is her name that we use most frequently when we say the Erinn Isles of Ireland.

III.

In old Erinn, the source of trouble, change, and inspiration came from an even older place, Lochlann. Originally, Lochlann was under the sea, or within a lake. It was an "other world" that could be the source of creation or destruction. Later, as invasions changed the face and imagination of Ireland, Lochlann came to mean the source of invaders, namely Scandinavia. Specifically, Lochlann came to refer to Norway.

Now, the reason we were in this little boat, unsteadily approaching this little island, was because Erica and I had read that Robert Bly, a widely known Norwegian-American poet, was interested in Irish mythology. We had read that this conference was to focus on Celtic myth and imagination and had written to Robert Bly telling of our performance of Celtic myth, poetry, and music. He sent back an invitation to attend part of the conference. Now that we were crossing from one land to the other to attend the gathering, I feared we were crisscrossing paths on the sea of memory, memories of Irish and Norwegian groups crossing from one land to invade the other.

There were frequent battles between Norway and Ireland, and periods of peace were insured by each group holding hostages from the royal families of the other. Eventually, the hostaging became fostering, and royal sons of Norway would be fostered in Ireland and the sons of Ireland sent to Norway to be raised to men. But outbreaks of battle couldn't be helped, as when Fiachna Finn went visiting from Ireland to Lochlann, and big Eolgarg was king then. Fiachna was well received because Eolgarg and Fiachna's father had long ago done deeds in common. It happened during that visit, though, that Eolgarg fell ill. None of the doctors or druids of the land could cure the king, and it turned up that nothing whatever would cure him except the soup made from the cooking of a cow that was pure white of body and scarlet red in the ears. It turned out that the only such cow was in the possession of the Black Hag of Lochlann. And it turned out that people tended not to visit her much. Actually, people tended not to look at her, not to speak to her, nor go anywhere near her at all because of the disturbing power of her looks and her dangerous speech. Actually, people tended to pretend that they didn't know her, or know of her or of the flaming cow.

Despite all that, Fiachna Finn went his way to the dwelling of the Black Hag and entered with averted eyes but determined will. The Hag would only relinquish the red-eared cow for a reward that she would name at a later date. Fiachna simply agreed to the bargain. A soup was made of the white cow, and that soup cured Eolgarg. After a time, a message came to Fiachna, telling him that the king of Ulster had died and he should return home. Upon his return, Fiachna was crowned the new king.

As king of Ulster, Fiachna would sit all day and hear the complaints and sufferings of the people. He prided himself that anyone seeking justice in his hall would not leave without gaining it. One day the Black Hag of Lochlann came and caused such consternation and commotion that she had to be admitted to the hall of the king. She demanded payment for the white cow with the red ears.

Fiachna offered the Hag her choice of Irish cows to replace her cow, but the Hag demurred. He offered a cow for each leg of her cow, but she refused. Fiachna offered all the cows in Ulster. The Hag demanded that the reward be of her choosing. What could Fiachna do but agree to whatever she chose? And, when the only payment the Hag would accept was that Fiachna make war on Eolgarg, king of Lochlann, what could Fiachna do at all?

Fiachna sent word to Eolgarg, the king who had fostered him, saying that he was coming to make a battle and bringing so many men and coming at such a time, and that Eolgarg should gather as many men and get ready himself. Eventually, two battles were fought. The men of Lochlann almost won, because . . . well, they almost won because they cheated. That is to say, they almost won because Eolgarg released a herd of venomous sheep which drove the Irish heroes from the field and caused them to roost in the trees like hens. The battle would have ended there except that Manannan mac Lir, the god of the sea and of all that turns the tides, came by with a dog in his coat of such severe temperament and such insatiable appetite that it could devour anything. All that Manannan required for the use of the dog was whatever was born back in Ulster that Fiachna hadn't seen. Sure, it was Fiachna's son that had been born in his absence, but he didn't know, did he? And what could he do with himself and his men roosting in the trees but agree to it all? The dog was released, and soon all the sheep were devoured, and when the sheep were finished, well, so were the men of Lochlann. So say the Irish, although the Norwegians may have a version of the story that differs in some details.

At any rate, we were talking of the crossing to Tanglewood Island, and as our little boat reached the weathered dock, there was Robert Bly waiting and looking for all the world like a white-haired Viking king extending the welcomes of Lochlann and helping us to land. The greeting was a warm one and did much to ease the misgivings I carried across the bow of the boat. Learning that the island was sheepless was encouraging, and getting sight of a dog with a permanent frown made me downright at ease.

IV.

This island was a tumult of stories that were being told publicly and privately, consecutively and congruently. When stories weren't being told, then they were being rehearsed, rehashed, argued over, analyzed, and compared. Robert Bly was telling the tale of a princess who had found fault with every suitor and had refused many. The king, her father, declared she must accept the next man who appeared. When that man appeared to be a beggar, the princess wandered out into the world. Gioia Timpanelli was telling a great love story of Ireland, wherein the young lovers are chased from place to place by an old king who would stop the maid from marrying her young lover. Each place where the lovers slept in each other's arms is still remembered, and held to be a sacred spot in Ireland. To this day, couples that are falling in love, or fear they are falling out of it, go to those spots to sleep together and absorb that old love from the earth.

Hearing those stories caused the hundred people gathered on the island to tell their own love stories, to write things furiously in journals, to look moon-eyed at each other or else move uneasily from place to place. People talked to each other rapidly, intently, passionately. People listened closely, intimately. You could hear the strange chatter that occurs when people find the common in each other. It is a humming, buzzing speech that begins to sound like an impromptu song or the buzz of a joyous marketplace. It sounds unlike any specific language, could be any language. It's speech that opens the ear all the way through. It's like the chatter of animals, or an assembly of migrating birds recounting their travels. Each day was full with the recitation of poems, the writing of poems, the telling of personal histories, the retelling of old tales. There were periods of meditation, too; but truly a buzzing, burning conversation was going on right above the heads of the meditators. You could hear it despite the silence. It confused them and caused the meditators to bump into each other when coming and going.

Maybe it was important that the string of language kept going through the meditations, through the night, in order to not lose the threads that held the conference together. When I rose before morning could peel back the cover of night, a figure was stepping out from between the trees. It was the poet Etheridge Knight, making his way in the dark as the pale light revealed only the tops of trees. He was chanting a quiet struggle of words, working his fingers as he walked. His eyes sang some old wound, his face scarred as if branches tried to hold him back from the light of morning. It was Etheridge defying spells, keeping vigil all night, protecting the place, keeping the language going. He invited me right into the poem he was walking out. It was a generosity he had. Generosity permeated the entire event. It was a generosity that started with Robert Bly's ready invitation and extended in all directions. For there was a generous entering into the conflict of ideas and the struggle for meaning. And there were hearts and ears open and listening.

We found the audience we had been seeking. The old battle of poetic incantation got a proper "hearing." Our uneasy blending of music and poetry, of masculine and feminine, of the handed-down and made-up, received a blessing from Robert, from the hundred gathered there. The band played on afterwards, tossing tunes as everyone danced impromptu reels and jigs. Like most bands, No Comhaile broke up, though it lives on in local legend. Etheridge Knight died one morning, but his poems work their way on from mouth to ear. Robert Bly and I began a conversation that still goes on. For years we had an "adolescent hot line" on which we called each other when we were baffled by our sons and daughters, or when they were hurting, or when we were. It was a kind of Lochlann-Erinn long-distance fostering phone line, Moose Lake to Vashon Island.

Frequently, I go to meet Robert somewhere or other, to tell poems and stories wherever we can find an audience to hear them. When we do there's always some music and laughter, and there's usually an argument. There's no desire to argue, it's just the fears and ferocities that accompany the tunes and poems. Anything venomous that occurs is fed to the dogs afterwards.

Erica Helm and I married each other somewhere in the turnings of the battle-poems of Amergin and Cessair. We still argue in order to maintain our indigenous totems; we still find harmonies in poetry and stories. We offer the poem to Robert Bly again in gratitude for many invitations and blessings he has given to us.

Amergin and Cessair
A Battle of Poetic Incantation

Amergin: I plant my foot on this land.
For I am Amergin
Son of Mil
Son of the People of the Sea
Peoples of ships and barks
Son of the builder of the Spiral Castle.
Foetus of the womb of the Earth
Son of the Hag of Beara
Builder of the Tower of Bregon
Climber through the Needle's Eye
Namer of names
Judge between combatants.

Cessair: Here I stand
Daughter of the Moon
Cessair.
Poet of Arianrhod
Daughter of Danae, the Mother and Queen
Keeper of the house of Sidh
Daughter of the Northwest Wind; I am
Cessair.
Navigator on water
Mistress on shore
Fair as a flower
Daughter of Darkness
Daughter of the House of Arianrhod.

Amergin: Who foretells the ages of the moon?
Who brings the cattle from the sea and segregates them?
For whom but me will the fish of the laughing ocean make
welcome?
Who but I knows the secret of the Unhewn Dolmens?

Who shapes weapons from hill to hill?
Who but myself knows where the sun shall set?

Cessair: I am a flash of sun on water.
I am the clash of battle swords.
I am the teeth in the sea-shark's mouth.
I am the blood of wild beasts.
I am fire in the witch's hearth.
I am the evening sky ablaze—
The red of serpents' tongues
The black of deepest night.
I am a mare that knows no reins.

Amergin: I am the roar of the sea.
I am a bull of seven fights.
I am a hawk on a cliff.
I rove the hills, a ravening boar.
I am lightning that blasts the trees.
I am the point of weapons.
I am thunder on the mountains.
I am a God that fashions fire for a head.
I am a dragon that eats the sky.

Cessair: I thread the stars across the sky.
I am the kiss of lover's lips.
I am the mortar and the stone.
I am the song of my homeland.

Amergin: I am the wind on the sea.

Cessair: I am the bow of every ship.

Amergin: I am ocean waves.

Cessair: I am the foam upon the sea.

Amergin: I am a lake on a plain.

Cessair: I am the green of the fairest hill.

Amergin: I am the dewdrop, a tear of the sun.

Cessair: I am a lily on a still pond.

Amergin: I am the son of harmony.

Cessair: I am a word of skill.

Amergin: I am the silence of things secret.

A gathering of men, with James Hillman and Michael Meade on Robert's left, 1988 (Daniel Rowe photo).

Marion Woodman

For Robert on His Sixty-fifth Birthday

HONORING ROBERT BLY is honoring masculinity in myself. It is honoring masculinity in countless men and women who have touched that lost part of themselves through his conferences and books.

When I began working with him four years ago at the Great Mother Conference, I was immediately ignited by a new energy balance between the men and the women. Since then, I have experienced new balances in every conference. Always a poet, Robert intuits what is going on in his audience, and mirrors that back in images so exact that people recognize what they had not known was in themselves.

With his say-it-like-it-is, gusty, and sensitive voice, he constellates the king, the warrior, the child, the trickster. That is why I feel so challenged working with him. I never know what will happen next. We move from swan shirts to mouse steak to leaping firebirds with alarming ease. We have even been known to disappear. We were once sitting on a raised platform on a stage—very civilized, very gracious—with perhaps a little too much king and queen in the air. Suddenly, I realized his chair was moving back as if two mighty hands were pulling from behind. I was so curious about his chair that I didn't realize my own had begun to move. The next thing I knew we were both flat on our backs behind the platform, buried under wires and microphones with four little stockinged feet waving in the air. That changed the archetypes at that conference!

In essence, Robert dares the edge, however far that edge moves, and he commits with his huge and loving heart. I see him sitting on a Persian rug, with David plucking the heartstrings on his sitar and Marcus fingering the heartbeat on his tabla. Sometimes Coleman is there with his sensuous, southern Rumi. As poetry and music begin to dance through his whole body, Robert takes us with him into that world where time and timeless meet.

With Marion Woodman at the filming of Bly and Woodman on Men and Women, *Belleville, Ontario, September 1991 (Applewood Communications photo).*

Michael Ventura

An Open Letter to Robert Bly on His Sixty-fifth Birthday

MAESTRO . . .

Went into my corner Mayfair supermarket the other week, and there was the new *Esquire* with Jeff Bridges in a tux looking like a very angry hippie, and across his forehead was written, "Wild Men and Wimps." The featured names were among others, Joan Jett, Erica Jong, Jackie Collins, Judy Tenuta, "AND Robert Bly." It's a big magazine stand, the *Esquire* was smack in the middle, a very prominent display. To its left was *Modern Bride,* and a *Vogue* featuring Michelle Pfeiffer looking almost as sullen as Jeff Bridges. To its right was *People,* with "TV's Daring Duo—Regis and Kathie Lee—Is There Anything They Won't Say?" Above the *Esquire,* an *Entertainment Weekly* on which Spock and Captain Kirk were celebrating the twenty-fifth anniversary of "Star Trek." To the side, in a separate stand, the *National Enquirer* regaled one and all with "Bald Burt Reynolds Almost Blinded As Toupee Catches Fire!"

You weren't outgunned, Robert, but you sure were outnumbered, not to mention surrounded. Which is another way of saying: this is the context—the level of discourse, if you like—to which you have been relegated by the media this last year or so. Unheralded in a *Rolling Stone* on the same rack, you'd written a lovely and, as always, uncompromised piece on Thoreau. It was as though you were speaking quietly within the hubbub and daring someone to hear.

An aside: Would Thoreau have WANTED to be written about in *Rolling Stone?* I doubt it, but I suppose we can't ask questions like that anymore, there's no point, for the answers leave us with no alternative but silence, and these days to be silent is too close to being hopeless. When I entertain hopelessness—and I must tell you it's become a frequent guest in my mind—a sentence of R. D. Laing's speaks up and puts me in my place: "Who are we to decide that it is hopeless?"

The day after seeing you so beleaguered at the Mayfair, a friend told me she was watching a sitcom and the name "Robert Bly" was either a set up for the joke or the punch line, she couldn't remember. So, Maestro, you have joined Carl Sandburg and Allen Ginsberg as one of the three legit American poets of the twentieth century to become a household name, or as near as poets get to that—for you can't get any more "household" than a sitcom. I don't know if that's what you wanted, but it sure is what you got.

Well, they did it to Joe Campbell, they do it to every presidential candidate, they do it to anyone who begins to make an impact, and they're doing it to you: sticking you in the most trivial contexts to strip you of your meanings.

If you don't mind me quoting myself, this is from a piece called "Report From El Dorado": "America is form opposed to content. Not just form INSTEAD of content. Form opposed. Often violently. There are few things resented so much among us as the suggestion that what we do MEANS. Other cultures have argued over their meanings. We tend to deny that there is any such thing, insisting instead that what you see is what you get and that's IT. All we're doing is having a GOOD TIME, all we're doing is making a buck, all we're doing is enjoying the spectacle, we insist. . . . Media is the American war on content with all the stops out, with meaning in utter rout, frightened nuances dropping their weapons as they run."

I feel ever-so-slightly responsible for the deconstructed spectacle of you on that magazine rack, Robert, since I believe I was the first to put you on the cover of a purely Pop publication—L.A. Weekly, in January 1982. My editor ran a coverline (without informing me) that went something like, "Robert Bly—Who Is He? Is He the Smartest Man in America Today?" I don't remember much about that piece now except that it was from the heart, and that the editor's unscrupulous headline was an attempt to subvert and trivialize what both you and I were trying to say—an attempt that was more reflexive than intentional. (There isn't an editor in the country who hasn't done the same to dozens, even hundreds, of pieces that unconsciously threaten them.)

They've squeezed you into a box, a context, that ignores so much about you. They don't seem to remember, for instance, that you were one of the earliest organizers against the Vietnam War. That you wrote lines like, "The Marines use cigarette lighters to light the thatched roofs of huts / because so many Americans own their own homes," and "I know that books are tired of us. . . . Books don't want to remain in the same room with us anymore . . . . [Plato] wants to hurry back up the river of time, so he can end as some blob of sea flesh rotting on an Australian beach." (Sometimes it seems even you don't remember, playing to the affluent as you so often do now. You speak of grief so beautifully, but perhaps not enough of rage?)

Neither the men nor the women who write about you seem to remember that back in 1973, a decade before most feminists caught on to Goddess-thinking, in *Sleepers Joining Hands* you wrote one of the finest essays on that subject, that pulse, that shape of things to come. Nor do the magazine writers know you as one of the great translators of the century. You gave us the finest English versions I know of Lorca, Jiménez, Neruda, Tranströmer, and Vallejo, before you gave us Kabir. (The men's gatherings could use a little more Lorca, not to mention Vallejo, the way they could use a long reading of "The Teeth Mother Naked at Last.")

And then, the complex phenomenon of the gatherings. We started to get to know each other at the first one you ever had in California—March of '82. I think it was only the second men's week you'd ever done. As always when a movement begins, it was funkier then. Now two or three teachers focus on one, maybe two old tales, and it's mixed with samba and movement work in a well-organized pattern that's repeated at every conference. Which is to say: it's an institution. But in '82 it was just you, working at fever pitch, so jazzed with this new material you'd discovered that you taught seven tales in as many days. And every day, all day, it rained, and the fifty-or-so of us stayed cooped in that not-very-large cabin. We were supposed to sleep out on the ground, but that was impossible. We all slept on the floor of that one cabin, inhaling each other's breath. It was hard to take, faces you couldn't turn away from, and the dampness melding all our smells into an aroma you couldn't escape, it even seeped into the food. We all got a little crazy, one guy got very crazy ranting and disappeared. And all our words never stopped, and everyone spoke so excitedly.

That week there weren't any martinets (there seem to be so many now) carefully instructing grown men to get wild only when the conference allows it and to go along with the program otherwise. There didn't seem to be ANY organizers: the food ran out on the fourth day and we had to eat peanut-butter-and-onion sandwiches (on white bread) because there wasn't anything else. I will always be grateful for that week. You won't like the metaphor, but it was like getting inside a Jimi Hendrix solo and not being able to (not wanting to) get out. Here are some of your sentences from my notes, sentences I keep returning to: "It's always almost too late in the psyche—but not QUITE too late." And: "In one way men are very lazy now. In ancient times men talked about what they loved—what they loved in this world. Now what do men dance about?" And: "You simply can't say that a woman has a male side and let it go. Which male is it?"

It's my nature to respond more deeply to your earlier, often raunchier, angrier work, but I don't feel that that work is better or more important than what you've done since. In your writing, certainly, there's no clear demarcation line. "Snowbanks North of the House," published in 1981, is a marvelously dark poem, streaked with light; as many of the love poems are. And I'm not saying your poetry is more important than the brilliant *Iron John;* nor that the men's movement, which you single-handedly originated, is less radical than the antiwar movement was. (What could be more radical than redefining manhood?) I do think the movement has lost something crucial since its beginning, but that's another letter. No, I'm writing all this to say that your new media fame has made even people who know your work well treat you as though you simply appeared, full-blown, a large white-haired bearlike troubadour wearing a vest and waving your arms in the air, exclaiming, exclaiming!

It is not attended to that you journeyed to this image, this persona; that it took hold of you just as much as you took hold of it, part choice, part fate; and that, quite apart from you, the journey you made follows you around and speaks through you.

This is all far away from a Robert Bly who once had to be searched for. No, not even searched for! Had to be found by accident. A Robert Bly whom friends, and even strangers, passed from one to the other as a gift. From the midsixties I'd devoured your translations as soon as they were published, but it was a lovely woman named Lee, who worked the cash register at a health food store in Austin in 1976, who pressed your Goddess essay on me. (I never saw her again.) Three years before, I was working in a bar in the Texas Panhandle, just outside the little town of Clarendon, and a woman who taught at a nearby junior college gave me the anthology *Naked Poetry,* where you printed the earliest version I've read (it's dated 1967) of the essay "Looking for Dragon Smoke." What a thing to read during those great Tornado Alley thunderstorms! I read it over and over—as I've read the book you later made of it, *Leaping Poetry.* How deeply that essay and book influenced the way I think of form, and the way I think of thought itself. Some of the sentences in that early, shorter version didn't make it to the later, more polished ones, like this passage, which still says itself in my mind often: "Blake took the first step: he abducted the thought of poetry, and took it off to some obscure psychic woods. His woods were real woods. Occult ceremonies took place in them, just as ceremonies had taken place in ancient poems."

Your woods are real woods, too. There are animal cries and birdsongs to be heard in your woods that can be heard nowhere else. There are gnomes at the bridges, witches at the crossroads, a strange man living at the bottom of a pond, and men and women on missions of life and death, all spoken of in one of the most tender voices in modern writing. And, as in all woods, people and other things get lost in yours sometimes—even some of your own poems get lost. My favorite of yours is one you didn't include in your *Selected Poems*—which means many will never see it, because once a "selected" is out that's all most folks tend to buy. So I'm going to give it back to you, by repeating it here. It's from *This Tree Will Be Here for a Thousand Years,* and it's called "Passing an Orchard by Train":

Grass high under apple trees.
The bark of the trees rough and sexual,
the grass growing heavy and uneven.

We cannot bear disaster, like
the rocks—
swaying nakedly
in open fields.

One slight bruise and we die!
I know no one on this train.
A man comes walking down the aisle.
I want to tell him
that I forgive him, that I want him
to forgive me.

In thanks and with love,
Michael Ventura

Appendix 1

Acceptance of the National Book Award for Poetry

By Robert Bly

I AM UNEASY at a ceremony emphasizing our current high state of culture. Cultural prizes, traditionally, put writers to sleep, and even the public. But we don't want to be asleep any more. Something has happened to me lately: every time I have glanced at a bookcase in the last few weeks, the books on killing of the Indians leap out into my hand. Reading a speech of Andrew Jackson's on the Indian question the other day—his Second Annual Message—I realized that he was the General Westmoreland of 1830. His speech was like an Administration speech today. It was another speech recommending murder of a race as a prudent policy, requiring stamina. Perhaps this coincidence should not have surprised me, but it did. It turns out we can put down a revolution as well as the Russians in Budapest; we can destroy a town as well as the Germans did Lidice—all with our famous unconcern.

As Americans, we have always wanted the life of feeling without the life of suffering. We long for pure light, constant victory. We have always wanted to avoid suffering, and therefore we are unable to live in the present. But our hopes for a life of pure light are breaking up. So many of the books nominated this year—Mr. Kozol's on education in the slums, Mr. Styron's, Mr. Mumford's, Mr. Rexroth's, Miss Levertov's, Mr. Merwin's—tell us that from now on we will have to live with grief and defeat.

We have some things to be proud of. No one needs to be ashamed of the acts of civil disobedience committed in the tradition of Thoreau. What Dr. Coffin did was magnificent; the fact that Yale University did not do it is what is sad. What Mr. Berrigan did was noble; the fact that the Catholic church did not do it is what is sad. What Mitchell Goodman did here last year was needed and in good taste. The sad thing is that the National Book Committee, in trying to honor those who told the truth last year, should have invited as a speaker Vice-President Humphrey, famous for his lies. Isn't the next step, now that individual people have committed acts of disobedience, for the institutions to take similar acts? What have our universities done to end the war? Nothing. They actually help the war by their defense research. What has the book industry done to end the war? Nothing. What has my own publisher, Harper and Row, done to help end the war? Nothing. In an age of gross and savage crimes by legal governments, the institutions will have to learn responsibility, learn to take their part in preserving the nation, and take their risk by committing acts of disobedience. The book companies can find ways to act like Thoreau, whom they publish. Where were the publishing houses when Dr. Spock and Mr. Goodman and Mr. Raskin—all three writers—were indicted? What the publishing houses do is up to them. It's clear they can have an editorial policy: they can refuse to pay taxes.

These concerns are not unconnected to such a ceremony as this. For if the country is dishonored, where will it draw its honor from to give to its writers? I respect the National Book Awards, and I respect the judges, and I thank them for their generosity. At the same time, I know I am speaking for many, many American poets when I ask this question: since we are murdering a culture in Vietnam at least as fine as our own, have we the right to congratulate ourselves on our cultural magnificence? Isn't that out of place?

You have given me an award for a book that has many poems in it against the war. I thank you for the award. As for the thousand-dollar check, I am turning it over to the draft-resistance movement, specifically to the organization called the Resistance. [Whereupon Mr. Bly handed the check to Mr. Mike Kempton, who was representing the Resistance.] I hereby counsel you as a young man not to enter the United States Army, not under any circumstances, and I ask you to use this money I am giving you to find and to counsel other young men, urging them to defy the draft authorities—and not to destroy their spiritual lives by participating in this war.

March 6, 1969

Appendix 2

War Is the Health of the State

By Robert Bly

President Bush's decision to attack Iraq is the greatest mistake ever made by an American president. Because the soul of the nation is still torn by the Vietnam War, the banking community is in desperate shape, research funds disappearing, schools being abandoned, the nation cannot afford this manic adventure, this inappropriate Good Friday of fireworks, this resolute walking off the cliff that "beetles o'er its brow into the sea."

The Mexican War, in 1846, was an ugly event, and we recall Abraham Lincoln saying of the then president, Polk: "His mind, tasked beyond its power, is running hither and thither, like some tortured creature on a burning surface, finding no position on which it can settle down and be at ease." The decisions to break the Indian treaties, to attack North Korea, to go off the gold standard, to fund "Star Wars" were all bad decisions, but none of them imperiled the republic as the attack on Iraq does. The Iraq operation is larger than the arms runs to the Contras, but it depends similarly on secretive governmental decisions for war, supported relatively by Congress when it is too late to change. The government decision gives no hint of shadow motives. Deception goes to the heart of the decision and deception is dangerous to the republic.

The president, speaking the other day to religious leaders, said, "We seek nothing for ourselves." Can one imagine Napoleon sending 500,000 troops across the plains to Russia and declaring, "We seek nothing for ourselves"? He got nothing, but he sought much. So do all sovereign states that enter war.

A revolting high-mindedness surrounds the decision. We say that Saddam is a demon, and we are angels. Saddam is a disgusting murderer—resembling in that respect Pinochet, Marcos, Franco,

Trujillo, and many old solemn friends of the United States.

We see Iraq's shadow, but not our own shadow. President Bush could mention that he used to be head of the local KGB—I mean the CIA—which kills secretly, close up and at a distance. I know that one may expect self-righteousness, pious rhetoric, hypocrisy, verbal chicanery, entire sheep pulled across one's eyes, outright lies from presidents and prime ministers, but this high-mindedness takes place in some new area. The media accept the hypocritical rhetoric and pass it on virtually without comment. They invite generals to discuss the morality of war.

Shadow-concealment on a large scale is going on, and that leads the nation to act out the myth of St. George and the Dragon. Curiously, the myth first entered Westerners' consciousness during the Crusades. In Mediterranean versions the hero *engages* the dragon for some ritual time, whereupon the Dragon transforms into human shape. But the Europeans perverted the myth into a killing myth. The knight kills the Dragon. Bush—strangely named George—has been turning Saddam Hussein into a dragon so he can kill him. Both Saddam and Bush have adopted the myth to blacken and demonize the other side. For a planet that can now be glimpsed whole from space, these incitements to tribal hatreds are too primitive. The perverted Dragon myth is driving Western and Near Eastern consciousness on to the coming disaster.

If we return to psychological thought for a moment, we notice that something we can't see in our own shadow prevents us from grasping Saddam's motives and thought. Bush, relying on contemporary up-to-date Beltline models, assured us that Saddam, sufficiently threatened, would withdraw. "I feel it in my gut." Four hundred thousand troops would do it; wrong. Security Council backing would do it; wrong. A deadline would do it; wrong. Congressional backing would do it; wrong. Who has ever, as a war leader, been so wrong?

Saddam is not operating in the Western psychological mode. He is apparently in the Crusader mode—ancient enmities, death for God, manic warriorhood, sacrifice, loss, advance, sacrifice, loss, advance. We behaved that way in 1100 also, so it is part of our shadow, but not now available to us. President Johnson, relying on attrition in the South, and bombing in the North, failed to grasp Vietnamese psychology. Bush is repeating this colossal error.

The United States, like every other nation, finds itself both a state and a country. The state has a valid interest in oil, whether or not oil continues to be sold in dollars, and how oil is funneled to Germany and Japan. The state's interests are international interests; Bush has always done best in representing the state. Randolph Bourne once said, "War is the health of the state."

In other words, if the state doesn't go to war for a while, it begins to feel sick. But included in the United States there is also a country, and in this decade the country has its concerns: helping millions of children in poverty, rebuilding bridges and highways, improving schools, sheltering the homeless, dealing with racism and explosive inequalities, strengthening families. The state has its demands, often contradictory to the country's needs.

The United States has always found it difficult to honor both these opposites, the state and the country, and to live in the resonating space between. If the opposites get too far apart, ungovernable forces flow into the gap.

During the sixties, the "sixties people," students, live-wires, populists, took us all toward the country, private delights, pleasures, country compassion. The state was despised. When too large a gap opens between state and country, forces connected to frontier mentality and mad individualism enter, and the nation is forced to experience the assassination of its greatest leaders. The Bush administration has now repeated that error, pulling the nation toward the state this time, giving war—the health of the state—full rein. That, alas, means increased sickness in the country. Psychologically, then, a dissolving of the opposites is taking place, no resonant space between, an empty place where complicated thought should be.

The United States, as we know from our own history, needs to beware of that gap and the forces it invokes. Sophocles expresses the danger in his great rendition of Agamemnon's dilemma on the way to the Trojan War. The winds, necessary for that war "that is the health of the state," will not come unless he sacrifices his daughter.

In private life, she is his chief joy, but he says, very pitifully, that as a public man he in effect has no desires. He sacrifices his daughter. In our terms, "daughter" would be the country and its human needs. His wife, Clytemnestra, watches this, and when he returns from the war, kills him ritually in his bath. President Bush has foolishly opened this gap between the state and the country, and he hopes that no evil forces will enter if he opens it only briefly. This will not be Vietnam. But the invisible forces care nothing for length.

In our war fever, we have already sacrificed our "daughter": that is, the human needs of the country, and the forces of this story have been set in motion. Bush and the Congress and the majority of the citizens have unwisely, like President Johnson, sacrificed the domestic program to the passions of the state, and the result will likely be the same sorrow and grief one feels at the end of a Sophocles play.

Minneapolis Star Tribune, *February 24, 1991*

Chronology

1926   Robert Elwood Bly born December 23 to Jacob Thomas Bly and Alice Aws Bly in Madison, Minnesota.

1944   Graduates from high school and enlists in Navy, where he is strongly influenced by men interested in poetry.

1946–47   Attends St. Olaf College in Northfield, Minnesota.

1947–50   Attends Harvard, graduating with a B.A., magna cum laude. Works on *Harvard Advocate* staff, delivers class poem.

1951–53   Lives alone in New York City, writing, reading, and supporting himself with part-time jobs.

1954   Moves to Iowa City and enrolls in M.A. program at University of Iowa.

1955   Marries Carolyn McLean. They move to a farm in Minnesota.

1956   Returns to Iowa City, where he submits book of poems *Steps Toward Poverty and Death* as master's thesis. Receives master's degree.

1956–57   Fulbright Fellowship in Norway. In Oslo library he discovers work of Spanish surrealist poets that will transform his own style.

1958   Publishes first issue of *The Fifties*; meets James Wright.

1959   Works on *Poems for the Ascension of J. P. Morgan,* some of which will turn up later in *The Light Around the Body.*

1961   Publishes first Sixties Press book, *Twenty Poems of Georg Trakl,* translated with James Wright.

1962   Birth of first daughter, Mary. First major book of poems, *Silence in the Snowy Fields,* published. *The Lion's Tail and Eyes: Poems Written Out of Laziness* and *Silence and Twenty Poems of César Vallejo* published.

1963   Birth of second daughter, Bridget. Amy Lowell Travelling Fellowship in England, France, and Spain. Guggenheim Fellowship.

1966   Organizes, with David Ray, national organization, American Writers Against the Vietnam War. Edits *A Poetry Reading Against the Vietnam War* and *Forty Poems Touching on Recent American History.*

1967   Birth of first son, Noah. *The Light Around the Body* published.

1968   Receives National Book Award for *The Light Around the Body* and turns prize money over to War Resisters League. *Twenty Poems of Pablo Neruda* published.

1969   *Forty Poems of Juan Ramón Jiménez* published. *Tennessee Poetry Journal* publishes special Bly issue.

1970   *The Teeth Mother Naked at Last* published. *Twenty Poems of Tomas Tranströmer* published. Lives with family in California, writes *Point Reyes Poems*.

1971   Birth of second son, Micah. *Neruda and Vallejo: Selected Poems* (with James Wright and John Knoepfle) published. Publishes first Kabir Versions, *The Fish in the Sea Is Not Thirsty*.

1972   Guggenheim Fellowship.

1973   *Sleepers Joining Hands* published. *Lorca and Jiménez: Selected Poems* published.

1974   Teaches course in hometown titled "The Discoveries of Freud and Jung and How They Apply to Life in Madison, Minnesota."

1975   Publishes first large collection of prose poems, *The Morning Glory*. Also publishes *Leaping Poetry* and *Friends, You Drank Some Darkness*. Organizes first annual Conference on the Great Mother.

1977   *This Body Is Made of Camphor and Gopherwood* published. *The Kabir Book* published.

1978   Bly is subject of two documentaries, *A Man Writes to a Part of Himself* by Mike Hazard, and a PBS Bill Moyers production.

1979   Robert and Carolyn Bly divorce; *This Tree Will Be Here for a Thousand Years* published.

1980   Marries Ruth Ray and moves to Moose Lake, Minnesota; *News of the Universe* and book of interviews *Talking All Morning* published.

1981   *The Man in the Black Coat Turns* and *Selected Poems of Rainer Maria Rilke* published. Special double issue of *Poetry East* published in honor of Bly. Friend and fellow poet James Wright dies.

1982   Teaches at first annual men's conference in Mendocino, California.

1983   Publishes *Times Alone*, translations of Antonio Machado. *Eight Stages of Translation* published.

1985   *Loving a Woman in Two Worlds* published.

1986   *Selected Poems* published. *A Little Book on the Human Shadow* (with William Booth) published.

1987–88   Leads, with Michael Meade, James Hillman, and Robert Moore, workshops and conferences for men, developing material that will eventually become *Iron John.*

1989   A Bill Moyers documentary on Bly, *A Gathering of Men,* brings men's work into public eye. Companion documentary with Bly and Michael Meade, *On Being a Man,* produced by KTCA-TV, St. Paul, Minnesota.

1990   *Iron John: A Book About Men* published. *American Poetry: Wildness and Domesticity* published.

1991   *Iron John* rises to top position on *New York Times* bestseller list. Bly is vocal critic of the Gulf War.

1992   Takes year off from public appearances. *What Have I Ever Lost by Dying? Collected Prose Poems* published. Edits book of poetry from men's work, *The Rag and Bone Shop of the Heart,* with James Hillman and Michael Meade. Revises edition of *This Tree Will Be Here for a Thousand Years.*

Selected Bibliography

PRIMARY SOURCES

1. Poetry

Silence in the Snowy Fields, Middletown, CT, Wesleyan University
    Press, 1962

The Light Around the Body, New York, HarperCollins, 1967

Sleepers Joining Hands, New York, HarperCollins, 1973

Jumping Out of Bed, Fredonia, NY, White Pine Press, 1973 (with
    Wang Hui Ming)

Old Man Rubbing His Eyes, St. Paul, Ally Press, 1975

The Body Is Made of Camphor and Gopherwood, New York,
    HarperCollins, 1977

This Tree Will Be Here for a Thousand Years, New York, Harper-
    Collins, 1979; revised 1992

The Man in the Black Coat Turns, New York, HarperCollins, 1981

Four Ramages, Daleville, IN, Barnwood Press, 1983

Loving a Woman in Two Worlds, New York, HarperCollins, 1985

Selected Poems, New York, HarperCollins, 1986

The Apple Found in the Plowing, Baltimore, Haw River Books, 1989

Angels of Pompeii (with Stephen Brigidi), New York, Ballantine, 1991

What Have I Ever Lost by Dying? Collected Prose Poems, New York,
    HarperCollins, 1992

2. Essays

Leaping Poetry, Boston, Beacon Press, 1975

News of the Universe, Poems of Twofold Consciousness, San Fran-
    cisco, Sierra Club, 1980

Talking All Morning, Ann Arbor, University of Michigan Press, 1980

The Eight Stages of Translation, St. Paul, Ally Press, 1983

Fifties/Sixties, Reprint Series, issues 1-10, Geneva, NY, Hobart and
    William Smith, 1984

The Wingéd Life: The Poetic Voice of Henry David Thoreau, New York, HarperCollins, 1986

The Pillow and the Key, St. Paul, Ally Press, 1987

A Little Book on the Human Shadow (with William Booth), New York, HarperCollins, 1988

American Poetry: Wildness and Domesticity, New York, Harper-Collins, 1990

When a Hair Turns Gold, St. Paul, Ally Press, 1989

Iron John: A Book About Men, Reading, MA, Addison-Wesley, 1990

Remembering James Wright, St. Paul, Ally Press, 1991

3. Translations

Hunger, Knut Hamsun, New York, Farrar, Straus and Giroux, 1967

Neruda and Vallejo: Selected Poems, Boston, Beacon Press, 1971

Selected Poems, Miguel Hernandez, Timothy Baland ed., Fredonia, NY, White Pine Press, 1972

The Kabir Book, Boston, Beacon Press, 1977

Twenty Poems of Rolf Jacobsen, Madison, MN, Seventies Press, 1977

I Never Wanted Fame, Machado, St. Paul, Ally Press, 1979

Truth Barriers, Tomas Tranströmer, San Francisco, Sierra Club, 1980

Night and Sleep (with Coleman Barks), Rumi, Cambridge, MA, Yellow Moon Press, 1981

Selected Poems of Rainer Maria Rilke, New York, HarperCollins, 1981

The Economy Spinning Faster and Faster, Göran Sonnevi, New York, SUN, 1982

Times Alone: Selected Poems of Antonio Machado, Middletown, CT, Wesleyan University Press, 1983

Mirabai Versions, Mirabai, New York, Red Ozier Press, 1984

When Grapes Turn to Wine, Rumi, Cambridge, MA, Yellow Moon Press, 1986

Light and Shadows, Juan Ramón Jiménez, Fredonia, NY, White Pine Press, 1987

Trusting Your Life to Water and Eternity, Olav H. Hauge, Minneapolis, Milkweed Editions, 1987

Ten Poems of Francis Ponge Translated by Robert Bly and Ten Poems of Robert Bly Inspired by the Poems of Francis Ponge, Alma, NB, Owl's Head Press, 1990

4. Audio Cassettes

Loving a Woman in Two Worlds, St. Paul, Ally Press #C101, 1985
Fairy Tales for Men and Women, St. Paul, Ally Press #C102, 1986
A Home in Dark Grass: Poems and Meditations on Solitudes,
    Families, Disciplines, St. Paul, Ally Press #C105, 1987
Iron John and the Male Mode of Feeling, Pacific Grove, CA, Oral
    Traditions, 1987
The Naive Male, St. Paul, Ally Press #C104, 1988
Men and the Wound, St. Paul, Ally Press, #C106, 1988
Poems of Kabir, South San Francisco, Audio Literature, 1988
An Evening with Robert Bly, Boulder, CO, Sounds True, 1989
Openings and Limitations, St. Paul, Ally Press #C107, 1989
Poems of Rumi (with Coleman Barks), South San Francisco, Audio
    Literature, 1989
Men and the Wild Child (with James Hillman), Boulder, CO, Sounds
    True, 1990
The Power of Shame (interview), San Francisco, New Dimensions
Magic Words (interview), San Francisco, New Dimensions
Into the Deep: Male Mysteries (interview), San Francisco, New
    Dimensions
William Blake and Beyond (interview), San Francisco, New
    Dimensions
Iron John (abridged, studio reading), New York, Random House, 1991
Men and the Life of Desire (with James Hillman and Michael
    Meade), Pacific Grove, CA, Oral Traditions, 1991
The Divine Child (with Marion Woodman), South San Francisco,
    Audio Literature, 1991
The Human Shadow, New York, Sound Horizons, 1991
The Inner King and Queen (with Michael Meade), New York, Sound
    Horizons, 1991
The Masculine Road (interview), San Francisco, New Dimensions,
    1991
What Stories Do We Need?, New York, Sound Horizons, 1991
We Make the Road by Walking, Chicago, C. G. Jung Institute, 1991
The Educated Heart, New York, Sound Horizons, 1992

5. Video Cassettes

A Man Writes to a Part of Himself, St. Paul, Ally Press, 1978
A Gathering of Men (with Bill Moyers), New York, Mystic Fire, 1990

On Being a Man (with Michael Meade), St. Paul, KTCA TV, 1990

SECONDARY SOURCES

Nelson, Howard, *Robert Bly, An Introduction to the Poetry*, New York, Columbia University Press, 1984

Peseroff, Joyce, ed., *Robert Bly: When Sleepers Awake*, Ann Arbor, University of Michigan Press, 1984.

Roberson, William H., *Robert Bly, A Primary and Secondary Bibliography*, Metuchen, NJ, Scarecrow Press, 1986

Sugg, Richard P., *Robert Bly*, Boston, Twayne Publishers, 1986

Davis, William V., *Understanding Robert Bly*, Columbia, University of South Carolina Press, 1988

Harris, Victoria Frenkel, *The Incorporative Consciousness of Robert Bly*, Carbondale, Southern Illinois University Press, 1992

All of this material is in print and available from a catalog published by the Ally Press Center, 524 Orleans St., St. Paul, MN 55107, 1-800-729-3002. Titles are listed by city, current publisher, and date of first known edition.

Walking Swiftly is also published in a hardcover edition by Ally Press. To order call the above number or send $19.95 plus $2.50 postage and handling.

Notes on Contributors

In the last fifteen years **Coleman Barks** has brought out nine volumes of translations of the thirteenth century Sufi mystic, Jelaluddin Rumi, including *Open Secret, Unseen Rain, Like This,* and *One-Handed Basket Weaving.* He is currently working on a volume of his own poetry, *Gourd Seed.* He teaches poetry at the University of Georgia in Athens.

William Booth lives in the north woods of Minnesota. He edits audio tapes—most recently *The Great Self Within* (Michael Meade, Robert Moore) and *The Educated Heart* (Robert Bly). He is the editor of *A Little Book on the Human Shadow* (Robert Bly). He and his wife Nancy have a small resort, Cry of the Loon Lodge.

Michael Dennis Browne has a new book of poems, *You Won't Remember This,* out from Carnegie Mellon, as well as an article on James Wright in *The Gettysburg Review.* He teaches at the University of Minnesota.

Lou Camp recently retired as editor of *The Painted Bride Quarterly* to spend more time on his own writing. He lives in Philadelphia and teaches at Bucks County Community College where for many years he coordinated the Poetry Reading Series.

A native of La Crosse, Wisconsin, **C. Owen Christianson** is a pastor in the Evangelical Lutheran Church in America. He lives in Moose Lake, Minnesota, with his wife and two children.

Noel Cobb is the editor of *Sphinx, a Journal for Archetypal Psychology and the Arts.* His book *Archetypal Imagination: Essays in Cultural Psychology* is being published in 1992 by Lindisfarne Press. He is author of an alchemical study of Shakespeare's "The Tempest," *Prospero's Island* (Sigo Press). As chairman of The London Convivium, he has regularly hosted poetry readings by Robert Bly during the latter's visits to England.

Philip Dacey's fifth book of poetry, *Night Shift at the Crucifix Factory,* winner of an Edwin Ford Piper Poetry Award, was published in 1991 by the University of Iowa Press. With David Jauss, he coedited *Strong Measures: Contemporary American Poetry in Traditional Forms* (Harper and Row, 1985). Recently he resigned from full-time teaching at Southwest State University in Marshall, Minnesota, in order to be able to write poetry a minimum of six months a year.

Marv Davidov is the founder of the Honeywell Project, a nationally known peace organization, considered the oldest project in the United States confronting management of a major multinational corporation through nonviolent civil disobedience. More recently he has founded the new Midwest Institute for Social Transformation.

John Densmore was drummer for the influential sixties rock band the Doors. He has recently published an autobiographical account of that experience, *Riders on the Storm* (Bantam). He will spend most of 1992 on the college lecture circuit speaking, reading from his book, and drumming.

Andrew Dick's problems with Robert Bly started in 1975. He stopped practicing law several years ago to write and serve as a neutral in alternative dispute resolution. Andrew is presently rearranging the basement walls of his Minneapolis home, and will postpone talking about how intelligent he might be until the job is finished.

Terry Dobson was an Aikido teacher who trained in Japan for many years. He taught Aikido in several schools in California, and began teaching with Robert Bly and Michael Meade in men's conferences in 1983. He published two books, *Aikido in Everyday Life* (North Atlantic Books) and *Safe and Alive* (Tarcher). He died unexpectedly in fall 1992.

William Duffy is a high school English teacher and poet. He was cofounder of *The Fifties* with Robert Bly, and shared a book of poems entitled *The Lion's Tail and Eyes* with Robert Bly and James Wright. He has also published in *Poetry* and the *San Francisco Review.* He lives in Grand Marais, Minnesota, and likes to eat Lake Superior herring.

Saul Galin, professor of English and Comparative Literature at Brooklyn College, is the director of the B.F.A. Program in Creative Writing and the

Brooklyn College London Summer Program in Shakespeare, Fiction Writing, Poetry Writing, and Playwriting. He lives in New York City.

After working ten years as a printer, **Paul Feroe** is now publisher of Ally Press full time. He lives in St. Paul with his wife Julie and daughters Kirsten and Rebecca and is the editor of *Silent Voices: Recent American Poems on Nature* (Ally Press).

James Haba's work was included in *Ten Love Poems,* edited by Robert Bly (Ally Press, 1981). He is presently an associate professor of English at Glassboro State College in New Jersey, and has had primary responsibility for organizing the Geraldine R. Dodge Poetry Festival, the largest in the country. He was series consultant for the 1988 Bill Moyers PBS series *The Power of the Word.*

Donald Hall met Robert Bly in the offices of the *Harvard Advocate* in February 1948. Hall lives in New Hampshire, where he makes his living by free-lance writing, and has published ten or eleven books of poems, including *Old and New Poems* in 1990.

Victoria Frenkel Harris is a professor in the English department at Illinois State University. Her book *The Incorporative Consciousness of Robert Bly* was published by Southern Illinois University Press in 1991. She is presently working on a book-length project focusing upon the presentation of subjectivity in contemporary American women's poetry.

Ex-theologian **Patrick Herriges** is executive director of the West Central Wisconsin Community Action Agency. He is a nightclub pianist and, with his musician sons Chris and Greg, operates a small music publishing company, Magnet Productions. He and his adopted cats, Margaret and Oshun, live in Glenwood City, Wisconsin.

James Hillman, one of America's most original and distinguished psychologists, is author of many books, including *Re-Visioning Psychology* (HarperCollins), *Anima: An Anatomy of a Personified Notion* (Spring), and *A Blue Fire: Selected Writings* (HarperCollins). Recently he collaborated with Michael Ventura on *We've Had a Hundred Years of Psychotherapy—And the World's Getting Worse* (HarperCollins). He has taught often at men's conferences with Robert Bly and Michael Meade.

Bill Holm still lives in Minneota, Minnesota, his hometown. He drives down the road when necessity calls and teaches at Southwest State University in Marshall, Minnesota. He has taught in Iceland and China. He has four books: two of prose, *The Music of Failure* and *Coming Home Crazy,* and two of poems, *Boxelder Bug Variations* and *The Dead Get By with Everything;* all are from Milkweed Editions. He misses his neighbor just to the north!

Chungliang Al Huang is founder-president of the Living Tao Foundation. He is author of *Embrace Tiger, Return to Mountain* and *Quantum Soup* and co-author (with Alan Watts) of *Tao: The Watercourse Way.*

David Ignatow has published fourteen books of poetry and is recipient of the Bollingen Prize, the Wallace Stevens Fellowship, the Guggenheim Prize, and many other awards. His most recent books are *Shadowing the Ground* (Wesleyan University Press) and *Despite the Plainness of the Day: Love Poems* (Mill Hunk Books). At present he teaches at Columbia University.

Ann B. Igoe was born and grew up in small towns in South Carolina. She received an A.B. degree in English and an M.F.A. in dance, studying with Martha Graham and Jose Simon. She has worked as a dancer, choreographer, and teacher, and has done a lot of painting. She is mother of two, wife of one.

Louis Jenkins's poetry has been published in a number of magazines and anthologies, including *American Poetry Review, Kenyon Review, Poetry East, Paris Review,* and *Virginia Quarterly Review.* His books of poetry include *An Almost Human Gesture* (Eighties Press and Ally Press, 1987) and *All Tangled Up with the Living* (Nineties Press, 1991). He lives in Duluth, Minnesota, with his wife, Ann, and son, Lars.

Jane Kenyon has four books of poems and translations: *From Room to Room, Twenty Poems of Anna Akhmatova, The Boat of Quiet Hours,* and *Let Evening Come.* Her work appears frequently in *The New Yorker, The New Criterion,* and other magazines.

Galway Kinnell teaches one semester a year in the Graduate Creative Writing Program at New York University. He is the State Poet of Vermont.

John Knoepfle is author of numerous books, including among the most recent *Dim Tales* (Stormline Press, 1989) and *Selected Poems* (University of Missouri, Kansas City Press, 1985). His translations of Neruda and Vallejo, along with those by Robert Bly and James Wright, are kept in print by Beacon Press. He teaches at Sangamon State University in Springfield, Illinois. (His friend Peter Simpson, source of many details of Robert Bly's visit for the interview in this book, died last January.)

Meridel Le Sueur, poet, writer, and activist, is one of the influential literary figures of the Midwest. She began publishing in the 30s, and her many books include *Rites of Ancient Ripening* (poetry, Vanilla Press), *The Girl* (novel, West End), and *Ripening* (selected work, Feminist Press).

Frederick Manfred is the author of many novels, including the contemporary classic *Lord Grizzly.* He has devoted his writing life to chronicling that part of the prairie Midwest he calls Siouxland. His recent publications include *No Fun on Sunday* (University of Oklahoma Press), *Flowers of Desire* (Dancing Badger Press), and *Of Lizards and Angels: A Saga of Siouxland* (University of Oklahoma).

Barbara McClintock is the executive director of the Joseph Campbell Archives and Library on the campus of Pacifica Graduate Institute, Santa Barbara, California. Over the past fifteen years she has hosted Robert Bly at readings, seminars, and conferences, including the (infamous) "Between the Horns and the Bull" conference with Joseph Campbell and James Hillman.

Michael Meade is an Irish-American mythologist, drummer, and storyteller in the Schanachie tradition. With Robert Bly and James Hillman, he has taught men at conferences and workshops for the past decade, and is working on a book, *Men and the Water of Life.*

Charles Molesworth is the author of *Marianne Moore: A Literary Life* (1990). He is chairperson of the Department of English at Queens College, City University of New York, where he also teaches at the Graduate Center. He has published books on Gary Snyder, Donald Barthelme, and contemporary American poetry, and is currently working on a study of the roots of cultural criticism in the 1920s.

Robert L. Moore, author and psychologist, is associated with the Jung Institute of Chicago and the Chicago Theological Seminary. With Douglas Gillette, he has written *King, Warrior, Magician, Lover: Rediscovering the Archetypes of the Mature Masculine* (HarperCollins), a seminal work in the emerging men's movement. He is series editor of the Paulist Press series on Jungian psychology and world spirituality.

Howard Nelson lives between two of the Finger Lakes in upstate New York. His book *Robert Bly: An Introduction to the Poetry* (Columbia University Press) appeared in 1984. He is also author of two collections of poems, *Creatures* (Cleveland State) and *Singing into the Belly* (FootHills Publishing).

Nils Peterson has taught at San Jose State University since 1963. He was coordinator of creative writing for more than twenty of those years. He has published many poems in journals and a chapbook entitled *Here Is No Ordinary Rejoicing.* He is at present circulating a manuscript entitled *The Heart Wants What It Wants.*

Michael Quam is professor of Anthropology and Public Health at Sangamon State University in Springfield, Illinois. He grew up in Madison, Minnesota, and is the author of "Through Norwegian Eyes: Growing Up Among the Snowy Fields," *Plainsong,* Fall 1981.

Milli Quam lives in Springfield, Illinois, where she is a psychotherapist in private practice. She has been a friend of Robert's for thirty years and attends the annual Great Mother Conference.

For five years **Fran Quinn** ran the annual Great Mother Conference with Robert Bly. He is a founding member of the Worcester (Massachusetts) County Poetry Association. His first chapbook, *Milk of the Lioness,* was published in 1982. He has a full-length manuscript in circulation now, and is presently living in Indianapolis where he is poet-in-residence at Butler University.

Kathleen Raine is editor of the British journal *Temenos,* which is about to be transformed into the Temenos Academy of Integral Studies. Her most recent books are *India Seen Afar* (autobiography, Green Books),

Golgonooza, City of the Imagination (last essays on Blake, Golgonooza Press), and *Living with Mystery* (poetry, Golgonooza Press).

David Ray graduated from the University of Chicago and has taught at universities in the United States, as well as in India and New Zealand. His recent books of poetry include *Sam's Book* (Wesleyan, 1987) and *The Maharani's New Wall and Other Poems* (Wesleyan, 1989). He has a new book of poems, *Wool Highways,* forthcoming from Helicon Nine. With Robert Bly, he founded American Writers Against the Vietnam War.

Rita Shumaker teaches at University of North Carolina-Charlotte and the Charlotte Country Day School. An artist who has exhibited her work nation-wide, she has participated as a teacher in the Great Mother Conferences, and her work embellished *Night and Sleep,* versions of Rumi by Robert Bly and Coleman Barks, published by Yellow Moon Press.

Thomas R. Smith is the author of a book of poems, *Keeping the Star* (New Rivers Press, 1988), and editor of *What Happened When He Went to the Store for Bread: Selected Poems of Alden Nowlan* (Nineties Press, 1992). He was a founding editor of *Inroads,* and works as an associate editor at Ally Press.

Ted Solotaroff recently retired after thirty years as a literary editor and is now a contributing editor for *The Nation.* He was a founding editor of *New American Review.*

William Stafford has recently published the following books of poetry: *Passwords* (HarperCollins), *A Scripture of Leaves* (Brethren Press), *Kansas Poems* (Woodley Memorial Press), and *How to Hold Your Arms When It Rains* (Honeybrook Press). A volume of selected poems edited by Robert Bly is due from HarperCollins this year.

John Stokes lives in Corrales, New Mexico. He has combined the arts of music, storytelling, and dance with the martial arts and traditional tracking and survival skills in a program called "The Arts of Life." Through his nonprofit organization, the Tracking Project, he and other artists carry their program to thousands of native youth in North America and Hawaii, as well as to nonnative youth and adults.

Gioia Timpanelli is considered, with Robert Bly, one of the earliest and most central figures in the modern revival of storytelling. She has won the Woman's National Book Association Award for bringing the oral tradition to the American public. She is currently working on a book of her own stories, in which "The Old Couple" is included, to be published by William Morrow.

Tomas Tranströmer is the most influential modern Swedish poet. In 1980, Sierra Club Books published his *Truth Barriers,* translated by Robert Bly. His *Selected Poems, 1954-1986,* edited by Robert Hass, is published by Ecco Press. He was 1990 winner of the Neustadt International Prize for Literature.

Michael True, author of *Ordinary People: Family Life and Global Values* (1991) and editor of *Daniel Berrigan: Poetry, Drama, Prose* (1988), teaches at Assumption College in Worcester, Massachusetts. His essay, "Robert Bly, Radical Poet," in *Win* described the poet's readings in the early 1970s.

Michael Ventura is a Los Angeles writer.

Judith Weissman is a professor in the English Department of Syracuse University, and has published many essays in scholarly and critical journals, including *The Georgia Review, The Sewanee Review,* and *The Southern Review.* Her two major works are her books *Half Savage and Hardy and Free: Women and Rural Radicalism in the Nineteenth-Century Novel* (Wesleyan, 1987) and *Of Two Minds: Poets Who Hear Voices,* forthcoming from Wesleyan.

Marion Woodman is a Jungian analyst in private practice in Toronto, Canada. She has written several books on contemporary women's psychology and has conducted workshops and conferences on emerging feminity. During the past four years, she has worked with Robert Bly in conferences bringing men and women together.

Annie Wright lives and works in New York City and Misquamicut, Rhode Island. She plans to edit an anthology of the letters of her late husband, James Wright, sometime in the future.

Acknowledgments

Grateful thanks to David Bly, William Booth, Mike Hazard, Patricia Olson, Anne Running, and Anthony Signorelli for their assistance in preparing *Walking Swiftly*.

Thanks to HarperCollins Publishers for their permission to reprint the following poems by Robert Bly: "Walking Swiftly" from *This Body Is Made of Camphor and Gopherwood,* copyright © 1977 by Robert Bly; "The Loon's Cry" from *Selected Poems,* copyright © 1986 by Robert Bly; and "Passing an Orchard by Train" from *This Tree Will Be Here for a Thousand Years,* copyright © 1979 by Robert Bly. All other writings by Robert Bly are reprinted here with his generous permission.

Thanks also to the editors of the following publications in which these pieces or excerpts originally appeared, sometimes in different form: *The Paris Review* for "Excerpt from the *Paris Review* interview with Peter Stitt" by Donald Hall; *Poetry East* for "Excerpt from 'Reflections Upon the Past with Robert Bly' " by David Ignatow; *Crab Creek Review* for "Robert Bly's Working-with-Things Project" by William Stafford; *Poetry East* for "Joining Hands with Robert Bly" by Annie Wright; and *The Nation* for "Captain Bly" by Ted Solotaroff.